Classic 'Burgh

CLASSIC SPORTS
Jonathan Knight, Series Editor

Classic Bucs: The 50 Greatest Games in Pittsburgh Pirates History
David Finoli

Classic Steelers: The 50 Greatest Games in Pittsburgh Steelers History
David Finoli

Classic Browns: The 50 Greatest Games in Cleveland Browns History
Second Edition, Revised and Updated
Jonathan Knight

Classic Cavs: The 50 Greatest Games in Cleveland Cavaliers History
Second Edition, Revised and Updated
Jonathan Knight

Classic Pens: The 50 Greatest Games in Pittsburgh Penguins History
Second Edition, Revised and Updated
David Finoli

Classic Bengals: The 50 Greatest Games in Cincinnati Bengals History
Steve Watkins and Dick Maloney

Classic 'Burgh: The 50 Greatest Collegiate Games in Pittsburgh Sports History
David Finoli

Classic 'Burgh

THE 50 GREATEST COLLEGIATE GAMES
IN PITTSBURGH SPORTS HISTORY

David Finoli

BLACK SQUIRREL BOOKS®

Kent, Ohio

BLACK SQUIRREL BOOKS® 🐿®

Frisky, industrious black squirrels are a familiar sight on the Kent State University campus and the inspiration for Black Squirrel Books®, a trade imprint of The Kent State University Press. www.KentStateUniversityPress.com.

For my parents,
Domenic and Eleanor,
who taught me three things in life:
be kind to others,
give back as much as you can,
and take care of your family.
They were lessons well taught.
You are both missed.

Contents

Acknowledgments

Every project I begin is the extension of a dream I've had since I was young: writing about the history of sports in a place I've always treasured. It's the extension of a dream I was inspired to pursue by my parents, Dom and Eleanor; by my grandparents, Inez, Tom, Maria, and Angelo; by my aunts and uncles, Vince, Betty, Maryanne, Louise, Norma, Jeannie, Libby, Mary, and Evie; and by my cousins, Tom Aikens and Eddie DiLello. It's a dream I am inspired to continue to pursue, thanks to my loving wife, Viv; my children, Cara, Matt, and Tony; my brother, Jamie, and his wife, Cindy; my nieces, Brianna and Marissa; my sister, Mary, and her husband, Matthew; my other cousins, Fran, Luci, Flo, Beth, Tom, Gary, Linda, Amy, Amanda, Claudia, Ginny Lynn, Pam, Debbie, Diane, Vince, and Richard; and, last but not least, my in-laws, Vivian and Salvatore Pansino.

There is my roundtable of Pittsburgh sports experts who provide insight into the teams of today as well as those of the past, a group that I call on to bounce ideas off when needed. They include Chris Fletcher, Bill Ranier, Dan Russell, Rich Boyer, Gary Kinn, Tom Rooney, Shawn Christen, Matt O'Brotka, Don Lavell, Gary Degnan, Robert Healy III, David Laza, Mark Franz, Frank Katz, Joe Magnu, Dave Pevarnik, and Mark Richard.

To get a project to reach its potential, you need a good publisher, and in this case I have one of the best. A press that I've had the honor to work with on five books. The fine people at The Kent State University Press include Will Underwood, Jonathan Knight, Rebekah Cotton, and Mary Young.

Finally, a thank-you to those whose generous help in securing the photos for this book were most essential in completing the project: Dave Saba from Duquesne; E. J. Borghetti from the University of Pittsburgh; Allegheny College's Jim Berger; Taylor Powers from St. Francis University in Loretto, Pennsylvania; Matt Kifer of the California University of Pennsylvania; and those who helped with some essential research such as Craig Britcher at the Western Pennsylvania Sports Museum.

Introduction

Most of my books have been about the national pastime and my favorite professional team, the Pittsburgh Pirates, so it comes as no surprise that many think it's my favorite sport. I certainly do love baseball as well as the Bucs, but, truth be told, my dirty little secret is that college football has always been my first love, and with it the trials and tribulations of the University of Pittsburgh football team, which has been my main sports passion.

There's just something special about college football, as well as collegiate sports in general. The unbridled excitement by those on the field of play just isn't replicated in professional sports. In college football, with only four teams in the playoff for the national championship, every game from Labor Day on is like a season-long elimination tournament. Every game counts. College basketball brings us a tournament unmatched in sports with March Madness. When it comes to college athletics in western Pennsylvania, you not only get the thrill of competition at every level in every sport, but you get a unique team history.

In the early twentieth century, a 2.7-mile drive down Forbes Avenue in the Steel City separated three of the top football programs in the nation. Carnegie Tech (a.k.a. Carnegie Mellon University) fielded teams that found ways to infuriate the great Knute Rockne and his legendary Fighting Irish of Notre Dame. In 1938 they won the Lambert Trophy, emblematic of the best team in the East, and battled top-ranked TCU in the Sugar Bowl, giving them all they could handle before falling late in the game. Duquesne University became a staple in the top 20 starting in the late 1930s, winning the precursor to the Orange Bowl, the Festival of Palms, before becoming Orange Bowl champions themselves in 1937.

As successful as both schools were, the one that stood between them, the University of Pittsburgh, is one of the great dynasties of all time. Between 1915 and 1937, the Panthers captured eight national championships, and when it looked like the program had dissolved into one of the nation's worst almost 40 years later, they rose like the Phoenix and shockingly captured a ninth, only four short years after coach Johnny Majors took over a 1–10 program.

If football were all that western Pennsylvania boasted of, its legacy would be fruitful; but when it comes to collegiate sports, football only scratches the surface. On the hardwood, Pitt won two national championships under the leadership of one of the game's great coaches, Doc Carlson. While on the Bluff at Duquesne, the Dukes spent three decades at the top of the sport.

Chick Davies and his successor, Dudey Moore, were often on the steps of a national championship at Duquesne, only to resemble the Buffalo Bills teams of the 1990s as they fell short several times. Though it was often frustrating at the end of the year, the program proudly helped integrate college basketball at a time when many schools refused to recruit some of the best African American players in the East. Finally, in 1955, when it appeared the team was highly flawed with only two stars leading a moderately talented team, they stunned the college basketball world by winning a Division I national championship—the only time a western Pennsylvania school ever triumphed in a tournament. Sixty years later the California (Pennsylvania) women's basketball did them one better by winning their second Division II title 10 years after capturing their first.

While football and basketball encompass most of the region's classic contests and titles, a relatively new sport on area college campuses, hockey, has become the major focus at both Robert Morris University and Mercyhurst, with impressive results for each school's men's and women's squads.

College sports in this area is often relegated beneath the headlines of two of the most successful professional franchises in the country, the Penguins and Steelers, not to mention the Pirates. Despite playing second fiddle to professional sports, which is an issue that usually plagues sports at schools located in a major market, college athletics have been a huge part of the successful legacy that is western Pennsylvania sports. It is the intention of this book to revive those remarkable moments and achievements, highlighting the stories of these great games.

#50

To Go Where No One Has Gone Before

While college basketball and football have historically dominated the headlines in western Pennsylvania, another sport has emerged during the past 30 years to join them as a front-page attraction. That sport is hockey, and both the men's and women's teams at Robert Morris University and Mercyhurst University have become a source of pride over the past two decades.

While the sport has thrived at the club level in the area for years, the Mercyhurst men's hockey team was the first to hit the modern NCAA landscape in 1987, when they began as a Division III squad. The team had great success at that level before moving up to Division II in 1992, where they reached the national championship in 1993 and 1995, losing both times. In 1999, the squad made the jump to Division I, where they won three conference tournament titles, won a regular-season conference championship, and appeared in the NCAA tourney three times.

In 2004 Robert Morris joined Mercyhurst at the Division I level with a new varsity program and since 2010 has been one of the Atlantic Hockey Conference's best programs, capturing two regular-season crowns and a tournament title in 2014. Robert Morris launched a Division I women's hockey program in 2005, and 12 years later they won their first regular-season and tournament conference crowns with a magnificent 24–5–6 mark, earning their first NCAA tournament bid. As successful as these programs have been, each team takes a backseat to the Mercyhurst women's club.

The Lakers first dropped the puck in 1999 and quickly have become the New England Patriots of women's hockey in the College Hockey America conference (CHA). Since they began the program, Mercyhurst captured three Great Lakes Women's Hockey Association (GLWHA) titles in their only three seasons in

1

that league before moving to the CHA in 2001. There they won 13 championships in their next 15 campaigns, including 11 conference tournament titles and 11 trips to the NCAA tournament, where they advanced to the Frozen Four on four occasions. For all the memorable moments they've provided over the years, a game in 2009 is considered one of the quintessential moments in western Pennsylvania collegiate hockey history: the day Mercyhurst took on Minnesota in the NCAA semifinals. It was a game that sent them where no other area hockey program had gone before or since, to the national championship contest with an exhilarating overtime win against the Golden Gophers.

Coming off a disappointing 2007–08 campaign in which the Lakers didn't win the regular-season championship in the CHA, head coach Michael Sisti—the only coach the program has known—and his squad wanted to get back to the top quickly. Led by junior Meghan Agosta's 41 goals and 78 points in 32 games, as well as stellar freshman goaltender Hillary Pattenden, who was 24–3 with a 1.95 goals against average, the Lakers were perfect in the conference with a 16–0–0 record before breezing through the CHA tournament, outscoring the opposition by a 14–3 mark to secure their fifth consecutive bid to the NCAA tourney.

Up to this point, Mercyhurst played well in their first four ventures into the NCAA tournament but lost each time by a single goal, with three of the contests going to overtime. As they took on St. Lawrence in the quarterfinals, the Lakers wanted to make sure they didn't end up with another close loss. Freshman Kelley Steadman netted a goal in the opening period before Agosta scored the game winner in the second on the way to a 3–1 victory. The Lakers' initial NCAA win paved a path to the program's first Frozen Four appearance against a school that had long been one of the true giants in the sport, whether it be the men's or women's program: the University of Minnesota Golden Gophers.

The second-seeded Gophers had already won two national championships and just finished a spectacular 32–5–3 campaign that included a 4–3 win over Boston College in the quarterfinals. Freshmen twin sisters Monique and Jocelyne Lamoureux, both of whom play for the US national team, headed a powerful young team with 30 and 23 goals, respectively, and they looked to continue their winning ways against the upstart Mercyhurst squad.

Ending the third-ranked Lakers season looked like a possibility when Minnesota's Gigi Marvin knocked home a power play goal 5:38 into the game to give the Gophers a quick 1–0 lead. But that momentum slipped through their hands as Mercyhurst dominated the next 10 minutes.

A little over 3 minutes later, the Lakers were on a two-person advantage when senior Valerie Chouinard took a pass from Hayley McMeekin and put it past Alyssa Grogan to tie the game at 1. With 5 minutes left, Mercyhurst had another power play opportunity when Bailey Bram took advantage of a turnover to give the Lakers their first advantage at 2–1. Agosta made the score 3–1 with 1:14 left in the frame with a blistering shot from the blue line that ended the day for Grogan as she was pulled at the end of the first intermission.

Despite the goalie change, the onslaught continued in the second period when Chouinard became the second player in the program's history to eclipse 200 points as she sent a shot toward the Minnesota goal that Meghan Corbett tipped in, increasing the Mercyhurst advantage to three. As time was running out in the second, it appeared a rout was on when Agosta scored with 5 seconds left to make it a seemingly insurmountable 5–1 lead.

While Lakers fans were excited, assuming they were only a period away from a spot in the finals, Minnesota was about to dampen their enthusiasm. Mercyhurst was still hanging on to their four-goal advantage with under 9 minutes left when the Golden Gophers decided to show the Lakers it wasn't over. Jen Schoullis, Gigi Marvin, and Monique Lamoureux all beat Pattenden for goals, cutting the seemingly insurmountable lead to a single goal with 1:17 left in the contest.

Minnesota dominated the third period, outshooting Mercyhurst 14–5, and kept the pressure on after pulling their goalie in the final minute of the game. But Pattenden refused to be beat as Mercyhurst held on for the 5–4 victory.

Even though the Lakers were shut out in the national championship game by Wisconsin 5–0, this Mercyhurst team went further than any other western Pennsylvania NCAA college hockey team had.

Scoring	1st	2nd	3rd	Final
Mercyhurst	3	2	0	5
Minnesota	1	0	3	4

Shots	1st	2nd	3rd	Final
Mercyhurst	10	7	5	22
Minnesota	10	13	14	37

Period	Scoring	Time
1	Minn—Marvin 29 (Drazen) Pp	5:29
1	Merc—Chouinard 21 (McMeekin, Scanzano) Pp	8:38
1	Merc—Bram 16 Pp	15:47
1	Merc—Agosta 40 (Jones, Scanzano)	18:46
2	Merc—Corbett 6 (Chouinard, Cockell)	3:40
2	Merc—Agosta 41 (Scanzano)	19:55
3	Minn—Schoullis 17 (Marvin) Pp	11:13
3	Minn—Marvin 30	15:24
3	Minn—M. Lamoureux 39 (Drazen, Marvin) En	18:43

Team	Goalie	Saves	Goals
Mercyhurst	Pattenden	33	4
Minnesota	Grogan	7	3
Minnesota	Lura	10	2

COMMUNITY COLLEGE OF BEAVER COUNTY TITANS 83,
PENN VALLEY COMMUNITY COLLEGE SCOUTS 81
MARCH 22, 1997
MEN'S DIVISION II NJCAA BASKETBALL

Snatching Victory from Defeat

Take a ride down the Parkway-West past the Pittsburgh International Airport and you'll begin to see signs as you enter the Beaver Valley, reminding you just how rich the history of football is in western Pennsylvania. Look to the right and there is a sign directing you to Hopewell, where the University of Pittsburgh's lone Heisman Trophy winner, Tony Dorsett, went to high school. Then comes Aliquippa, the home of Iron Mike Ditka, a Hall of Fame NFL tight end, who led the Chicago Bears to a Super Bowl victory as a head coach. A few miles from there is Beaver Falls, which produced "Broadway Joe" Namath, one of the most legendary quarterbacks in NFL history. There are many more great football names from this region to add to the mix.

For all the glory, one thing you won't see is a sign celebrating the memorable champions from a different sport: the thrilling run that gave the Community College of Beaver County (CCBC) the 1997 National Junior College Athletic Association (NJCAA) Division II men's basketball national championship. While they may not be commemorated by any signs along the highway, these champions are nonetheless remembered fondly by those lucky enough to have witnessed their efforts in 1997.

The Titans were led by coach Mark Javens, who, like legendary Pitt football coach Johnny Majors, inherited a mess when he came into the job. The big difference was that after Majors's initial season, you could see he was building something special. That same feeling was not there for the Titans coach. Javens's first campaign in 1993–94 ended in the embarrassment of a 2–19 mark. While difficult to see at that time, the fortunes of the program would soon turn around. A year later, CCBC stood at 24–10 before improving to 27–6 in 1995–96. Like

Majors did two decades earlier, Javens used his fourth campaign with the Titans to launch them into the national spotlight.

Before 1997, the most interesting aspect of the team was the rather unique building they called home. The Golden Dome, as it's known in Beaver County, is a geodesic dome—a hemispherical thin-shelled structure that was built in 1975, seating 5,000 for basketball. The dome was painted gold and remains today as not only one of eight such structures in the country but one of the area's most notable landmarks. In 1997 it housed the No. 1 Division II junior college team in the land as the Titans, with an undefeated 22–0 mark, faced their rivals, the Community College of Allegheny County (CCAC).

It was certainly an important Western Pennsylvania Collegiate Conference matchup, but one that most thought would end in a lopsided win for the Titans. But CCAC had other plans. It was a close contest that went to overtime before Larry Richardson and Jim Miller hit three free throws for CCAC in the final 16 seconds to secure the upset win and knock CCBC from the ranks of the undefeated. While upset, Javens considered it a wake-up call for his team. After eventually winning the WPCC championship, the coach remarked, "I'd like to publicly thank CCAC for beating our behinds. I don't think we could have gone all the way through the state tournament, the regional tournament and the national tournament without a loss. That was a good loss for us."[1]

The Titans dominated their remaining opponents not only to capture the conference crown but to emerge victorious at the state and regional level and secure a spot in the national tournament, where they weren't exactly respected by their opponents despite their sparkling record. Star guard Wayne Copeland recalled that "when we got down there we were the laughing stock of the tournament. Teams were just laughing at us."[2]

CCBC was an undersized team who many thought had no business making it this far. But the Titans were a close unit that knew how to win, and a big part of that was playing great defense. Javens prepared the team to play aggressive defense, and their opponents weren't prepared for the all-out full-court press the Titans displayed. The coach felt that since center Al Franklin was his biggest player at a relatively small 6'6", it was the only chance the team had to succeed. The strategy had a bigger effect than anyone could have imagined, as CCBC battled their way through the preliminary rounds and surprisingly found themselves in the national championship game against the defending champions, Penn Valley Community College from Kansas City, Missouri.

Like it did against their previous opponents, the full-court press confused Penn Valley at the outset as the Titans raced to an early 11–2 lead. As defending national champs, the Scouts had faced adversity before and came back to take a 25–24 advantage. CCBC had forced 11 turnovers in the first 20 minutes but could only turn it into nine points, which kept the Titans from taking a significant lead. The two teams went back and forth the rest of the first half, but when Penn Valley's Laron Daniels buried an outside shot as time expired before the intermission, the Scouts forged ahead 43–42.

It continued to be a close game in the second half, but Penn Valley was finding ways to beat the pressure. With time winding down, the score was tied at 81. CCBC was unable to take the lead, and the Scouts had the ball with a chance at winning the game with the last shot. With under 10 seconds left, a potential last-second loss quickly turned into a chance for a stunning victory. Copeland stole the ball with 5 seconds left and tossed a pass at midcourt to Jeff Benson, who sprinted down underneath the basket. Benson snagged the long toss and scored with only a second remaining to snatch victory from defeat with a dramatic 83–81 win for the national title.

Copeland was stunned: "All I remember is that I was running around hugging everybody. I was hugging people I didn't even know. It was just the greatest feeling."[3] Senior Jim Cottrill's last game was better than he ever could have imagined. He said, "Even if I never play another game of basketball again, I can't think of a better way to end a career than with a national championship."[4]

Javens, who would collect more than 300 wins in a career at the school while winning an achievement award presented by the Beaver Valley Sports Hall of Fame, knew the special effort it took to get to this point. "The beauty of it was, this was a whole team effort," Javens said. "You don't just win a national championship with seven or eight guys. Everyone contributed something, from the players, to the coaching staff, to the trainer."[5]

It was a complete effort that led to a moment that stands proudly next to the accomplishments of the football legends who grew up in the area; a basketball team who took a victory away from defeat to give Beaver Valley its only collegiate basketball national championship.

CCBC

Player	Fg (3pt)	Ft	Pts
Franklin	13 (1)	0	27
Copeland	3 (1)	0	7
Walker	5 (2)	2	14
Patterson	2	0	4
Davidson	2	0	4
Benson	10 (1)	4	25
Cottrill	0	0	0
Foust	1	0	2
Totals	34 (5)	10	83

Penn Valley

Player	Fg (3pt)	Ft	Pts
Mottesheard	2	0	4
Daniels	0	0	0
Knight	3 (1)	0	7
Ray	4(2)	1	11
Williams	7	0	14
Moore	3	0	6
Turner	5	2	12
Howell	1	0	2
Jones	1	0	2
Johnson	10	1	21
Green	1	0	2
Totals	37 (3)	4	81

Team	1st	2nd	Final
CCBC	42	41	83
Penn Valley	43	38	81

IUP CRIMSON HAWKS 76, ST. CLOUD STATE HUSKIES 70
MARCH 25, 2010
MEN'S DIVISION II NCAA BASKETBALL

The Basketball Haven

For the first decade of the twenty-first century, when you thought of men's collegiate basketball in western Pennsylvania, you thought of the University of Pittsburgh, one of the nation's best programs. Ben Howland had turned around the fortunes of the Panthers program and handed it over to Jamie Dixon, who continued its winning ways. One of Dixon's right-hand men was assistant coach Joe Lombardi, who was responsible for recruiting and brought in some of the important pieces of the 2009 Elite Eight squad, which included Gilbert Brown and Sam Young. Lombardi left the school in 2006 before he had a chance to enjoy the spoils of his work at Pitt, moving 55 miles east of Pittsburgh to become the head coach at the Indiana University of Pennsylvania (IUP) in hopes of mirroring the Panthers' success and turn what has always been a football-first university into a basketball haven.

It wasn't a great situation that the new coach walked into. Only a short time into his tenure, it was announced that the program had been placed on probation for violations committed between 2000 and 2006. The Crimson Hawks were stripped of two scholarships, and the new staff would have their recruiting time away from campus reduced. In basketball, two scholarships can be crucial to the success of a rebuilding team and devastated IUP in Lombardi's first season. The team limped to a 6–21 mark in 2006–07 before improving to 13–15 the next season.

Lombardi's third edition of IUP basketball was drastically different, ending with a 22–8 mark and a spot in the NCAA Division II tournament field. After defeating Virginia Union 69–63 in the first round, IUP lost to Pennsylvania State Athletic Conference (PSAC) foe Kutztown 86–82. With their confidence at a high level going into the 2009–10 campaign, the Crimson Hawks rolled off

9

11 consecutive victories to begin the season before an 88–84 upset at Cheney. They stood at 18–1 when they traveled to Clarion and played their worst game of the season, dropping a 71–62 decision.

Rather than lament about a bad loss to an undermanned team, Lombardi refocused his Crimson Hawks as they won the final seven games of the regular season to enter the PSAC championships with a 25–2 record. After easily defeating Gannon in the quarterfinals, IUP traveled to East Stroudsburg for a semifinal matchup. With the score tied at 63 and only 2:19 remaining, the Crimson Hawks' defense took over, shutting out East Stroudsburg the rest of the way as they hit four foul shots in the 67–63 victory. Their struggles continued in the PSAC finals, falling behind Kutztown 35–33 at the half, but they turned it around in the second half as the Hawks gained revenge for the loss in the NCAA tourney the year before with an 84–73 victory.

The reward for capturing the PSAC tournament was home-court advantage throughout the NCAA Atlantic Regional tournament. To make it through to the Elite Eight in Springfield, Massachusetts, they would have to defeat three schools from the state of West Virginia. After a comeback win against Fairmont State in the first round (a game they were behind by 2 points with 1:29 left in the contest before pulling out a 71–67 victory), they went on to handily defeat West Virginia State and West Liberty to capture the Atlantic Region crown and a spot in Springfield.

In their quarterfinal matchup against Valdosta State, Julian Sanders and Darryl Webb each led IUP with 17 points as five Crimson Hawks scored double digits in a contest that saw them rebound from a poor first half. They trailed by 12 but then outscored Valdosta 54–26 in the second half on their way to an 80–64 victory and a spot in their first Final Four since 2002 against St. Cloud State.

While IUP may have been the favorite, St. Cloud was a formidable foe. The Huskies' Matt Schneck hit a free throw to tie the game at 6 for the underdogs, but right after the free throw the Crimson Hawks' defense took over. Webb hit the next 4 points and grabbed a rebound leading IUP on a 13–0 run, giving them a 19–6 advantage at the midpoint of the first half.

The situation did not improve for the Huskies as IUP continued to pressure them, pulling ahead by 15 when Sanders notched a three-pointer at the 5:42 mark to make the score 30–15. Unfortunately for the Hawks, St. Cloud finally got back into the contest as Schneck connected on four consecutive free throws to bring the Huskies to within seven, 32–25, as the half ended.

After the Huskies made it a one-point contest at 36–35, IUP asserted their dominance. The team once again opened a comfortable lead when Ashton Smith hit a layup with 9:24 left in the contest to make the score 54–42. But

St. Cloud came right back with a 20–8 run as they tied the score at 64 after Brett Putz scored on a layup of his own. With only 3:31 left in the game, the Crimson Hawks' magical season was in jeopardy.

Not wanting it to end, Sanders immediately hit a clutch three-point shot. Then Thomas Young connected on 5 consecutive points for IUP to give the Hawks a 75–70 lead with only 19 seconds left. The defense held firm and Webb made one last free throw to send IUP to their first national championship contest with a 76–70 victory. Unfortunately, the dream ended there with Cal Poly Pomona beating the Hawks 65–53 for the national crown, but it didn't put a damper on the incredible 33–3 campaign. Thanks to the gift from Pitt in head coach Joe Lombardi, IUP could now proudly say it was a basketball school too.

IUP

Player	Fg (3pt)	Ft	Pts
Stewart	4 (3)	0	11
Webb	4	4	12
Young	5	5	15
McClain	5	0	10
Smith	4 (1)	5	14
Sanders	3 (2)	0	8
Renkin	1	2	4
Estrella	1	0	2
Totals	27 (6)	16	76

St. Cloud State

Player	Fg (3pt)	Ft	Pts
Rothstein	1 (1)	0	3
Witt	7 (1)	1	16
Ortmann	2	2	6
Bernstetter	2 (1)	0	5
Schneck	9	11	29
Putz	3 (2)	2	10
Phillips	0	0	0
Bergstraser	0	1	1
Totals	24 (5)	17	70

Team	1st	2nd	Final
IUP	32	44	76
St. Cloud State	25	45	70

DUQUESNE DUKES 57, VILLANOVA WILDCATS 54
MARCH 5, 1977
MEN'S DIVISION I NCAA BASKETBALL

The Last Time

At Duquesne University, the men's basketball players had been the kings on the Bluff since the late 1930s. There had been somewhat of a malaise after their National Invitation Tournament championship in 1955, but as the school entered the 1970s, it looked like there was about to be a resurgence. Head coach Red Manning took the team to two NCAA tournaments in three seasons, advancing to the Sweet Sixteen in 1969.

After Manning retired following a subpar 1973–74 campaign, his assistant, John Cinicola, took over and struggled with two sub-.500 seasons in his first three campaigns. The Dukes were not playing well as they entered the 1977 Eastern Collegiate Basketball League (ECBL) postseason tournament, more popularly known as the Eastern Eight (a precursor to the Atlantic 10). It was the Dukes' first season in a conference after being an independent since their initial campaign in 1913, and while their first postseason conference tournament would end in a memorable fashion, no one could have guessed it would be the last time this program would find its way into an NCAA tournament.

The team's first venture into conference play had been a bumpy one, to say the least. They finished in next-to-last place in the Western Division with a 3–9 mark that included a 64–56 loss to crosstown rival Pitt in the final regular-season contest, giving the Panthers their only conference victory of the season. Duquesne's roster included a great player in Norm Nixon, but Nixon wasn't enough to make this team a winner despite his 22-points-per-game average.

As they limped into the ECBL postseason tournament, they faced the Penn State Nittany Lions, who shared the Western Division championship with West Virginia the first round. While Penn State was the division champion, the West was by far the weaker division and the Nittany Lions ended conference play with a 5–5 mark to go with an 11–14 overall record. The Dukes easily dispatched the Lions 65–55, but they got another break when fourth-seeded Massachusetts upended top-seeded Rutgers 78–74 and became their opponent in the semifinals. While it was an upset, Massachusetts was a formidable foe, finishing with a regular-season record of 19–10.

A member of the school's all-century team, Norm Nixon, shown here shooting in a game against Pitt, led the Dukes to their final NCAA tournament appearance in 1977 with an Eastern Eight tournament championship. Nixon went on to a great NBA career with the Los Angeles Lakers in the 1980s. (Courtesy of Duquesne University Athletics)

It was safe to say that the Minutemen were favorites in the semifinal, but Duquesne was playing their best ball of the year and easily downed Massachusetts 82–65, setting up a championship clash with second-seeded Villanova, with the winner securing a spot in the NCAA tournament.

Despite the fact that they were second in the division, the Wildcats were arguably the best team in the league. Led by legendary coach Rollie Massimino and his top two players—brothers Keith and Larry Herron, who scored 19.8 and 14.7 points per game, respectively—the Wildcats had a 20–8 record that included a 64–62 victory over then eighth-ranked Notre Dame.

With the fact they were considered a better team and that the tournament was in Villanova's home town of Philadelphia, not many fans or experts gave Duquesne much of a chance to pull off what would amount to an incredible upset. Then again, most experts didn't know about 6'5" forward Don Masur and the role he was about to play in helping to turn this disappointing campaign into a special one.

In the first two rounds of the tournament, the Dukes got lucky playing a substandard Western Division champion in Penn State and then avoiding top-seeded Rutgers. They caught another break for the championship game when Villanova's Keith Herron sprained his right ankle in the semifinal victory over the West Virginia Mountaineers. While he would suit up for the championship, he was limited physically and proved to be ineffective in the short time he played.

Herron had been the glue to the Wildcats' tournament run to this point, scoring 45 points in two contests, and his loss certainly hurt Villanova's title ambitions. Before the contest, he stated, "It doesn't feel very good. I'm hoping the shot (to numb the pain) and it being wrapped real tight will do the job."[1]

After Herron tested his ankle in warm-ups, Massimino decided to start Reggie Robinson in his place—telling everyone that Herron wasn't anywhere near 100 percent. Luckily for the Wildcats, promising freshman Rory Sparrow helped lead their attack early on.

Sparrow scored the team's first 6 points, but a surge by Nixon, Don Gambridge, and Masur pulled the Dukes ahead 14–10. The Wildcats battled back, going on a 6-point run to take the lead once again by 2 after Larry Herron netted an 18-foot shot.

The close game was tied at 24–24 with 7 minutes remaining in the first half when Massimino inserted Keith Herron into the contest for the first time. The Cats' leading scorer was not himself and was held scoreless in the first half. But Sparrow and Robinson had combined for 18 points in the first half and the home team scored the final six points of the half to turn a 28–26 Duquesne lead into a 32–28 advantage.

Following the break, the Dukes battled back to tie it at 38 before Villanova appeared to take control, scoring 6 quick points to pull ahead, 44–38. As it looked like Duquesne's Cinderella run was about to end, Nixon led a Duquesne surge with his aggressive defense as Cinicola called for a tight full-court press that the favorites couldn't handle.

The Dukes defense forced turnovers that resulted in fast-break baskets that sent the men from the Bluff up by 3, 47–44, led by Nixon scoring 10 points in the first 9 minutes of the second half. The desperate Massimino once again inserted his injured star to try to jump-start the Wildcats' offense. Herron immediately hit an outside shot to bring Villanova back within one. It was a tightly fought game after that as the two teams battled back and forth in a tension-filled final 5 minutes.

The Dukes eventually crept to a slim 1-point lead and had possession of the ball with 6 seconds left. The Wildcats fouled Masur, who was having one of his best games of the year with 10 points. It was an especially rewarding night for Masur since, just two years earlier, doctors had diagnosed a kidney issue and told him he'd never play basketball again. He fought back and was able to continue his career with the Dukes, so it was remarkable he was in this position as this point. Masur calmly hit both free throws, which gave Duquesne a 57–54 advantage that they would not relinquish.

The win sent the Dukes to the NCAA tournament for the first time since 1971, where they faced the Virginia Military Institute, who went on to finally end Duquesne's surprising season 73–66. The Dukes hoped that this was only the beginning and that they would be a regular in the NCAA tourney over the next few seasons. But more than four decades later, the program is still waiting for that next bid.

Duquesne

Player	Pts
Cotten	4
Masur	12
Gambridge	4
Nixon	27
McClain	8
Hubbard	2
Baldwin	0
Felix	0
Total	57

Villanova

Player	Pts
L Herron	10
Robinson	18
Olive	4
Sparrow	8
Rigsby	6
Rogers	2
K Herron	6
Underman	0
Total	54

Team	1st	2nd	Final
Duquesne	28	29	57
Villanova	32	22	54

#46

DUQUESNE DUKES 12, MONMOUTH HAWKS 10
NOVEMBER 22, 2003
MEN'S DIVISION 1-AA NCAA FOOTBALL

Unfinished Business

Truth be told, in the modern era of Duquesne University football, the 2002 squad is considered the program's undisputed best team.

The team that season was the most dominant football team to play on the Bluff since 1941. The Dukes dominated almost every opponent to take the field against them, with only Dayton (35–28) and Lafayette (23–22) coming within single digits. They outscored their 11 opponents 397–91, including a remarkable 237–17 in their final five regular-season matchups, easily capturing their fourth consecutive Metro Atlantic Athletic Conference (MAAC) championship. One would find few who would dispute the fact that they were the best I-AA non-scholarship squad ever assembled at that point. Their prize was to play the Northeastern Conference (NEC) champion in the Eastern College Athletic Conference Bowl, more commonly known as the ECAC Bowl. The two conferences alternated home sites year to year for the event, and the Dukes would have to travel to Albany, New York, to face the University of Albany, who won the NEC with a 7–4 mark.

The Dukes were confident, even bringing players who hadn't traveled to away games all season so they could celebrate the moment as a team. It was a snowy, bitterly cold day in Albany, which affected the favorites greatly. Bob Healy, who was an offensive lineman on that team, remembered it clearly: "The game was lost on the opening coin toss. I've never been as cold as I was on that November day in Albany. I'm not kidding. Snow up to our ankles. And Albany's stadium back then was wide open, with the wind wreaking havoc on our high-powered offense that featured all-everything Jeremy Conley (WR), Niel Loebig (QB), Mike Hilliard (RB) and others."[1] With a victory, they not only would capture the I-AA non-scholarship national championship but

Bob Healy was an incredible two-sport athlete at Duquesne during the early part of the twenty-first century. The starting right guard for the 2003 national champions Duquesne Dukes football team, Healy was also a terrific track and field athlete, winning three medals at the 2006 Atlantic 10 Track & Field championships. (Courtesy of Duquesne University Athletics)

would most likely be the first non-scholarship school ever invited to the I-AA NCAA tournament.

Albany won the toss and kicked off, taking the savage wind at their back to start the game. They scored the game's first 17 points as the Dukes never recovered in a disastrous 23–0 defeat. The loss not only cost them a shot at the playoffs but the national championship itself, as Dayton, a team they defeated in the season, walked off with the title.

Despite the fact that the Dukes would begin the next year losing some of the better players from that team, they had Loebig and Hilliard returning, and the inspiration to seek retribution for not being awarded the trophy they thought was rightfully theirs. Healy reflected the thoughts of the 2002 squad when he said, "An incredible team, including an incredible senior class, was stunned. Duquesne was shut out for the first time since 1997, and the Sports Network voters gave the Cup and national championship to the 11–1 Pioneer champs, the Dayton Flyers, whom we beat at their place earlier in the season. We were also 11–1. It didn't seem right. It still doesn't."[2]

The 2003 Dukes weren't dominant by any stretch of the imagination, losing three contests, including a 51–10 drubbing at the hands of Penn, but all three losses came against I-AA schools that offered scholarships. They were dominant in the conference and finished the season as MAAC champs again with a 7–3 mark following a thrilling 33–28 victory over rival Robert Morris. Loebig had been terrific, throwing for 3,086 yards and 25 touchdowns, while Hilliard again showed his dominance, rushing for 1,544 years while scoring 15 times.

They faced the NEC champion Monmouth Hawks in the ECAC Bowl, this time at Rooney Field, and while the weather was more conducive to playing a different type of football than the year before, it was nonetheless a tough, closely fought battle.

Duquesne opened the scoring after a bad Hawks snap on a punt was recovered by the Dukes. But they couldn't find their way into the end zone as Francisco Uribe kicked a 34-yard field goal 9:57 into the first period to put the Dukes on top, 3–0. Monmouth's Steve Andriola tied the game at 3 with a 30-yard field goal, and the score would hold up until the half. Then the Hawks went ahead 5 minutes into the third quarter as quarterback Brian Boland completed a 44-yard pass to Tim Hiltwine, which gave the underdogs great field position. Boland finished the job, finding Michael McClelland for a 4-yard scoring strike to give the Hawks a 10–3 lead. Duquesne rebounded with a 31-yard Uribe field goal on the next possession, but as the game entered its final quarter, the Dukes needed a spark on offense that so far had alluded them.

With time running out and the team facing a second consecutive humbling bowl game defeat, the spark they needed came from Loebig. Great players make great plays in clutch moments, and Loebig showed why he was one of the best quarterbacks in the program's history. With 13:27 remaining in the game, he found Michel Warfield for a 60-yard scoring bomb to give the team a 12–10 lead. Uribe missed the crucial extra point, which put the defense in the position of having to hold Monmouth scoreless if they wanted to win the contest.

They were put to the test midway in the fourth when the Hawks' Kevin Hutchinson intercepted a Loebig pass and returned it to the Duquesne 20. The defense stiffened and forced a 40-yard field goal attempt with 4:29 remaining. Luckily for the Dukes, Andriola's kick sailed wide left and the Duquesne offense took over. Needing to run down the clock, Loebig led them on a time-consuming drive, holding the ball until there were only 23 seconds left. Monmouth's slim chance ended when Antoine Bullock sacked Boland to end the game.

The team finally had a chance to celebrate after having endure the horrible memory of the Albany game for 12 months. To have a chance at a national title, they would have to root for Valparaiso to defeat Morehead State (who beat the Dukes 15–10 in the regular season) in the Pioneer League championship game.

In the post–World War II modern era of Duquesne University football, its best player was Leigh Bodden. The all-time leader in career interceptions with 28, Bodden was an All-American in 2002 when the Dukes disappointedly lost the national championship to Dayton. He went on to an eight-year NFL career with Cleveland, Detroit, and New England. (Courtesy of Duquesne University Athletics)

Valparaiso came through, and two days later the retribution for the 2002 squad was complete when Duquesne was named the Division I-AA non-scholarship national champions unanimously by all three polls.

Healy, who was injured for the bowl game, recalled, "Maybe it was karma, but whatever it was, it helped Valparaiso beat Morehead State that day in that year's Pioneer League championship game. We didn't know the result of the Morehead game when Gord brought down the Monmouth quarterback, but we embraced all over Rooney Field in that sack's wake anyway. I told a few players 'I love you' that day. I meant it. Especially the seniors. I heard it back from a few, too. 'Go Valpo' was the other popular chorus. And when we found out later that Valpo had won, we knew we at least had a chance. The Sports Network poll came out on Monday as usual and it was beautiful."[3] It certainly was a beautiful moment as the unfinished business was finally finished.

Team	1	2	3	4	Final
Monmouth	3	0	7	0	10
Duquesne	3	0	3	6	12

Team	Play	Score
Duquesne	Uribe 34-Yard Field Goal	0–3
Monmouth	Andriola 30-Yard Field Goal	3–3
Monmouth	McClelland 4-Yard Pass From Boland (Andriola Kick)	10–3
Duquesne	Uribe 31-Yard Field Goal	10–6
Duquesne	Loebig 60-Yard Pass To Warfield (Kick Failed)	10–12

Rushing—Monmouth

	Att	Yds	Ave	Td
Migliore	26	110	4.2	0
Smith	4	11	2.8	0
James	1	3	3.0	0
Boland	9	-11	-1.2	0

Rushing—Duquesne

	Att	Yds	Ave	Td
Hilliard	25	97	3.9	0
McCullough	2	4	2.0	0
Loebig	3	-9	-3.0	0

Receiving—Monmouth

	Rec	Yds	Ave	Td
Austin	4	39	9.8	0
Lynn	3	32	10.7	0
Hiltwine	2	61	30.5	0
McClelland	2	18	9.0	1
Lutz	1	6	6.0	0
Boland	1	-2	-2.0	

Receiving—Duquesne

	Rec	Yds	Ave	Td
Warfield	6	144	24.0	1
Vulakovich	6	56	9.3	0
Brantley	6	54	9.0	0
Hilliard	4	18	4.5	0
Cooley	1	13	13.0	0

Passing—Monmouth

	Comp	Att	Pct	Yds	Td	Int
Boland	13	25	52.0	154	1	1

Passing—Duquesne

	Comp	Att	Pct	Yds	Td	Int
Loebig	23	41	56.1	285	1	1

#45

ST. VINCENT BEARCATS 7, EMORY & HENRY WASPS 6
JANUARY 2, 1950
MEN'S NCAA FOOTBALL

Tangerine

Outside of the fact that it's a fruit, probably the one thing most think of when they hear the word *tangerine* is the famed song written by Victor Schertzinger and Johnny Mercer and sung by such legends as Frank Sinatra, Dean Martin, and Tony Bennett. To the alumni at a small Catholic college in Latrobe, Pennsylvania, by the name of St. Vincent, the word reminds them of something else entirely: the greatest moment in their school's football history.

While many in the football world know St. Vincent College for its affiliation as the home of the Pittsburgh Steelers summer training camp, the school played football from 1923 until 1962, when it discontinued the program before returning at the NCAA Division III level in 2007. Before resurrecting the program 45 years later, the Bearcats enjoyed only moderate success on the gridiron. They continued to mire in mediocrity until a disciple of Knute Rockne, Gene Edwards, was hired in 1932.

St. Vincent became competitive under Edwards, and in 1936 finally built Bearcat Stadium, an on-campus stadium that the administration felt rivaled any that its competitors played in. With the combination of Edwards and a new facility, the program took off two years later with an 8–1–1 mark. The phenomenal '38 campaign was the beginning of a successful era, with the Bearcats going 20–8–5 before World War II forced the program to shut down for three seasons.

When the war ended, Edwards chose not to return, so the school decided to continue its football program under former St. Vincent legend Baptiste "Bap" Manzini. But, unfortunately, the school returned to its mediocre ways; Manzini finished his two-year tenure at his alma mater at 7–10–1 before deciding to resume his NFL career with the Detroit Lions. At that point, the school

The 1950 St. Vincent College Bearcats were the greatest team ever to grace the Latrobe, Pennsylvania, campus. They finished the season with the only undefeated record in the school's history, 9–0, and with the first postseason bid a Bearcats team would receive. It would be 61 years before they were invited to another postseason contest. (Courtesy of St. Vincent College Athletics)

administration decided to look toward another area Catholic university when they tabbed the former Duquesne Dukes' Al DeLuca to restore the success the school enjoyed before the war.

DeLuca was inventive, installing an offense that combined three of the most successful formations at the time—the Notre Dame Box, the single wing, and the T formation—to develop what he called the Adaptable T. The results of his innovation were immediate, as St. Vincent reversed their record from 3–6 in 1947 to 6–3 in 1948, a mark that included a one-sided 26–0 victory over St. Francis.

With the program on an upward swing, in 1949 captains Frank DiMilio and future Pitt head coach Dave Hart led St. Vincent in a campaign that would be the greatest in school history. The Bearcats began the season outscoring the Indiana State Teachers College (IUP) and Steubenville by a combined 60–0 count, and by the time they hosted West Virginia Wesleyan they stood at 6–0, outscoring their opponents by a 111–0 margin.

The Bearcats rolled out to a 33–0 lead that day until Wesleyan's Charles Shepard did what no one else had or would do in the regular season against the stout St. Vincent defense—score a touchdown. It was the only highlight for the visitors in a 52–6 St. Vincent triumph. They went on to shut out Mount St. Mary's and Westminster to conclude the year 9–0.

With their most successful season in hand, the Bearcats had a chance to do something they never had before in the program's history: pick a postseason contest to play in. They had two choices: the Mountain Bowl against New England College or a newer bowl that eventually would become one of college football's most notable bowl games, the Tangerine Bowl in Orlando, which today is called the Buffalo Wild Wings Citrus Bowl. St. Vincent chose the Tangerine, facing the Emory & Henry College Wasps.

Coach Conley Snidow's Wasps finished the year 10–0 and ran an effective Split-T offense that Snidow hoped would find a way to break through the vaunted Bearcats' defense. DeLuca was confident, though, going into the matchup. "My team is ready to go," he said. "You can't ever tell what's going to happen in a football game, especially against a fine team like Emory and Henry, but my boys should give a good account of themselves. I believe they are in as good trim for this Tangerine game as they have been for any game this season."[1]

The two combatants took the field in a night game, which was unusual for the time, as a record crowd for the contest at that time of 10,000 fans jammed Orlando Stadium, including 1,200 who traveled from western Pennsylvania and Virginia to see their schools play. Most expected a tough battle, and they were not disappointed.

While both squads were effective offensively during the season, it was the defenses that would control this game. Early on, it was apparent that St. Vincent was the better team, as they were dominating statistically, yet the Bearcats had nothing to show for all their hard work as the first quarter ended scoreless. Early in the second, the Bearcats stopped Emory & Henry on their own 17 when the Wasps' Bob Miller came in to punt. He launched the kick to the St. Vincent 42, where Vince Sundry ripped through the coverage, running for 41 yards to the Emory & Henry 17. The Bearcats took the ball to the 1, where the Wasps stopped them on three straight plays.

DeLuca knew he had a great offensive line and gambled by going for it. Fullback Don Henigin rewarded the coach for his faith by bolting over the goal line to give St. Vincent the lead. While it might have seemed insignificant at the time, the extra point would prove to be the biggest of this contest as Jack Heimbeucher converted, making the score 7–0.

The Bearcats and their fans were confident since the defense had only surrendered six points all season. But the Wasps were the best team St. Vincent had played all season and quickly went down the field as quarterback Chick Davis led them on a 64-yard drive. Davis finished the impressive drive with an 8-yard scoring toss to Bob Howard to bring Emory & Henry to within a single point. Bill Pippen missed the extra point wide left but got a second

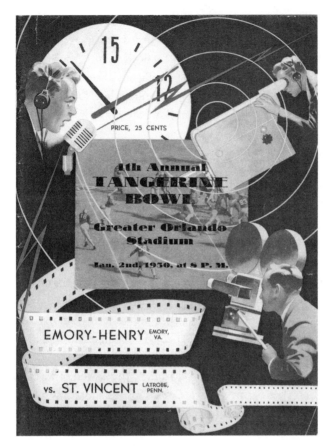

Pictured here is the program to the 1950 Tangerine Bowl in Orlando. St. Vincent College faced off against Emory & Henry. The only scoring was in the second quarter, when a Jack Heimbeucher extra point was the difference in a 7–6 victory. (Courtesy of St. Vincent College Athletics)

chance when the Bearcats were called for jumping offside. The second kick was a carbon copy of the first, going wide left as the two teams ended the exciting half with St. Vincent up, 7–6.

As well as the Bearcats played in the first half, the Wasps played even better in the second, thoroughly dominating play while threatening to score time and time again. Bearcats defensive back Nick Troila intercepted two passes while Emory & Henry tailback Jesse James fumbled as he was about to break the goal line in the fourth quarter with Hart diving on the ball for a touchback. In the end, the Wasps just blew too many chances as the Bearcats hung on to their slim advantage, winning the Tangerine Bowl 7–6 to finish the season 10–0.

Sixty-eight years later, *tangerine* is the most notable word in the St. Vincent athletic department. The trophy for winning the Tangerine Bowl still is displayed there proudly. Recently, following the death of Henigin, the man who scored the lone touchdown, his family returned the game ball he was given after the contest to the school. Henigin's daughter, Dawn Ann, spoke of the ball's importance to her father: "Our dad was presented the ball in the locker room right after the game by the coaches. It was in his bedroom for the rest of his life."[2]

Both daughter and father knew of the importance of that moment on January 2, 1950, which is still the most significant moment in the school's athletic history.

Team	1	2	3	4	Final
Emory & Henry	0	6	0	0	6
St. Vincent	0	7	0	0	7

Team	Play	Score
St. Vincent	Henigin 1-Yd Run (Heimbeucher Kick)	0–7
Emory & Henry	David 8-Yard Pass To Howard (Kick Failed)	6–7

Stat	St. Vincent	Emory & Henry
First Downs	8	21
Rushing	134	192
Passes Comp-Att	4–13	16–27
Passing Yards	34	142
Total Yards	168	334
Punt Average	37.5	33.5

ST. FRANCIS RED FLASH 82, DUQUESNE DUKES 72
JANUARY 8, 1955
MEN'S DIVISION I NCAA BASKETBALL

Maurice!

It's been a long time since the legendary Maurice Stokes dominated the hardwood at St. Francis University in Loretto, Pennsylvania, but so memorable was his time there that you can't walk too far around the campus without being reminded of this incredible Hall of Famer. There is the Stokes Club (an athletic booster club at the school), the Maurice Stokes Athletic Center, and the Stokes Soccerplex. On a national level, the NBA gives an award to the player it feels is the best teammate in the league; the Twyman-Stokes Award is named after the St. Francis star and his teammate with the Cincinnati Royals, Jack Twyman, who helped inspire Stokes to work hard in his rehabilitation following a tragic incident.

The story that Maurice Stokes is most noted for came in his NBA career with Cincinnati. After becoming a legend at St. Francis, where he accumulated 2,282 points and 1,819 rebounds for his career there, Stokes was drafted by the Rochester Royals as the second overall pick. He quickly established himself as a star, scoring 32 points while garnering 20 rebounds and eight assists in his first NBA game before receiving the 1955–56 Rookie of the Year award and being selected to play in the All-Star Game in both 1957 and 1958. In the final game of the 1957–58 season, Stokes crashed to the ground and hit his head in a win against the Minneapolis Lakers. Then three days later, following a playoff loss at Detroit, he collapsed on the trip home. He was sent to the hospital, where he was diagnosed with post-traumatic encephalopathy. Even though he never regained the ability to walk, Stokes, with Twyman by his side, fought valiantly over the next 12 years, often going through five hours of grueling rehab on a given day. Despite the fact it was such a tragic situation, he maintained a tremendous inspirational attitude until his death in 1970. Twyman said, "I never saw him feel sorry for himself. I never, ever in twelve

Shown going up for a basket is Maurice Stokes of St. Francis University. Stokes ended his career as the school's leading scorer (2,282) and rebounder (1,819). In 1955 he not only led the Red Flash to a surprising spot in the NIT final four, garnering the tournaments MVP award in the process, but he led his team to an incredible upset over second-ranked Duquesne earlier in the season. (Courtesy of St. Francis University Athletics)

years saw him have a bad day, never, ever not have a smile on his face; not be more interested in you than he was in himself. He never pitied the situation he was in. And that's the uniqueness of the individual."[1]

Before coming to Loretto in 1951, Maurice Stokes was an outstanding high school basketball player at Westinghouse High School in Pittsburgh. Playing for perhaps the greatest coach in Red Flash history, Dr. William Hughes, the team started a very successful four-year run in which they went 36–12 in the first two seasons. In the following campaign, Stokes helped the Red Flash to their initial postseason appearance in 1953–54, when after a 22–9 campaign they received a bid to the National Invitation Tournament (NIT). It was there that St. Francis defeated BYU in the first round before losing to Duquesne 69–63 in the quarterfinals.

They began the next year with a 4–4 mark that included an embarrassing loss to Mount St. Mary's and then went into a contest against the second-ranked team in the country, their rivals from Duquesne. While they were rivals, the Dukes came into the game at Johnstown's War Memorial Arena beating St. Francis 14 consecutive times, including a 71–58 defeat earlier in the season.

Tragically, Maurice Stokes (*left*) would suffer a career-ending injury after hitting his head on the floor while playing for the Cincinnati Royals. He spent the rest of his life paralyzed but was supported by his friend and teammate Jack Twyman (*right*), who became his legal guardian. After 12 years of being an inspiration and working hard in his rehabilitation, Stokes died in 1970 at age 36 of a heart attack. (Courtesy of St. Francis University Athletics)

While the Red Flash was struggling, Duquesne was playing incredibly well. They were coming off a victory in the prestigious Holiday Tournament at Madison Square Garden in New York, where they defeated the defending national champion LaSalle Explorers in the final. Unfortunately, one of the Dukes' two stars, Dick Ricketts, hurt his ankle against LaSalle and would be playing at a reduced effectiveness.

Stokes, who had come into this contest averaging 32 points and 24 rebounds per game, would show the heavily favored opponents that he was the equal of the two Dukes All-Americans: Ricketts and Sihugo Green.

Close to 5,000 fans jammed the War Memorial for this contest and were treated to an exciting battle during the first 20 minutes. The Red Flash was outstanding at the beginning, racing to a 27–16 lead midway through the first. Despite the fact that he was injured, Ricketts poured in 12 of his 16 first-half points after that to give Duquesne a 32–30 lead. The two teams went back and forth the rest of the half with Hughes, who was coaching his first game of the season after sitting out the previous eight with an ulcer, leading his club into the locker room with a 36–34 advantage.

The second half would shape up to be a marvelous battle between Green, who finished with a game-high 26 points, and Stokes, who was right behind him with 24. The ankle injury neutralized Ricketts, especially in the second half when he was held scoreless and was pulled by Duquesne coach Dudey Moore with 5 minutes left.

Green started off the scoring in the final 20 minutes by tying the contest at 36 before St. Francis rattled off 7 consecutive points to take a 43–36 lead. Green and point guard Mickey Winograd were both in foul trouble and not playing with the same aggressiveness, but Stokes began to take control. The Dukes pulled within 3 midway through the second but never were able to get any closer.

Stokes was remarkable at that point, either scoring or assisting on the next 12 points as the Red Flash stretched their lead to 73–60 with 5 minutes left. Green fouled out soon after, and Winograd joined him a minute later as the Dukes were unable to mount a comeback. St. Francis completed the upset, with Stokes leading the team to an incredible 82–72 upset.

It was a win that inspired St. Francis, as they closed the season with a 16–3 run after the remarkable upset win, and garnered a second NIT bid. The Red Flash made it to the semifinals, as Stokes continued his amazing play, capturing the tournament's MVP award. It was a season that showed St. Francis fans why Stokes is the greatest player the program ever produced, a fact that Duquesne and the nation experienced that evening.

Duquesne

Player	Fg	Ft	Pts
Green	11	4	26
Da. Ricketts	1	1	3
Da. Ricketts	3	10	16
Winograd	2	2	6
Fallon	4	0	8
Severine	2	0	4
Schneider	0	2	2
Lojpersberger	0	0	0
Totals	29	14	72

St. Francis

Player	Fg	Ft	Pts
Stokes	8	8	24
Puschauver	3	12	18
Watro	4	6	14
Wandishin	4	0	6
Milinski	1	0	2
McClellan	5	6	16
Totals	25	32	82

Team	1st	2nd	Final
St. Francis	38	44	82
Duquesne	34	38	72

DUQUESNE DUKES 2, TENNESSEE VOLUNTEERS 0
DECEMBER 23, 1946
MEN'S BASKETBALL

And Justice for All

As the United States entered the post–World War II era, race relations were beginning to progress, but there was still much more that needed to improve. On August 28, 1945, Jackie Robinson took the first step toward breaking the color barrier in professional baseball by signing with the Brooklyn Dodgers' organization. Eight months later, he began his historic journey by playing for the Dodgers' top farm team in Montreal. While Robinson was just finishing his time in Montreal before embarking on his historic career in Brooklyn, freshman Chuck Cooper was helping to integrate college basketball at Duquesne University, when the Dukes were about to host the Tennessee Volunteers in a game that made it seem like no change was taking place at all.

Cooper came from Westinghouse, the same Pittsburgh high school that would later produce the legendary Maurice Stokes. After developing into a star at the school, Cooper decided to attend a college that was famous for recruiting some of the great African American players of the day: West Virginia Wesleyan, where he made an impact before deciding to enroll in the armed forces during the latter stages of World War II. He served a year on the West Coast before returning to resume his basketball career—this time, deciding on Duquesne University, a school closer to home and one of the premier programs in the country. Cooper showed early on that he had the potential to be a force with the Dukes, scoring 17 points in a contest against Miami of Ohio. Two days later, Cooper and the Dukes would face a southern power, the University of Tennessee Volunteers at the McKeesport High School Gymnasium, a facility they were using at the time after selling the bleachers to their own home gym during the war.

The Volunteers were led by head coach John Mauer, who would go down as one of the greatest, if not the greatest, head coach in school history. Orphaned

A true pioneer in basketball as the first African American to be taken in the NBA draft in 1950, Chuck Cooper had a tremendous career at Duquesne. Probably the most memorable moment occurred in his freshman season at the school when Duquesne forfeited a game against Tennessee in 1946 after the Volunteers told Dukes coach Dudey Moore they wouldn't play if Duquesne used an African American player. (Courtesy of Duquesne University Athletics)

by the time he was 13, Mauer eventually attended the University of Illinois, where he roomed with a more celebrated athlete, Red Grange. Mauer may not have been the same caliber of athlete as Grange, but he was nonetheless still good. One of the first to use a one-hand shot, Mauer was named the Big Ten's Scholar Athlete of the Year his senior season.

After his collegiate career, he was named head coach of the University of Kentucky, a position he held until the legendary Adolph Rupp took over. Mauer then moved on to Miami (Ohio), where he had the honor of coaching future Dodgers manager Walt Alston. It was also a school that he struggled at for seven seasons before turning the program around in 1936–37.

Following that campaign, Mauer was hired by Tennessee as not only the head basketball coach but also the baseball coach and an assistant football coach under the great Gen. Robert Neyland. Mauer thrived in Knoxville with a 127–41 mark in seven seasons, capturing two Southeastern Conference (SEC) championships. It was his final season in 1946–47 when he would be the other lead character on this evening in McKeesport.

Over 2,600 fans were jamming into the small gymnasium, not yet aware of the controversy they were about to witness. On hearing that the Dukes had an African American player on their roster, Mauer sent a letter to the school requesting they not play him. Mauer said, "About two weeks ago I heard Duquesne University had a Negro player. I wrote Coach (Chick) Davies but received no answer. We left on a trip last Tuesday and played Long Island in Madison Square Garden last Saturday night, losing 43–32. Now last year Long Island had two Negro players and I informed their coach Clair Bee that we wouldn't play against them. So he agreed before the game not to use them and kept his promise."[1]

Mauer heard nothing from Duquesne, but he assumed they would agree to his wishes. Davies did receive the letter but turned it over to his graduate manager, Jack Davis. After he handed it off, he said, "I guess they (Duquesne) took no action so I had to make the decision just before game time tonight."[2]

Davies tried to compromise, telling Mauer that he wouldn't use the freshman unless he had to, but the Tennessee coach refused that compromise, saying that his players would not take the court with an African American player. Sam Weiss, the chairman of the Duquesne Athletic Council and a graduate of the university who became a US Congressman before being elected as a judge, was not so hospitable. He announced to the fans that Duquesne would not yield to Mauer's demands. As a result, there would be no game this night, and their money would be refunded.

Weiss said that "speaking as a Duquesne Athletic Council official, I insist that no player be barred from this game by reason of race, color, or creed. The principle of this entire matter means more to us than a mere basketball game."[3] Weiss further went on to insist he had responded to Mauer's letter, noting that Duquesne did, in fact, have an African American on the roster but never suggesting they wouldn't use him. While Mauer claimed he never received this letter, Duquesne decided not to give Tennessee its guaranteed money for the contest, claiming the school didn't live up to its contractual agreement.

Not wanting to put Cooper in this situation again, the school decided to cancel its other contest against a Deep South school. Duquesne had scheduled a trip on January 15 to Miami, where they were to participate in the Orange Bowl basketball tournament but decided against it.

The history books show that this December 1946 game was recorded as a victory by Duquesne as a 2–0 forfeit, but it was more than just winning a game. It was a victory for Judge Weiss and Coach Davies, who stood up to the prejudice that was still rampant in America despite the advances the country seemed to be making. On this evening, they insisted on justice for all.

#42

CARNEGIE MELLON TARTANS 24, DAYTON FLYERS 21
NOVEMBER 18, 1978
MEN'S DIVISION III NCAA FOOTBALL

Goliath Goes Down

Western Pennsylvania has had a rich tradition when it comes to college football at the Division II and III levels. Washington and Jefferson, Indiana University of Pennsylvania (IUP), California University of Pennsylvania, and Allegheny College, just to name a few, have enjoyed great success. But in 1978 much of the small college tradition had yet to be written, and the first pages of it were about to be penned by Carnegie Mellon University.

A major college program in the first half of the twentieth century, when, under their former name of Carnegie Tech, the Tartans battled and sometimes defeated the likes of Pitt and Notre Dame. The school deemphasized the program after World War II and hadn't played a postseason game since a loss to top-ranked TCU in the 1938 Sugar Bowl.

After enjoying some success in the 1950s, the program had struggled afterward with only five winning seasons between 1960 and 1975. The school administration looked to West Virginia University before the 1976 campaign and hired a Mountaineers assistant coach by the name of Chuck Klausing with the hope of moving the program in the right direction. Klausing already had success in western Pennsylvania at the high school level, first as a coach for Pitcarn and then at Braddock, where he won five consecutive western Pennsylvania Interscholastic Athletic championships. He then moved on to IUP, where he went 46–11 in four years and earned a berth in the 1968 Boardwalk Bowl against Delaware.

Klausing proved to be a wise selection, as he immediately turned CMU around. The Tartans went 14–2–1 in his first two seasons and won their first Presidents Athletic Conference championship in 1977. The success continued in 1978 as the Tartans went 9–1, losing only to Hiram 10–8 in the third week of the season. They reeled off six consecutive victories to end the campaign, outscoring their opponents 184–81 in the process. The impressive finish garnered their first spot in the NCAA Division III playoffs. While there was an initial excitement in the achievement, it was tapered when they found out their opponent in the quarterfinals was going to be the University of Dayton.

It had only been two seasons since the Flyers had deemphasized their own program, moving down from Division I, but they still had a full staff of coaches, compared to Carnegie Mellon's two, and 12 scholarship players who were recruited at the D-I level. They were faster, bigger, and stronger than the Tartans. The game appeared to have the makings of a mismatch.

Klausing was certainly very concerned about this matchup. When asked what his chances were of beating his opponent, the CMU coach responded, "Mighty tough. They're bigger and faster than us in every way. I feel like David going up against Goliath."[1]

At that time, home field wasn't necessarily given to the higher rated seed, so CMU was given the home game. With a formidable task in front of the team, against what appeared to be a superior opponent, the athletic department did all it could to make sure the stands were full of enthusiastic fans, giving CMU a true home-field advantage. The department convinced the Dole Fruit Company to give the school more than 2,000 bananas to distribute to the fans. The promotion was called "Go Bananas over CMU."[2]

The promotion helped, as more than 4,500 fans showed up to cheer on the Tartans. With bananas in hand, they saw a prepared Tartans team give Dayton all they could handle. The Flyers' defense used everything in their arsenal, including calling out defensive signals loudly to try and prompt the Tartans into false start penalties. An irritated Klausing asked the referees to quiet down the Dayton players. They obliged, and the Tartans' quarterback Bob Kennedy immediately directed the team on a 79-yard, 13-play drive that ended when running back Bob Gasior went into the end zone from a yard out to give CMU a surprising 7–0 lead, one they held onto going into the locker room at the half.

The Flyers tied the game in the third quarter, but then, after being ineffective for most of the contest, Kennedy once more took his offense on another long drive. This one was 70 yards and ended when Gasior again vaulted in from a yard out to put the Tartans up 14–7 with 5:38 left in the game. The fans were beside themselves, throwing quite a few of the bananas on the field. But they quieted down when Dayton quarterback Claude Cheney found Al Laubenthal for a 48-yard touchdown to tie the score again with under 2 minutes remaining. CMU couldn't answer in the final minutes, sending the game into an overtime procedure, one that looked very similar to the system that all of college football would eventually adopt. Instead of the sudden-death scenario that the NFL used, each team received the ball on their opponent's 15-yard line and received one opportunity to outscore the other until a winner was decided.

Dayton got the ball first and quickly scored to take a 21–14 advantage. CMU was unable to move on their first two plays, and it looked like their season was about to come to an end before receiver Bob Samsa pulled in a clutch third-down pass for a first down at the 1. Gasior once again bolted into the end zone to tie the contest. Receiving the ball first for the second overtime period, the Tartans had to settle for a 27-yard Denny Postufka field goal to take a 24–21 lead.

With a touchdown, the Flyers would move on to the semifinals. The smaller CMU defense was tiring, but David had just enough left to sling one last stone toward Goliath. Linebacker (and future Tartans coach) Rich Lackner bolted toward Dayton running back Brian Dorenkott on a handoff and knocked the ball away. CMU's Gregg Gailey pounced on the fumble to end the game as his teammates descended on him to celebrate the unlikely upset.

Klausing was emotional at the end of the contest. He looked toward his players and, while holding back tears, stated, "This is one of the proudest moments of my life. You fellows . . . you . . . you were just great." He told reporters later, "I am emotional, I just don't show it . . . but today . . . this was different. These kids are tremendous in the classroom, in practice, everywhere. And this game . . . this game. . . . If this game had been played in the pros or on a high school level it would have been called one of the greatest games of all time."[3]

Even at the Division III level, it was one of the greatest games this city has ever seen, one in which David boldly took aim at Goliath and took him down.

Team	1	2	3	4	OT	OT	Final
Dayton	0	0	7	7	7	0	21
Carnegie Mellon	0	7	0	7	7	3	24

Team	Play	Score
CMU	Gasior 1-Yard Run (Postufka Kick)	0–7
Dayton	Dorenkoff 3-Yard-Run (Strecker Kick)	7–7
CMU	Gasior 1-Yard Run (Postufka Kick)	7–14
Dayton	Laubenthal 48-Yard Pass From Chaney (Strecker Kick)	14–14
CMU	Gasior 1-Yard Run (Postufka Kick)	14–21
Dayton	Dorenkoff 1-Yard Run (Strecker Kick	21–21
CMU	Postukfa 27-Yard Field Goal	21–24

Rushing—CMU

Player	Att	Yds	Ave	Td
Gasior	26	70	2.7	3
Colosimo	12	44	3.7	0
Kennedy	18	21	1.2	0

Rushing—Dayton

Player	Att	Yds	Ave	Td
Dorenkoff	16	79	4.9	2
Monroe	26	72	2.8	0
Chaney	8	27	3.4	0
Batts	3	28	9.3	0
Pruitt	2	15	7.5	0

Receiving—CMU

Player	Rec	Yds	Ave	Td
Digioia	4	55	13.8	0
Starr	1	16	16.0	0
Samsa	1	9	9.0	0
Colosimo	1	6	6.0	0

Receiving—Dayton

Player	Rec	Yds	Ave	Td
Pruitt	4	61	15.3	0
Labanthal	2	53	26.5	1
White	1	12	12.0	0
Terry	1	10	10.0	0

Passing—CMU

Player	Comp	Att	Pct	Yds	TD	Int
Kennedy	7	11	63.6	86	0	0

Passing—Dayton

Player	Comp	Att	Pct	Yds	Td	Int
Chaney	8	18	44.4	136	1	2

#41

The 16-Year Wait

In the 1970s and 1980s, when college football fans talked about the greatest rivalries in the country, the annual Pitt-Penn State contest was always on the list. Unfortunately, in the late 1990s, the sports administrations at the warring schools could not come to an agreement to continue the rivalry into the twenty-first century.

The fact that the two universities played in different conferences was a factor, but the primary issue was Pitt seeking a long-term contract to continue the annual game, while Penn State never wanted to make more than a two-year commitment. There were rumors that longtime Penn State coach Joe Paterno wanted two home games to Pitt's one as a staple of any agreement, something that Panthers officials wouldn't agree to. Former Pitt coach Walt Harris blamed Paterno for the rivalry ending, claiming that "I don't think there will be any communication on playing (Penn State) as long as one man is running the program."[1]

With no agreement, the last game in the series was played in 2000 with Pitt winning, 12–0. Following the Jerry Sandusky scandal in 2011, Paterno was no longer in charge of the program. Whether this was a factor, the two schools finally would sign a new contract to play in 2012, albeit only a four-year one, but on September 10, 2016, the 16-year wait would end, as the two teams would finally meet again at Pittsburgh's Heinz Field.

Unlike the late 1970s and early 1980s when the two were among the best programs in the country, Pitt and Penn State went into this contest having hit some major roadblocks. The University of Pittsburgh never seemingly recovered after letting Jackie Sherrill go to Texas A&M following the 1981 campaign and was still looking to return to their days as a nationally prominent program. Meanwhile, Penn State University was still suffering from the fallout of the Jerry Sandusky trial, the most horrific college scandal in the history of collegiate sports. While neither program was as strong as in their glory days, area fans were so thirsty for this rivalry to renew that a record crowd for a sporting event in the city of Pittsburgh—69,983—showed up at Heinz Field.

The Panthers were 1–0 after a 28–7 win over Villanova, while the Nittany Lions won 33–13 against Kent State in their opener. As with the two state rivals took the field and the game began to unfold, it looked like the dominance the Lions had over their nearby rivals since Joe Paterno took over in 1966 was going to continue. They pinned the Panthers at the 1 for their first possession after driving into Pitt territory on theirs.

Pitt running back James Conner, who had heroically returned from cancer treatments, bolted up the middle for 24 yards on the second play of the drive, setting an early tone. Inspired, the Panthers continued to march on a drive that was highlighted by a 38-yard run by Quadree Henderson on a jet sweep. Eventually, they completed the 99-yard drive in 10 plays to take a 7–0 lead on a George Aston 1-yard touchdown run. Pitt quickly doubled the advantage following a fumble recovery by Mike Caprara after Ejuan Price sacked Penn State quarterback Trace McSorley at his own 12. Nate Peterman found Henderson from 7 yards out two plays later to make the score 14–0.

Two possessions later, the Nittany Lions' John Reid returned a Ryan Winslow punt 59 yards to the Pitt 15 before Saquon Barkley ran it in from the 3 to cut the lead in half. Pitt responded quickly and took control of the game when Peterman found Scott Orndoff with a 2-yard scoring pass capping a nine-play, 74-yard drive. Soon after, Price caused another turnover deep in Penn State territory, and the Panthers took advantage of it once again as Aston scored his second touchdown of the day to give Pitt a commanding 28–7 lead.

Stunned, the Lions were able to respond and embarked on a long touchdown drive of their own. The teams went to the locker rooms at the half with the Panthers up 28–14 following Barkley's second short scoring run.

Penn State gained confidence on the second play of the second half and whittled the lead to a single touchdown after McSorley found Barkley from 40 yards out. Once again Pitt responded, methodically going down the field, with Conner scoring for the second time from a yard out, restoring their 14-point halftime lead.

Penn State's attempt at a response went awry when Barkley fumbled the ball at the Pitt 35 and Narduzzi's troops had a chance to add onto the lead. But Pitt kicker Chris Blewitt missed a 50-yard field goal attempt and the score stayed at 35–21.

Given new life, the Nittany Lions began finding the soft spots in the Panthers' secondary. McSorley kept finding open receivers to move Penn State down the field, and Barkley scored again to make it 35–28 early in the final quarter. Pitt fans were even more nervous after Conner fumbled on his own 11, leading to a Tyler Davis 38-yard field goal as Penn State crept to within four points.

Just when it appeared Penn State was in control, Henderson returned the ensuing kickoff 84 yards to set up a Conner 1-yard scoring run that gave Pitt a seemingly comfortable 42–31 advantage.

McSorley was not done with his memorable day, once again quickly moving the Lions down the field to set up Barkley's fourth touchdown run. When the young quarterback, who threw for 332 yards on this afternoon, found DaeSean Hamilton for the two-point conversion, the Lions had pulled to within 3 points with 5 minutes left.

Now rattled, Pitt went three-and-out and punted the ball back to Penn State, which would start from their own 29. With the Pitt defense holding strong, the Lions faced a fourth-and-16 at their own 34. With his back to the wall, McSorley found DeAndre Tomkins for a 34-yard gain for a first down at the Panthers' 32. But two plays later, the sophomore quarterback then lofted an ill-advised pass into the end zone, where Panthers defensive back Ryan Lewis pulled it in for the game-clinching interception.

After the game, Conner brought together his offensive line—which helped pave the way for 343 yards rushing—and told the media, "This is a day me and my brothers, everybody on the team, will never forget. We wanted to run downhill and just get into a rhythm. That's what we did today."[2]

There was a celebratory atmosphere at Heinz Field as Pitt won their second consecutive game against the Lions—16 years apart.

Team	1	2	3	4	Final
Penn State	7	7	7	18	39
Pitt	14	14	7	7	42

Team	Play	Score
Pitt	Aston 1-Yd Run (Blewitt Kick)	0–7
Pitt	Henderson 7-Yd Pass From Peterman (Blewitt Kick)	0–14
Penn State	Barkley 3-Yd Run (Davis Kick)	7–14
Pitt	Orndoff 2-Yd Pass From Peterman (Blewitt Kick)	7–21
Pitt	Aston 3-Yd Run (Blewitt Kick)	7–28
Penn State	Barkley 1-Yd Run (Davis Kick)	14–28
Penn State	Barkley 40-Yd Pass From McSorley (Davis Kick)	21–28
Pitt	Conner 1-Yd Run (Blewitt Kick)	21–35
Penn State	Barkley 1-Yd Run (Davis Kick)	28–35
Penn State	Davis 38-Yd Field Goal	31–35
Pitt	Conner 12-Yd Pass From Peterman (Blewitt Kick)	31–42
Penn State	Barkley 2-Yd Run (McSorley To Hamilton For 2-Pts)	39–42

Rushing—Penn State

Player	Att	Yds	Ave	Td
Barkley	20	85	4.3	4
Robinson	1	4	4.0	0
Allen	1	2	2.0	0
McSorley	9	-17	-1.9	0

Rushing—Pitt

Player	Att	Yds	Ave	Td
Conner	22	117	5.3	1
Henderson	4	58	14.5	0
Peterman	8	52	6.5	0
Ollison	9	36	4.0	0
Hall	4	33	8.3	0
Whitehead	1	28	28.0	0
Aston	4	14	3.5	2
Ford	1	6	6.0	0

Receiving—Penn State

Player	Rec	Yds	Ave	Td
Thompkins	3	87	29.0	0
Hamilton	8	82	10.3	0
Gesicki	4	47	11.8	0
Barkley	2	45	22.5	1
Goodwin	4	36	9.0	0
Johnson	1	27	27.0	0
Allen	1	4	4.0	0
Polk	1	4	4.0	0

Receiving—Pitt

Player	Rec	Yds	Ave	Td
Henderson	3	47	15.7	1
Conner	4	29	7.3	1
Orndoff	4	15	3.8	1

Passing—Penn State

Player	Comp	Att	Pct	Yds	Td	Int
McSorely	24	35	68.6	332	1	1

Passing—Pitt

Player	Comp	Att	Pct	Yds	Td	Int
Peterman	11	15	73.3	91	3	1

PITT PANTHERS 90, PROVIDENCE FRIARS 56
JANUARY 25, 1988
MEN'S DIVISION I NCAA BASKETBALL

The Dunk

Most games are included in this book either because they were exciting or because of their historical aspect. Defeating the Providence Friars by 34 points on a cold January evening is neither exciting nor historic. This game is remembered for one play, a single basket that had little impact on the game's outcome, yet it is considered one of the most iconic moments in the history of college basketball: when the Panthers' Jerome Lane ripped down the backboard after a monstrous dunk. It's a moment that 30 years later is still talked about and viewed with the reverence reserved for elite moments in the sport's history.

A 6'1" junior power forward from Akron, Ohio, Lane was a rebounding machine and a physical force under the board for the Panthers. While he went on to be well known in the NBA for his poor free throw skills at Pitt, Lane was a star. (Lane hit on only 37.9 percent of his free throws over the course of his career, making him the rare player who had a higher field goal percentage than free throw percentage.) He averaged a double-double for his career with 13.1 points per game and 10.4 rebounds per game, one of only five players in the program's history to achieve such a feat. He was also the shortest player in almost 30 years to lead the country in rebounding in 1986–87. Perhaps his most notable moment at the school before this evening was his 20-point, 21-rebound performance against Connecticut the previous season. While his overall performance against UConn was much more impressive, it was this night that he would be most remembered for.

Led by Charles Smith, Pitt came into this game as one of the best teams in the country, winning 12 games in a row on their home court at Fitzgerald Field House. They were 13–2 overall on the season, losing only to national powers Georgetown and Oklahoma. Providence was an average squad with an 8–7 mark, 2–3 in the Big East. It was expected to be a one-sided affair, especially since the Panthers were irritated at losing the game before against the Sooners 86–83. But the Pitt-Providence game found its way onto ESPN's Big Monday national broadcast. While the Friars had hung tough in the early going, trailing only 6–5 almost 5 minutes into the game, most in the crowd expected Pitt to quickly take control before too long. Then it happened.

As Providence in-bounded the ball under the Panthers' basket, Pitt's freshman point guard Sean Miller picked off the pass. As a three-on-one break emerged, Miller was looking for the right player to pass to for what should have been an easy basket to give the Panthers a three-point lead. "On a three-on-one," Miller would say later, "I think one of the things you learn as a point guard is you look and you choose your better finisher."[1] The better finisher he chose was Lane.

Lane recalled, "I knew if he gave it to me I was going to dunk it."[2] The aggressive power forward did dunk—so hard that the backboard shattered as the rim ripped away and glass rained down on the court. Teammate Jason Matthews described the moment: "When Jerome broke the backboard, it literally sounded like someone threw a brick through a huge glass window."[3]

The sold-out throng at the Field House rose to their feet cheering. Legendary broadcaster Bill Rafferty added his name to the game with his memorable call. He first just screamed "OHHHHHHHHHHHHH!" before simply shouting the call that most remember, "Send it in, Jerome!" Rafferty recalled his thought process at the time: "When I finished the call, I'm sitting here and I'm going, 'This is incredible.' Over the years, guys have used different ways of describing a dunk and it just made sense to say, 'Send it in, Jerome.'"[4]

The game was delayed 29 minutes as the staff at the Fitzgerald Field House had to replace the shattered backboard. It was those 29 minutes that made this play even more of a phenomenon. The announcers spent the entire time showing one replay after another. Studio host Bob Ley bemused how Lane's play sent a national sports channel's schedule into chaos with the delay. Had the game not been on national TV, it certainly would not have been the iconic national moment it has become.

As far as the game went, Lane and Smith finished with game-high 17 points apiece as Pitt thoroughly dominated their Big East opponent 90–56. The game itself has been long forgotten, but the moment lives on. ESPN named it as one of its 100 greatest sports highlights. On each milestone anniversary it is celebrated in the national media.

It was the prefect storm: a national game, announced by a Hall of Fame broadcaster who made one of the most memorable calls of his long career. Put together, it turned Jerome Lane into a national figure and made this relatively boring game one for the ages.

Providence

Player	FG (3pt)	Ft	Pts
Burton	3	0	6
Shamsid-Deen	1	2	4
S. Wright	6	2	14
Brooks	3(2)	1	9
Lindsay	0	0	0
Murdock	4 (1)	0	9
Screen	2	0	4
Ford	0	0	0
Foster	1	1	3
Watts	1 (1)	0	3
D. Wright	2	0	4
Benham	0	0	0
Totals	23 (4)	6	56

Pittsburgh

Player	Fg (3pt)	Ft	Pts
Gore	6	1	13
Lane	6	5	17
Smith	7	3	17
Matthews	4	4	14
Miller	0	2	2
Bailey	0	0	0
Colombo	1(1)	0	3
Cavanaugh	1	0	2
Porter	2	0	4
Maslek	1	1	3
Rasp	0	0	0
Martin	2	11	15
Totals	30 (3)	27	90

Team	1st	2nd	Final
Providence	28	28	56
Pittsburgh	39	51	90

#39

ROBERT MORRIS COLONIALS 3, MIAMI (OH) REDHAWKS 1
JANUARY 8, 2010
MEN'S DIVISION I NCAA HOCKEY

The Breakthrough

When a young sports program is trying to transform itself into a successful one, it can be a frustrating venture. It seems every light at the end of the tunnel turns out to be just a mirage. Finally, there comes that moment when everything seems to work and an unexpected victory against a major opponent can be the turning point. For one of western Pennsylvania's newest men's Division I programs, the Robert Morris Colonials hockey team, the breakthrough came against the biggest opponent possible—the No. 1 team in the nation—on the biggest possible stage—Mellon Arena, home of the then three-time Stanley Cup champion Pittsburgh Penguins.

Hockey began at Robert Morris in 2004, as the Colonials began playing in the College Hockey America conference (CHA), a league that was considered one of the worst in NCAA Division I hockey. It was a good circuit to start in, but even in the least-respected conference in major college hockey, RMU was at the bottom. Coach Derek Schooley improved the squad little by little until 2007–08, when they reached the .500 plateau with a 15–15–4 mark that included a 10–7–3 record in the CHA. It was a temporary surge, as the Colonials dropped to 10–19–7 in 2008–09.

As they entered their sixth season of varsity hockey, their last in the CHA before beginning play in the more formidable Atlantic Hockey conference, they struggled to a 3–12–3 record near midseason. There would be no relief in sight as they would face the No. 1 team in the nation, the Miami University Redhawks, in the fourth annual Pittsburgh Hockey Showcase contest at Mellon Arena. It was a yearly opportunity for the program to play in an NHL rink. Most years, it was an exciting evening for the school and the players. But in this instance, with the team playing so poorly, there was a genuine fear within the ranks that they'd be embarrassed in front of their biggest crowd of the season. Miami's season was heading in the exact opposite direction, as the Redhawks came into the game with a 13–2–5 record, 10–1–3 in the difficult Central Collegiate Hockey Association (CCHA). This would be the first of a home-and-home series that would shift to Oxford, Ohio, two days later.

As game time was coming close there was the possibility that the contest would not take place at all, when a crane outside the facility had malfunctioned, making the entrance to the arena unsafe. It was removed at 3:00 P.M., a few hours before the contest was to begin. As the game started, 3,654 college hockey fans came in to the arena to watch what appeared to be a mismatch. It was apparent early on that the Redhawks were the dominant team on the ice. They launched seven of the first eight shots and 11 overall at the Colonials' stalwart goalie, Brooks Ostergard, in the first period. Unfortunately for the nation's top-ranked team, Ostergard was having the game of his life, stopping every shot.

With their goalie keeping the game scoreless, Robert Morris finally took advantage as the period was coming to an end. The Redhawks were on the power play with under a minute left to go when the puck caromed to an open spot near center ice. The Colonials' Chris Kushneriuk raced to the puck and broke in on Miami goalie Cody Reichard. Kushneriuk brought the puck from his backhand to forehand, completely fooling Reichard. With the goalie out of position, Kushneriuk easily lifted the puck into the empty net, giving Robert Morris a stunning 1–0 advantage.

Early in the second, the Colonials had an opportunity to add to their lead as Miami's Cameron Schilling was called for high-sticking at the 3:45 mark. Less than a minute later, the Colonials' Furman South was given 2 minutes for interference, and a half a minute after, RMU's Denny Urban went into the box with a hooking call that gave Miami a two-man advantage. With the numbers skewed in their favor, the Redhawks finally got a puck past Ostergard, as Carter Camper scored the tying goal.

In the second period, RMU was outshot 15–13, but with 20 minutes left they were now tied with the heavy favorites as they were hoping for a miracle in the third. The third period seemed to be in the Colonials' defensive end for the most part as the Colonials were outshot 15–4, but games are won with pucks going into the net, not with teams outshooting their opponents.

With a little under 5 minutes gone in the final period, Robert Morris broke in once again on Reichard. Cody Crichton came down on a break with J. C. Velasquez and fed him with a perfect pass. Velasquez put the pass into the top of the opposite side of the net to once again give RMU the lead. Instead of going onto a defensive shell, the Colonials stayed aggressive. Stefan Salituro came in on a breakaway a minute later but was stopped by Reichard. With the goalie unable to secure the rebound, Urban fired another shot on goal, but it was stopped by the Miami netminder once again. The puck popped out to Salituro, who was parked in front of the net, and he stuck a shot behind Reichard to increase the Colonials' margin to two goals.

Irritated at the prospect of being upset, Miami dominated possession the rest of the way, but Ostergard was incredible, turning each shot aside as the Mellon Arena crowd was ecstatic, sounding more like a sellout crowd at a Penguins game than one that filled barely a quarter of the facility. As the final seconds ticked down, the sound multiplied as the fans began to understand what they had just witnessed.

Two nights later, they proved it was no fluke as they once again defeated the Redhawks 2–1. As it turned out the game at Mellon Arena proved to be a breakthrough. They went 7–7–3 the rest of the season and only suffered one losing record since (2018), winning one Atlantic Hockey tournament title as well as two regular-season championships to go along with the first bid ever to the NCAA tournament in 2014. It was a legacy of success that began on an evening in which they showed the nation's best team this was a losing program no more.

Scoring	1st	2nd	3rd	Final
Miami (OH)	0	1	0	1
Robert Morris	1	0	2	3

Shots	1st	2nd	3rd	Final
Miami (OH)	11	15	14	40
Robert Morris	6	13	5	24

Period	Scoring	Time
1	RMU—Kushneriuk	19:39
2	Miami—Camper (Wideman, Wingels)	5:54
3	RMU—Velasquez (Crichton, Chiavetta)	5:02
3	RMU—Salituro (Urban, Lewis)	6:13

Team	Goalie	Saves	Goals
Miami	Reichard	21	3
Robert Morris	Ostergard	39	1

#38

DUQUESNE DUKES 33, MIAMI (FL) HURRICANES 7
JANUARY 1, 1934
MEN'S NCAA FOOTBALL

Bowl Bound, or Something Like It

Football at Duquesne University in the mid-1920s was played in the shadow of the superior programs of their two neighbors: the University of Pittsburgh and Carnegie Tech (now Carnegie Mellon University). To try to compete on a more even level, they hired Elmer Layden, one of the great running backs in college football history, to take over the program in 1927. Six years later, they were closing in on Pitt and Tech as Layden led the Dukes to their first-ever postseason game: the second annual Festival of Palms game, a precursor to the Orange Bowl.

It would be incorrect to say that the Dukes were bowl-bound for the first time. While it seems like the contest should be remembered as a bowl game, the NCAA doesn't recognize the contest as such because the University of Miami (Florida) was guaranteed a spot in the contest regardless of record. But the Hurricanes were a formidable football team, deserving of the bid. Tom McCann took over the program in 1932, turning around the struggling team in only one season. The Hurricanes finished over .500 in McCann's first year, defeating Manhattan 7–0 in the first edition of the Festival of Palms. In 1933 the turnaround was complete. They entered this year's festival with an undefeated 5–0–2. Their opponent from the Steel City was coming off a season of similar success as the Dukes were hoping to use their first postseason bid to publicize their football program as more than just a third wheel next to their other Pittsburgh rivals.

It took Layden only a season to make the Dukes a viable program. After a 4–4–1 finish in his first season, Duquesne went 24–4–1 over the next three before slipping at 3–5–3 in 1931. They rebounded with a 7–2–1 mark a year later, but unfortunately one of their two losses was a 33–0 blowout defeat

Elmer Layden (*right*) is shown being honored by Duquesne University after deciding to return to his alma mater, Notre Dame, as head coach. With the Dukes, Layden was 48–16–6, leading them to their first postseason contest, the Festival of Palms game in 1933, his final game on the Duquesne sideline. (Courtesy of Duquesne University Athletics)

to Pitt. As good as the Dukes were becoming, they seemed light years away from their more nationally renowned neighbors on Forbes Avenue. In 1933 things looked to be changing. They were 8–0 after they once again defeated the Mountaineers before going into their annual contest against the Panthers. While they failed to score, as they always seemingly did against the Panthers, they only allowed a single touchdown, losing their only contest of the season, 7–0. Following the close loss, Duquesne beat Geneva 26–0 to end the season 9–1. Their fan base was excited to hear that they were being considered to play in the Festival of Palms, with the committee also looking at Mercer as the opponent for Miami. A day later it was official as Layden was given the opportunity to prepare his club for one more game for the 1933 campaign.

New Year's Day 1934 was a sun-drenched one in South Florida as 6,000 fans showed up at the Hurricanes' home stadium, Moore Park. After a scoreless first half, which was dominated by both defenses, it looked like the visitors may be in for a tough second half against a difficult opponent. The Dukes would also be at a disadvantage not being used to the Florida sun.

The Dukes had played a much tougher schedule than the Hurricanes in 1933, and it would prepare Duquesne for the second-half battle. The score remained 0–0 until late in the third quarter. After stopping the Miami offense, the Hurricanes punted into Duquesne territory, where Joe Gates, the speedy returner, took it 20 yards into Hurricanes territory at the 42. The men from the Bluff methodically took the ball down the field on the strength of Jim McDonald's passing, eventually getting to the 5-yard line for a first-and-goal situation. After three unsuccessful plays, Ed Zaneski rambled over right tackle to give the Dukes a 6–0 lead as the quarter was coming to an end. The score inspired Duquesne, and they turned this close contest against their undefeated hosts into a rout.

Layden became a gambler, calling for an onside kick after scoring the touchdown, which Duquesne recovered. After taking over at the Miami 40, Toots Fillingham ran for 20 yards on the first play, which helped set up a 5-yard scoring gallop by Zaneski to make it 12–0. The Hurricanes temporarily made it close, recovering a Marin fumble at the Dukes' 34, which led to a score that cut the visitors' lead to five. But Duquesne was not about to let this game slip through their hands. Al DeLuca took the ensuing kickoff 45 yards to the Miami 21 to set up a reverse from Cutrella to Sil Zanielli that became a 7-yard touchdown that made the score 19–7.

At that point, the game was well in hand, with the Dukes looking for the recognition that a rout over an undefeated team would give them. DeLuca would launch a 22-yard touchdown strike to Gerald Baker before Art Strutt put the finishing touches on this big win with a 55-yard toss to DeLuca to make it 33–7.

Having achieved one of the greatest victories in the program's history, Duquesne would receive some difficult news not long after the win: this would be Layden's last game as the Dukes' coach. Following the contest, he was given the chance to go back to his alma mater and lead the famed Notre Dame Fighting Irish.

Despite the fact Layden was now leaving, it was a win that would soon lift the Dukes into the national consciousness when it came to college football. Three years later they would get a bid to a "real" bowl game, beating Mississippi State 12–7 in the 1937 Orange Bowl, which is what the Festival of Palms would be renamed in 1935, recognition that came in a season when they were bowl-bound for the first time, or something like it.

Team	1	2	3	4	Final
Duquesne	0	0	6	27	33
Miami (FL)	0	0	0	7	7

Team	Play	Score
Duquesne	Zaneski 1-Yd Run (Kick Failed)	6–0
Duquesne	Zaneski 5-Yd Run (Kick Failed)	12–0
Miami (FL)	Ott 5-Yd Pass To Reichgott (Petrowski Kick)	12–7
Duquesne	Zanielli 7-Yd Run (Niccolai Kick)	19–7
Duquesne	Deluca 22-Yd Pass To Baker (Niccolai Kick)	26–7
Duquesne	Strutt 55-Yd Pass To Deluca (Niccolai Kick)	33–7

Stat	Duquesne	Miami (FL)
First Downs	15	4
Passes Comp-Att	8–19	7–10
Total Yards	264	68
Punt Average	50.3	42.3
Penalties	12–110	1–5

#37

ROBERT MORRIS COLONIALS 59, KENTUCKY WILDCATS 57
MARCH 19, 2013
MEN'S DIVISION I NCAA BASKETBALL

Our House

By the twenty-first century, the National Invitation Tournament (NIT), which crowned national champions six decades earlier, had been reduced to an event where mid-majors and lower-end power conference teams met to determine who was the 69th best team in the country. It was a tourney that most times was void of excitement. In 2013, when the Kentucky Wildcats were unable to host a first-round NIT contest against Robert Morris Colonials, the game was moved to the RMU campus in Moon Township near the Pittsburgh International Airport. Because one of the most powerful programs in the country was coming to Robert Morris, for the first time in a while the NIT bred a contest that captivated college basketball fans everywhere.

On the surface, this game seemed to be a mismatch. The Kentucky Wildcats were the defending national champions while the Colonials were a good Northeastern Conference (NEC) program whose main goal every year was to win the NEC tournament, affording them an opportunity to play a first-round NCAA tournament matchup where most likely they would lose easily to a much higher seed.

Despite the fact that Kentucky was the defending national champion, they were also a youthful rebuilding team who lost arguably their best player, Nerlens Noel, with a late-season ACL tear. The Wildcats played poorly down the stretch, costing them an opportunity to defend their national title. Instead they were given the consolation prize as the first overall seed in the NIT. Robert Morris, however, finished the campaign by winning the regular-season NEC championship. Unfortunately, a 69–60 loss to Mount St. Mary's on the Colonials' home court in the conference tournament derailed RMU's NCAA tourney hopes. As a regular-season conference champion that did not win their tournament or receive an at-large bid to the NCAA tournament, the Colonials were given an automatic bid to the NIT, albeit only as an eighth seed, the lowest in the bracket.

While it seemed an unfair situation, giving Robert Morris a home game was actually a decision made by Kentucky. The odds of Kentucky playing in this tournament before Noel went down were long indeed. The NCAA had already scheduled games for its own tournament at the Rupp Arena in Lexington, making it unavailable for this matchup. For successful Kentucky head coach John Calipari, the trip to Pittsburgh would be a homecoming. He grew up in Moon Township before playing his college ball at Clarion University. Even though the Wildcats were forced to travel, most expected this to be an easy affair for the defending champions.

But Robert Morris certainly took it seriously. It was an opportunity for a small program that rarely received any attention to shine on national TV. The game was sold out in short order, a rarity, and the school canceled all classes that evening so every student would have the opportunity to enjoy the moment. Normally NIT games weren't in the national limelight, but because of the circumstances—the defending national champions coming to a small western Pennsylvania school—this one was.

Lucky Jones, the Colonials' star player, saw it as an incredible opportunity. "I was shocked," he said. "I didn't think we were going to play them, especially here. I have confidence in my team that we're going to come out and play hard, play strong and play together, and the best man wins."[1] RMU coach Andy Toole added, "We have an incredible opportunity in front of us, maybe the best opportunity any of us has ever had in the world of basketball, and to not prepare ourselves and take advantage of that opportunity would be foolish. You're talking about bringing one of, if not the elite program in college basketball into your home facility. It is something that very few teams have the opportunity to do, ever."[2]

Calipari relished the opportunity to come home to an excited atmosphere and get his young squad focused on an NIT title. "Every game we play is someone's Super Bowl," he said. "Every game we play, when we come to the shootaround, students are lined up for the tickets. We don't play in anything except sold-out arenas. But that's the challenge. The greatest thing to be able to do is going on the road, in a hostile environment, play a team that's going to play their best, because they all play their best against us, and still win. But you've got to fight, you've got to compete, you've got to battle. It's going to be nuts, and I'm excited for it."[3]

It was going to be nuts, indeed, just not the way Calipari envisioned. Toole had spoken confidently about his team's chances since the matchup was announced, claiming many times the Colonials were likened to the famed movie hero Rocky Balboa. Hoping to see life imitate art, a record 3,444 excited fans jammed the 3,056 seat arena, some paying almost $75 outside the facility before the contest.

RMU came out playing better than anyone could have imagined, while the defending national champions were flat. Jones led his team to a 10–0 start before extending it to 14–2, holding the Wildcats without a basket for almost 5 minutes. The avid college basketball fans would certainly expect Kentucky to come roaring back; and though the Wildcats did, they had trouble overcoming the aggressive Robert Morris squad. While senior Jarrod Polson came off the bench for the Wildcats to help them close the Colonials' lead to a single point at the half, 28–27, Robert Morris was not intimidated and bounced back as the second half unfolded.

The Colonials were aggressive and shooting incredibly well, hitting eight of 12 shots in the middle of the second half to turn a close score back into a comfortable advantage, 49–36. They battled back to make this game close. Down 53–42 with only 6:32 remaining, they scored 11 unanswered points to tie it at 53. And when Jones, who scored a team-high 15 points despite only playing 18 minutes due to foul trouble, finally fouled out after a flagrant foul at the 3:41 mark, the Colonials' fairy-tale run appeared to be ending.

Toole had his team inspired as they continued to play tough down the stretch, going back and forth with their favored foes. Kentucky once again tied the contest 57–57 with only seconds left, but Robert Morris never allowed the defending champs to take the lead. While there was a feeling that somehow the Wildcats would find a way to pull this out, they fouled the Colonials' Mike McFadden with 8.7 seconds left and the score tied. McFadden, who had only 6 points in the contest coming into this incredible moment, sank both shots, making Robert Morris a perfect 14-for-14 from the foul line, and giving Robert Morris a 59–57 advantage. Calipari chose to not call a timeout, not wanting the Colonials' defense to set up properly. Kentucky rushed down the floor, and Kyle Wiltjer tossed up a 3-point shot as time expired. The ball bounced off the rim and fell away, sending the record throng into hysterics as the students rushed the floor.

While it was disappointing to miss out on the NCAA tournament, a victory against the defending national champions had a much more satisfying ending. "It's probably the greatest consolation prize you can possibly have," Toole said.[4]

While disappointed with his homecoming, Calipari was gracious in defeat. "This is a shot in the arm for them and they deserve to win the game," he said.

"If we'd have won at the buzzer, it would have been a shame."[5] Instead, the Colonials had the biggest victory in program history.

Kentucky

Player	FG (3pt)	Ft	Pts
Caukey-Stien	4	1	9
Poythress	3	0	6
Goodwin	5	8	18
Harrow	2(1)	0	5
Mays	1(1)	2	5
Hood	1	0	2
Polson	4	2	10
Wiltjer	1	0	2
Totals	21(2)	13	57

Robert Morris

Player	Fg (3pt)	Ft	Pts
L. Jones	4(1)	6	15
McFadden	3	2	8
Johnson	5(2)	2	14
Williams	2(2)	0	6
Myers-Pate	3	0	6
V. Jones	3	2	8
Appolon	0	0	0
Anderson	0	2	2
Bennett	0	0	0
Armstrong	0	0	0
Totals	20(5)	14	59

Team	1st	2nd	Final
Kentucky	27	30	57
Robert Morris	28	31	59

PITT PANTHERS 31, TEXAS A&M AGGIES 28
DECEMBER 30, 1989
MEN'S DIVISION I NCAA FOOTBALL

False Hope

It had been a thrilling day in El Paso, Texas, for the Pitt Panthers. A new coach, Paul Hackett, who had taken over after the controversial firing of successful head coach Mike Gottfried, had just led his squad to an exciting victory over a tough Texas A&M team. There was excitement from all involved in the firing, as they felt vindicated for their decision. Coaches and fans alike were optimistic that the Panthers would return to the days of glory that they enjoyed only seven years earlier. As it turned out, the joy was short-lived, and the John Hancock Bowl victory in 1989 would prove to be a case of false hope for fans and alumni of the program.

As the 1989 football season was unfolding at Pitt, there was real hope that the team's fortunes were about to change. The school had lured Mike Gottfried away from Kansas before the 1986 campaign with the hope of repairing the once nationally renowned program that had fallen into disrepair under Foge Fazio. Gottfried had turned around programs at Murray State and Kansas and looked like he was doing the same at Pitt. Victories over Penn State and Notre Dame in Gottfried's tenure going into 1989 gave hope to the fans that maybe this was the season they would finally be back among the nation's elite.

The Panthers started out with a 5–0–1 mark that included a win over nationally ranked Syracuse at home 30–23 and a dramatic 31–31 tie against West Virginia after the Mountaineers had built a 31–9 advantage in the fourth quarter. As the season went on, the team began to struggle, getting soundly defeated by Notre Dame and Miami before losing to Penn State, 16–13, in the next to last game of the season. They would finish the year by beating Rutgers 46–29 in Dublin, securing a bid to the John Hancock Bowl (formerly the Sun Bowl) against the always strong Texas A&M Aggies. But unbeknownst to Pitt fans, there was discord between Gottfried and his athletic director Ed Bozik as well as the academic community.

The school was set on making the academic requirements much tougher on the athletic program, which Bozik endorsed, making the standards higher than most major programs in the country. The head coach would often find himself at odds with the school and Bozik's new tougher standards. Gottfried felt they were giving his football team a disadvantage compared to other programs. He went to bat against the administration to try to save the eligibility of some of his better players, such as quarterbacks Darnell Dickerson and Gary Clayton, losing on both occasions. Gottfried was an intense man who often would reportedly irritate the players by belittling them, telling them how inferior they were to Notre Dame, Miami, or Penn State, rather than making them proud to be from Pitt.

Following the loss to the Nittany Lions, Gottfried gave a terse speech to the team who had chancellor Wesley Posvar, among others, upset. Gottfried had constantly argued with the administration, and not long before the end of the season he kicked the dean of the College of General Studies, John Bolvin, out of his office, saying he hated him and never wanted to see him again. After the rant following the loss to Penn State, Bozik and Posvar had enough. Once the regular season ended, they decided to end their relationship with a coach who looked like he was on the way to making Pitt a perennial top 25 program. Gottfried was stunned, as was a good deal of the Pitt community.

Offensive coordinator Paul Hackett was installed as the interim coach to prepare the team for the bowl game. He was highly respected as an offensive coach but, as time would tell, would not be a successful Division I head coach. Feeling Hackett was the right man for the job at the time, Posvar wasted little time in announcing that the team had found their permanent head coach; he announced the decision to the team in the locker room before the contest. The squad seemed happy with the choice and came out to the field inspired to take on the Aggies.

Pitt started the scoring when star running back Curvin Richards, who would amass 156 yards in the contest, ended a 63-yard drive with an 8-yard touchdown to give the Panthers an early 7–0 lead. After Texas A&M rebounded, the game stood at 10–10 late in the second quarter. Then freshman Pitt quarterback Alex Van Pelt, who had a phenomenal first season under the tutelage of Hackett—breaking Dan Marino's school record for passing yards in a season with 2,881—hit receiver Orlando Truitt with a 59-yard completion that set up an 8-yard scoring toss to Ronald Redmon. It gave Pitt a 17–10 lead with only 18 seconds left in the half.

The late score seemed to inspire the Panthers, who kept the momentum on the first drive of the second half by going 63 yards in 10 plays. Highlighted by a 32-yard completion to Truitt, the drive ended when Van Pelt bolted over from the 1 to give Pitt what seemed like a comfortable 24–10 lead. But the Aggies quickly fought back. The Texas A&M defense began to slow down what had been an effective Pitt offense, while their own offense began to rip through the Panthers' defense. The Aggies scored three unanswered touchdowns, failing on three straight 2-point conversions, to pull ahead of the Panthers 28–24 with 9:32 left in the game.

Pitt regained possession at their own 16-yard line but moved nowhere and faced a third-and-10 with under 4 minutes left. Van Pelt's third-down pass was tipped, and for a split second it looked like the Panthers would be faced with fourth-and-long. But Pitt tight end Lionel Sykes, who'd dropped a touchdown pass earlier, caught the tipped pass and took it 28 yards to the 44, giving the Panthers a first down and new life. Soon after, Van Pelt found receiver Henry Tuten for a 44-yard touchdown pass that gave Pitt a 31–28 lead with 2:19 left. The Pitt defense finally was able to stop the Aggies' offense as the Panthers hung on for a thrilling 31–28 victory.

After all the turmoil, the players were excited and the administration felt it had the right man to lead the Panthers to a successful program while raising its academic standards. Pitt finished 17th in the final Associated Press poll in 1989, and it appeared there was a bright future ahead. Hackett believed in the school's effort to improve the academic standards, releasing nine starters from the 1989 team before the 1990 campaign started; he just wasn't the right man to lead a winning program. The team failed under Hackett, going only 13–20–1 in two seasons. The John Hancock Bowl victory made Pitt fans believe the winning ways were back, but time would tell them that high academic standards and winning major college football are a combination that do not always mix well together.

Team	1	2	3	4	Final
Pitt	7	10	7	7	31
Texas A&M	7	3	12	6	28

Team	Play	Score
Pitt	Richards 12-Yd Run (Frazier Kick)	7–0
Texas A&M	Pavias 9-Yd Run (Talbot Kick)	7–7
Pitt	Frazier 24-Yd Field Goal	10–7
Texas A&M	Talbot 39-Yd Field Goal	10–10
Pitt	Redmon 8-Yd Pass From Van Pelt (Frazier Kick)	17–10
Pitt	Van Pelt 1-Yd Run (Frazier Kick)	24–10
Texas A&M	McAfee 31-Yd Run (Run Failed)	24–16
Texas A&M	McAfee 1-Yd Run (Pass Failed)	24–22
Texas A&M	Simmons 5-Yd Run (Run Failed)	24–28
Pitt	Tuten 44-Yd Pass From Van Pelt (Frazier Kick)	31–28

Rushing—Pitt

Player	Att	Yds	Ave	Td
Richards	23	156	6.8	1
Walker	8	29	3.6	0
Van Pelt	5	-20	-4.0	1
Redmon	2	1	0.5	0
Lewis	1	8	8.0	0
Bundy	1	2	2.0	0

Rushing—Texas A&M

Player	Att	Yds	Ave	Td
Wilson	16	145	9.0	0
McAfee	15	94	6.2	2
Simmons	9	41	4.5	1
Pavias	3	-1	-0.3	1
Osgood	1	-12	-12.0	0
Payne	1	-15	-15.0	0

Receiving—Pitt

Player	Rec	Yds	Ave	Td
Truitt	4	124	31.0	0
Tuten	4	96	24.0	1
Sykes	3	44	14.7	0
Moore	4	43	10.8	0
Jackson	2	35	17.0	0
Redmon	2	11	5.5	1
Richards	1	1	1.0	0

Receiving—Texas A&M

Player	Rec	Yds	Ave	Td
Waddle	6	105	17.5	0
Patterson	3	24	8.0	0
Jones	2	28	14.0	0
Wilson	2	31	15.5	0
Simmons	1	8	8.0	0
Carter	1	5	5.0	0
McAfee	1	-5	-5.0	0

Passing—Pitt

Player	Comp	Att	Pct	Yds	Td	Int
Van Pelt	20	40	50.0	354	2	1

Passing—Texas A&M

Player	Comp	Att	Pct	Yds	Td	Int
Pavias	10	20	50.0	152	0	2
Osgood	6	12	50.0	44	0	1
Jones	0	1	00.0	0	0	0

#35

One for the Ages

In the lower reaches of southwestern Pennsylvania are Greene County and Washington County, two areas that border each other. That section of western Pennsylvania is also the home of a pair of colleges with NCAA Division III football programs: Waynesburg University and Washington & Jefferson College. For the better part of their histories, W&J has dominated the headlines, including a dramatic 0–0 tie against the heavily favored University of California Bears in the 1922 Rose Bowl. For all the success that Washington & Jefferson has had, there is one moment late in 1966 when the Yellow Jackets did something that the W&J Presidents have never accomplished: captured a football national championship in a tournament.

While Waynesburg currently is an NCAA member, in the 1960s they belonged to the National Association of Intercollegiate Athletics (NAIA), an organization that many smaller schools joined since they had no championship to play in—until the NCAA established the more organized divisional structure that it has today. Even though the NAIA is not as prominent in collegiate sports as the NCAA is today, it has a great history. It began in 1937 with the formation of the first intercollegiate basketball tournament, an event that was put together by a group that included the father of basketball, Dr. James Naismith. Eventually this tournament would be the inspiration for the NCAA tournament. The NAIA was also the first association to invite historically African American colleges into its ranks, as well as the first to offer women's sports. In 1966 some of the best small colleges in the nation played for its national championships, where the football program at Waynesburg had its seminal moment.

As the 1950s were coming to an end, the Yellow Jackets were a struggling football team. Pete Mazzaferro had just taken over as head coach in 1959, winning only one contest over the next two seasons. Finally, in 1961 they had their first breakout season, rebounding from a 0–8–1 campaign in 1960 to finish 6–2. The winning continued throughout the decade, but not to the level that a young coach named Carl DePasqua took them to in his first season six years later.

DePasqua had played his college ball at the University of Pittsburgh before becoming an assistant at his alma mater in 1958 under John Michelosen, coaching the defensive backs until Michelosen was relieved of his job in 1965. DePasqua would not be out of work for long. Waynesburg was looking for someone to replace Mike "Mo" Scarry, who had left the university following the 1965 campaign to take a job as defensive line coach with the Washington Redskins.

DePasqua inherited a team with few weaknesses. They had an incredible defense that finished 1965, allowing only 47 points in nine contests, while his offense would be headed by All-American running back Rich Dahar. The team dominated their first six opponents, outscoring them 199–21, including wins over perennial western Pennsylvania powers Slippery Rock, 31–0, and the California University of Pennsylvania Vulcans, 20–7. Waynesburg struggled in their final three regular-season games, defeating West Virginia Wesleyan, Findlay, and Westminster by a combined eight points. Despite their issues at the end of the season, the Yellow Jackets were undefeated and received a bid to the NAIA national championship playoffs.

In 1966, only four teams received bids. Waynesburg was ranked sixth in the nation but received the bid when top-ranked Northwest Louisiana and Clarion turned down the ones they received. According to officials at Clarion, who had just won the Pennsylvania State Athletic Conference title against West Chester, they turned it down because the team would have to travel to New Mexico only five days later to play New Mexico Highlands. According to DePasqua, though, neither team wanted to face the powerful Wisconsin-Whitewater Warhawks in the final, should they make it that far. While they may not have been the first choice for the fourth bid, the Yellow Jackets were determined to make the most of it.

After slipping by New Mexico Highlands 30–27 in the national semifinal, the Yellow Jackets faced favored Wisconsin-Whitewater—who had thrashed Central (Iowa) 41–18 in the semifinals—for the national championship in Tulsa, which the NAIA called the Champions Bowl. Whitewater was ranked second and was considered the heavy favorite. Warhawk quarterback Bob Berezowitz was one of the best small college quarterbacks in the country and became the focus of DePasqua's defensive strategies. DePasqua was right to be concerned, as Berezowitz tossed two touchdown passes in the first half, both to Dennis Williamson. But the Waynesburg offense was playing well, scoring twice, including the second touchdown on a 1-yard run by quarterback Don Paull to take a temporary 13–7 lead. After Williamson's second scoring catch put the Warhawks back on top 14–13, the Jackets took over.

Late in the second quarter, receiver Dan Dvorchak caught a 15-yard touchdown pass that was followed by a Dahar 3-yard scoring run early in the third that gave the Yellow Jackets a surprising 26–14 advantage. Wisconsin-Whitewater closed to within 5 points following a 51-yard touchdown bomb to running back Jim Knoblauch, but the Waynesburg defense would stiffen and hold the potent Warhawks' offense scoreless the rest of the way. A rout was on—just not the way the experts had predicted.

Dahar, who set an NAIA Champion Bowl record with 233 yards on 41 carries, scored two more times—sandwiched in between a safety—to round out the scoring and give Waynesburg a surprising 42–21 victory in front of 6,070 fans to win the national championship. DePasqua was beside himself, amazed at what his young squad had achieved despite the odds. "They wanted to be the number one team," he said. "The kids did a magnificent job. It was magnificent ball control. It was a typical Waynesburg performance for a team that has to be considered a Cinderella team."[1]

It was a dramatic victory but turned out to be the only championship Waynesburg ever won. As a result, this team is celebrated by Waynesburg football fans, and the story is constantly retold about their win for the ages—one that college football fans in Greene and Washington Counties hold on to dearly as their shining moment in the collegiate football sun.

Team	1	2	3	4	Final
Waynesburg	13	7	6	16	42
Wisc-Whitewater	7	7	7	0	21

Team	Play	Score
Way	Ripepi 1-Yd Run (Kick Failed)	6–0
Wisc-Wh	Williamson 20-Yd Pass From Berezowitz (Hansen Kick)	6–7
Way	Paull 1-Yd Run (Falcone Kick)	13–7
Wisc-Wh	Williamson 20-Yd Pass From Berezowitz (Hansen Kick)	13–14
Way	Dvorchak 15-Yd Pass From Dahar (Falcone Kick)	20–14
Way	Dahar 3-Yd Run (Kick Failed)	26–14
Wisc-Wh	Knoblauch 51-Yd Pass From Berezowitz (Hansen Kick)	26–21
Way	Dahar 5-Yd Run (Falcone Kick)	33–21
Way	Safety, Williams Tackled In The End zone	35–21
Way	Dahar 2-Yd Run (Falcone Kick)	42–21

Stat	Waynesburg	Wisconsin-Whitewater
First Downs	22	9
Rushing Yards	349	-39
Passing Yards	68	225
Passing Comp-Att-Int	4–5–0	14–31–2
Punts No-Ave	5–36	6–37
Fumbles Lost	1	0
Penalty Yards	5	17

PITT PANTHERS 74, CONNECTICUT HUSKIES 56
MARCH 15, 2003
MEN'S DIVISION I NCAA BASKETBALL

On Top of the Big East Mountain

As the twenty-first century began, so did a basketball renaissance at the University of Pittsburgh, led by head coach Ben Howland and later his protégé, Jamie Dixon. Starting in 2001 when the Panthers surprised many by reaching the Big East final, the team would reach seven Big East tournament championships in eight years. But for all their consistency, only twice did they manage to capture the conference title. It was 2003, though, that was the highlight for the program during their amazing run in what was arguably the toughest conference in the country, the year when they were finally on top of the Big East mountain for the first time.

The program had suffered under the watch of Howland's predecessor, Ralph Willard, enduring four losing seasons in Willard's five-year tenure. When Willard was dismissed, the athletic department turned to the Lebanon, Oregon, native to revive the program's fortunes. Howland learned the defensive philosophy he would be known for in his coaching career as a player at Weber State, where he twice was named the team's defensive MVP.

He began his head coaching career at Northern Arizona, where, after two tough seasons, he turned the Lumberjacks around. He was named the Big Sky Coach of the Year in 1997, helping the team improve from seven to 21 wins in the space of one season. The next year, Northern Arizona won the conference tournament and a spot in the NCAA tournament. Following three consecutive 20-win seasons, Pitt athletic director Steve Pederson decided Howland was the man to rebuild his program and hired him before the 1999–2000 campaign.

In his first season at Pitt, the team showed little progress, but improvement was evident in his second campaign although they did suffer a late-season slide. The team found their confidence in the Big East tournament, collecting shocking victories over Miami (Florida), Notre Dame, and Syracuse before falling to Boston College in the first Big East tournament championship appearance in the history of Pitt basketball.

The 2001–02 Panthers showed that the tournament success of the year before was not a fluke, as they captured the regular-season West Division championship but only to lose once again in the tournament final, this time to Connecticut. But they secured their first NCAA bid under Howland and made it to the Sweet Sixteen before an upset loss to Kent State ended their phenomenal 29–6 breakout season. Howland was named the National Coach of the Year. The 2002–03 season would see the team try to improve on their success as they began playing in their new state-of-the-art facility.

For 51 years, the Fitzgerald Field House had been the home of the University of Pittsburgh basketball program. What it lacked in size it made up for in intimidating atmosphere. When it was full, there were few facilities in college basketball that could match its volume. Pitt Stadium was demolished following the 1999 football season to clear room for a 12,508-seat arena named after its main benefactors, John and Gertrude Peterson, who donated $10 million toward the project, giving the school a much-needed increase in revenue over its previous home facility.

The Panthers opened their new arena with an impressive 82–67 victory over crosstown rival Duquesne and kept their momentum going, finishing the regular season at 23–4—good enough to tie for the Big East West Division title for the second consecutive year. They were ranked fifth in the nation in the final Associated Press poll going into the conference tournament. After dominant victories over Providence and Boston College, Pitt earned a third-consecutive shot at the Big East tournament title against a team than not only defeated them the year before but had won the prestigious title five times: the University of Connecticut Huskies.

The Huskies had finished the season tied for the championship of the East Division and came in with a confidence that only the defending champions would have. But the Panthers had one of the great leaders in college basketball, a point guard who had been a major factor in the program's incredible turnaround: Brandin Knight. If ever there was a player who could get them over the hump, most figured it would be Knight.

Coach Jim Calhoun's UConn club had a reputation for having incredible mental toughness and a physicality that could wear you down by game's end, especially when it came to the postseason; on this day, they would meet their match. Pitt had developed one of the most physical defenses in the country. While UConn kept fighting, Pitt's defense was doing enough, especially against Huskies star Ben Gordon, and held a 36–35 advantage at the half.

Despite trailing, UConn had one big advantage. Knight had hurt his ankle against Boston College in the semifinal, and even though he had played well in the beginning of the game, he winced in pain 9 minutes into the contest and went to the Panthers' bench. Pitt trainer Tony Salesi taped the ankle well enough that the star guard could go back into the game.

Howland saw Pitt's slim lead evaporate when the Huskies tied the score at 40 after Denham Brown hit a jumper while being fouled by Carl Krauser, then completing the 3-point play with a free throw. Pitt once again vaulted into the lead as Jaron Brown and Julius Page scored quickly. Pitt continued to push hard, moving the advantage to 8, 52–44, after Krauser knocked down two free throws.

Connecticut wouldn't quit and battled back to within 4 points following a Marcus White free throw with 5:58 left on a play in which Pitt's Ontario Lett fouled out of the game. While Lett was a physical presence that was hard to replace, the Panthers' defense still began to wear down their opponents without him. The defense made it difficult on the defending champion Huskies for most of the game, forcing them to rely on one-on-one plays because the Panthers were disrupting their offensive flow so effectively.

Howland's stout defense held UConn to only 5 points in the final 6 minutes, while the Panthers scored 19. Calhoun had no options that were working. Even Gordon struggled, as he was limited to only 13 points by Page, who was named the tournament's MVP. Brown led the attack with 19 points while Page and Knight had 16 apiece.

With only 20 seconds remaining, the Panthers were running out the clock, and with the outcome decided, the Huskies had backed off defensively. With the shot clock about to expire, Brown launched a three-pointer instead of just handing the ball back to UConn, which is generally what the winning team does when the game is out of hand. The ball went through the hoop for the game's final basket, which irritated Calhoun. "I think when everyone backs off each other, you let the shot clock run out, that's kind of the unwritten rule," he said. "Ben Gordon did that once and I pulled him out and reprimanded him and went to the other team's locker room to apologize."[1]

It seemed like a backhanded shot at Howland for not doing what Calhoun thought he should in the situation, but it was obviously a frustrating moment for the legendary coach who saw his team thoroughly dominated by a Pitt team who was finally on top of the Big East mountain.

Pittsburgh

Player	FG (3pt)	Ft	Pts
Brown	6(1)	6	19
Zavackas	1	3	5
Lett	2	0	4
Knight	4(3)	5	16
Page	7(2)	0	16
Troutman	5	2	12
Krauser	0	2	2
Morris	0	0	0
Totals	25(6)	18	74

Connecticut

Player	Fg (3pt)	Ft	Pts
Anderson	0	0	0
Armstrong	1	0	2
Okafor	4	0	8
T. Brown	6	3	15
Gordon	5(2)	1	13
D. Brown	3(1)	1	8
Robertson	3(1)	0	7
White	1	1	3
Hayes	0	0	0
Wise	0	0	0
Totals	23(4)	6	56

Team	1st	2nd	Final
Pittsburgh	36	38	74
Connecticut	35	21	56

#33

PITT PANTHERS 31, WEST VIRGINIA MOUNTAINEERS 31
SEPTEMBER 30, 1989
MEN'S DIVISION I NCAA FOOTBALL

Never Too Late

There may be no more intense rivalry in college football than the Backyard Brawl between the University of Pittsburgh and West Virginia University. Fans from Pitt have a special distaste reserved for Mountaineers fans, while in West Virginia you don't hear the word "Pitt" unless "Eat Shit" is placed right in front of it. There may be no worse feeling for a winning home team than when the visiting team figures out it's never too late to mount a comeback. The 1989 Pitt-West Virginia game may go down in the annals of this legendary rivalry as a tie, but all who saw this classic contest knew that it was a high point for Panthers fans and a huge disappointment for their WVU counterparts.

The Backyard Brawl—a term that both schools jointly have trademarked—began on October 25, 1895, as WVU defeated the Western University of Pennsylvania (the original name of the University of Pittsburgh), 8–0, to begin what is the 14th oldest collegiate football rivalry in the country. Through the years, except for a period between 1924 and 1951 when the Panthers won 23 of 25 meetings, it's been a back-and-forth series with Pitt leading 61–40–3. There were many memorable battles in this classic, perhaps none more so than the 1989 tussle at Mountaineer Field in Morgantown.

The late 1980s were a time when the programs were going in different directions. Starting in 1973, when Johnny Majors came to Pitt from Iowa State, the Panthers were extremely successful, eventually winning the national championship in 1976 and becoming one of the more powerful programs in the nation. With Majors returning to coach his alma mater at Tennessee and Jackie Sherrill leaving after the 1981 campaign, Pitt had slipped. While they were enjoying a bit of a renaissance under Mike Gottfried in 1989, they were still not at the same level as West Virginia.

Hired in 1980 following a nine-year run at Bowling Green, head coach Don Nehlen quickly turned around the West Virginia program, leading it to three consecutive nine-win seasons between 1981 and 1983. WVU had fallen off a bit in 1986 and 1987, going 4–7 and 6–6, respectively, but it would be a quick rebuilding process. The Mountaineers stunned the college football world in 1988, completing an 11–0 regular season that earned them a trip to the Fiesta Bowl to face the Notre Dame Fighting Irish for the national championship. They would lose that game decisively, 34–21, but still managed to finish fifth in the final Associated Press and United Press International polls.

Despite the disappointing ending to an otherwise perfect season, the Mountaineers had established themselves as one of the best programs in the nation. After three decisive wins against Ball State, South Carolina, and Louisville and then a close 14–10 victory over their rivals at Maryland, they stood 4–0 and looked like they would have another opportunity to win the school's first football national championship. With the way the Mountaineers played against the Panthers on this evening through the better part of three quarters, it looked like the lofty expectations were reasonable.

Pitt had also been impressive early in the season, defeating Pacific and Boston College handily before upsetting nationally ranked Syracuse at home in front of a national TV audience to remain undefeated. The Panthers found an exceptional quarterback in freshman Alex Van Pelt, but in this contest, only 21 miles from his hometown of Grafton, West Virginia, he was having his worst game of the season, completing only five of 18 passes in the first half with two interceptions.

The Panthers' secondary would be rattled for most of the game, as Pittsburgh native and WVU quarterback Major Harris hit the speedy James Jett for a 41-yard score to give the Mountaineers a 7–0 lead. Pitt cut the margin to one with a Curvin Richards 8-yard scoring run, but two Harris touchdown passes to Reggie Rembert, sandwiched between an Ed Frazier field goal, would turn a close game into a potential rout by the end of the first half. On the first touchdown, Rembert took a short pass in the flat, then faked Panthers defensive back Steve Israel, and ran 38 yards into the end zone to put WVU up, 14–6. With 21 seconds left in the half and Pitt expecting the Mountaineers to run out the clock, Harris tossed a long pass to Rembert that set up a 4-yard scoring toss and a 21–9 halftime lead. After a fourth Harris scoring toss, this one a 4-yard toss to Rico Tyler, and a West Virginia field goal, the score stood at 31–9 as the third quarter came to an end.

It appeared to be one of the most embarrassing moments for the Panthers in the long rivalry, but right as it appeared to be over, Pitt's freshman quarterback rose to the occasion. Starting at his own 20, Van Pelt drove the Panthers downfield, highlighted by 20-and 13-yard passes to Henry Tuten before running back Adam Walker took it in from 2 yards out to make it 31–15 with 9:20 left in the game. Five minutes later, it was a 10-point game following a 9-yard scoring toss to Tuten and another missed 2-point opportunity.

Momentum was now clearly on Pitt's side, as the Panthers' defense was frustrating Harris and the WVU offense. After taking over once again with good field position, Van Pelt found Olanda Truitt for 23 yards and then Ronald Redmon for 21 more, pushing Pitt to the Mountaineers' 6 with a little over 3 minutes left. Richards would bolt in for another score that closed the seemingly insurmountable West Virginia lead to 31–28.

WVU regained possession with 2:55 left and once again moved the ball downfield. Pitt's comeback attempt appeared to be done with no timeouts left and Harris completing a first-down pass to Aaron Evans on a third-and-11 play deep in Pitt territory. Just as the 68,939 fans were about to celebrate the narrow victory, they saw a penalty flag on the field; the Mountaineers were called for an ineligible receiver downfield. Harris threw an incompletion on the next play with the Panthers taking over at their own 40 with 49 seconds remaining.

Van Pelt had rebounded from a first-half disappointment to throwing for 366 yards, the third-most total in school history at the time. Once again, he calmly took Pitt down the field, hitting Tuten for 25 yards to highlight the drive. The Panthers reached the WVU 25 with time for only one more play. Knowing the odds for a touchdown were long, Gottfried chose to go for a game-tying field goal. He sent his 19-year-old redshirt freshman kicker into the game to try to cap this unbelievable turnaround with a 42-yard field goal. Ed Frazier had a calmness about him not usually seen in such a young player and easily sent the ball through the uprights as time expired. The field goal devastated the home crowd as it gave Pitt a tie that felt like a win.

The enthusiastic kicker was thrilled. "We have to consider this a victory," Frazier said. "The way we came back in this game has taken my feet right off the ground."[1] In the other locker room, the Mountaineers were devastated. Nehlen was abrupt in the postgame press conference, answering only three questions and then ending it after being asked how the WVU players felt. He responded tersely, "They're not jumping up and down, swinging from the rafters if that's what you mean."[2]

Frazier was correct—though it wasn't a loss for either team, it certainly seemed like a win for the Panthers, who showed the college football world that's it's never too late for a comeback.

Team	1	2	3	4	Final
Pittsburgh	6	3	0	22	31
West Virginia	7	14	10	0	31

Team	Play	Score
WVU	Jett 41-Yd Pass From Harris (Carroll Kick)	0–7
Pitt	Richards 8-Yd Run (Kick Failed)	6–7
WVU	Rembert 38-Yd Pass From Harris (Carroll Kick)	6–14
WVU	Rembert 4-Yd Pass From Harris (Carroll Kick)	6–21
WVU	Carroll 20-Yd Field Goal	6–24
WVU	Tyler 4-Yd Pass From Harris (Carroll Kick)	6–31
Pitt	Walker 2-Yd Run (Pass Failed)	15–31
Pitt	Tuten 9-Yd Pass From Van Pelt (Pass Failed)	21–31
Pitt	Richards 6-Yd Run (Frazier Kick)	28–31
Pitt	Frazier 42-Yd Field Goal	31–31

Rushing—Pitt

Player	Att	Yds	Ave	Td
Richards	20	128	6.4	2
Redmon	13	36	2.8	0
Walker	5	7	1.4	1

Rushing—WVU

Player	Att	Yds	Ave	Td
Napoleon	11	60	5.5	0
Harris	10	28	2.8	0
Ford	9	24	2.7	0

Receiving—Pitt

Player	Rec	Yds	Ave	Td
Tuten	7	142	20.3	1
Redmon	6	74	12.3	0
Seaman	3	39	13.0	0
Jackson	2	33	16.5	0
Williams	2	30	15.0	0

Receiving—WVU

Player	Rec	Yds	Ave	Td
Rembert	5	145	29.0	2
Tyler	3	11	3.7	1
Jett	2	81	40.5	1
Dykes	1	16	16.0	0

Passing—Pitt

Player	Comp	Att	Pct	Yds	Td	Int
Van Pelt	26	50	52.0	366	1	4

Passing—WVU

Player	Comp	Att	Pct	Yds	Td	Int
Harris	12	23	52.1	250	4	1
Ford	0	1	00.0	0	0	0

#32

ALLEGHENY GATORS 21, LYCOMING WARRIORS 14
DECEMBER 8, 1990
MEN'S DIVISION III NCAA FOOTBALL

The Last of Its Kind

They were just two small colleges, Allegheny and Lycoming, as they met for the NCAA Division III national football championship in Bradenton, Florida. The victory by Allegheny College, known more for academics than athletics, caught the imagination of the sports public, even inspiring an article in *Sports Illustrated* the following week that raved of this tiny school's impending national championship. Located in Meadville, a town on Route 79 between Pittsburgh and Erie, Allegheny was best known to this point for being the 32nd oldest college in the country and for counting President William McKinley, Clarence Darrow, US Senator Thomas Tipton from Nebraska, and famed journalist Ida Tarbell as its most famous alumni. Perhaps the most amazing thing about the win is that in a football-rich area like western Pennsylvania, no team at any level of college football has since won another national championship in a tournament. Allegheny's 21–14 victory that afternoon turned out to be the last of its kind for the area.

Lycoming, a small liberal arts institution with 1,272 undergraduates, is located in Williamsport, Pennsylvania, a town better known for its history in Little League baseball than its liberal arts college. About 210 miles to the west is another liberal arts college, Allegheny College, a school somewhat larger than Lycoming at 1,931 students.

The Allegheny Gators had some previous success, winning the North Coast Athletic Conference (NCAC) twice in 1987 and 1988 under coach Peter Vaas, but all they had to show for the two titles was a first-round NCAA overtime loss to Washington & Jefferson, 23–17. Voss would leave at the end of the 1989 campaign, giving way to 37-year-old coach Ken O'Keefe. O'Keefe understood that developing football players was not as important as it might be in a big-time

Pictured here is the winning touchdown in the 1990 NCAA Division III national championship game as Kurt Reiser snags a pass from Jeff Filkovski to win the title for Allegheny College in a 21–14 victory over Lycoming. (Courtesy of Allegheny College Athletics)

Division I conference, but finding ways to have them reach their potential on
the field and win contests was still the ultimate goal.

The team started out his initial campaign with a tough 30–30 tie against
Juniata before winning their next nine games, including a 51–0 thrashing of
Duquesne University, to capture their third NCAC crown. After finishing
undefeated, the Gators were given a bid to the NCAA Division III playoffs
and a first-round matchup against Mount Union College.

While Mount Union eventually would become one of the great dynasties in
college football, winning 13 national championships between 1993 and 2017,
they were just at the beginning of their budding dynasty, and the Gators triumphed, 26–15. Allegheny went on to beat the defending national champions,
the Dayton Flyers, 31–23, before handing Central (Iowa) a 24–7 loss in the
national semifinal, securing their first bid to the Amos Alonzo Stagg Bowl to
play for the national title.

Lycoming was undefeated also but not a favorite to move on to the national
championship. They defeated two formidable western Pennsylvania foes in the
playoffs, beating Carnegie Mellon 17–7 in the first round and then a shutout
win over Washington & Jefferson in the second, putting Lycoming into the

semifinals. There, the Warriors defeated Hofstra, 20–10, to set up the championship showdown.

O'Keefe told his players that if they played aggressively for four quarters, they could win the game. But Lycoming dominated play in the first 30 minutes, holding the potent Gators' rushing attack to only 39 yards on 22 attempts in the first half to forge a 14–0 lead. O'Keefe and his players were irritated with their performance and decided they wouldn't repeat it in the second half. O'Keefe told them, "Be more aggressive this second half than you've ever been. Heck, be more aggressive than you have ever thought of being."[1]

Finding running lanes that hadn't been there in the first half, Allegheny started putting together longer drives. The first scoring drive was in the third quarter when the Gators moved 72 yards on 16 plays. The drive appeared stalled when Allegheny faced third-and-15 on their own 47. Quarterback Jeff Filkovski tossed a shovel pass to running back Jerry O'Brien, who sprinted toward left end for a nice gain but came up 1 yard short of a first down. The Gators converted on fourth down to keep the drive going, eventually culminating in Filkovski's ramble up the middle for an 11-yard touchdown run to cut the Warriors' lead in half.

As the game was winding down, Allegheny found themselves at their own 27, needing a long drive against the stout Warriors' defense to tie the contest. The Gators once again began moving through the Lycoming defense but then faced another third-and-long at the Lycoming 25. With 9 yards to go for the first down, Filkovski couldn't find an open receiver but saw open space in the middle of the field, so he took off scrambling for 17 yards and a first down at the 8. Three plays later he hit Julio Lecayo for the game-tying touchdown with 1:38 left.

The Gators' defense held firm the remainder of regulation, sending the game into overtime tied at 14. Overtime in 1990 was a rarity reserved for tournament play in the NCAA; it relied on a system that is currently used at all levels of NCAA play today: each team gets the ball at the opponents' 25 on alternate possessions until there is a winner. Allegheny got the ball first and quickly scored as Filkovski hit tight end Kurt Reiser with a 15-yard touchdown pass to make the score 21–14. Lycoming's offense had been stifled during the second half and did no better in the overtime period. When Allegheny's Tony Bifulco picked off a fourth-down pass from the Warriors' Ed Dougherty to end Lycoming's overtime possession, the Gators had done something no one had expected as the season began: they'd become national champions.

Back in Meadville, hundreds of students ran into town to celebrate. A few days later, thousands were on hand as the champions were given a parade

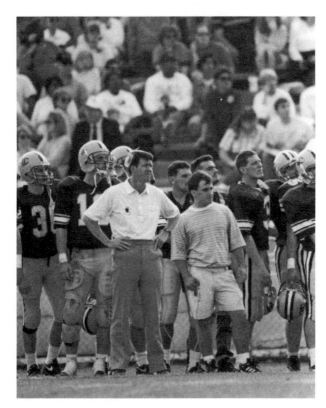

Ken O'Keefe, pictured wearing the head set, had a magnificent first season as the head coach at Allegheny College in 1990, going 13–0–1 while winning the Division III national championship. O'Keefe went 79–10–1 in eight seasons at Allegheny, leading them to six NCAA tournaments. Currently, he is the quarterbacks coach at the University of Iowa. (Courtesy of Allegheny College Athletics)

through the streets of the city. Through it all, the rookie coach kept things in perspective, knowing that sports wasn't the driving force for Division III schools. "This is a perfect example of what people can do when they believe in themselves and they believe in each other," he said. "Athletics are only an extension of the classroom. Young people are playing because it's fun and coaches can focus not on wins and losses per se, but on helping our players reach their full potential on the field and off."[2]

While O'Keefe tried to underscore the importance of academics over sports, it was a thrilling victory that has truly been the last of its kind.

Team	1	2	3	4	Ot	Final
Lycoming	7	7	0	0	0	14
Allegheny	0	0	7	7	7	21

Team	Play	Score
Lycoming	Sheridan 4-Yd Run (Phillips Kick)	7–0
Lycoming	Marion 10-Yd Run (Phillips Kick)	14–0
Allegheny	Filkovski 11-Yd Run (Boucher Kick)	14–7
Allegheny	Lacayo 7-Yd Pass From Filkovski (Boucher Kick)	14–14
Allegheny	Reiser 15-Yd Pass From Filkovski (Boucher Kick)	14–21

Stat	Lycoming	Allegheny
First Downs	12	21
Rushes-Yds	33–93	57–223
Passing Yds	165	115
Comp-Att-Int	16–33–2	15–26–2
Total Yards	258	338
Punt Average	37	48
Fumbles-Lost	1–0	4–1
Penalties	3–25	3–45

PITT PANTHERS 26, NORTH CAROLINA TAR HEELS 20

MARCH 21, 1941

MEN'S DIVISION I NCAA BASKETBALL

On to the Final Four

Pitt's basketball legacy in the twenty-first century has been one of a successful team falling short of reaching college basketball's elite event, the Final Four. While there are two national championship banners that hang in the Peterson Events Center, both were won before the NCAA tournament came into existence, having been awarded retroactively when the Helms Athletic Foundation chose Pitt as national champions for the 1927–28 and 1929–30 campaigns. In the history of a program that included so many disappointing endings in March Madness, there was one Pitt squad did that did manage to cross over the threshold into a Final Four appearance: the 1940–41 squad.

Legendary Panthers coach Doc Carlson had an experienced yet relatively small team for the time at his disposal as he started five seniors: Eddie Straloski, who led the team in scoring with a 9.1 points-per-game average; Sam Milanovich; Mel Port; George Kocheran; and Jimmy Klein. The team may have been small, but it was tough, garnering such nicknames as the Rinkydinks and Little Toughies. Other than going to the Final Four, this team was also noted for an off-the-court achievement: the team members all went overseas to fight in World War II, including reserve Harry Matthews, who was killed in action.

While it was a significant achievement even then, the 1940–41 team is not remembered as one of the premier clubs in school history. They finished the campaign with a decent 12–5 mark that included victories over second-ranked Wisconsin, Illinois, who was 23rd, and split the season series with 16th-rated Penn State. Despite the impressive wins, Pitt was not the first choice of the NCAA selection committee to represent the region in the eight-team tournament.

There were four teams in the area that were considered worthy of the District II bid to the tournament: Pitt, Duquesne, Penn State, and Westminster,

Like Jock Sutherland, Henry Clifford "Doc" Carlson was an All-American on the 1917 football team and earned a doctorate at the school. He would go on to become arguably the greatest coach to have ever been on the bench of Pitt basketball, leading his team to the school's only two national championships. (Courtesy of the University of Pittsburgh Athletics)

who was 20–1 in a season that included a 41–36 victory over the Panthers. The committee that was headed by Penn athletic director H. Jamieson Swartz (and actually included Carlson) cut the field down to two possible teams. Duquesne, who was 17–2—losing only to Ohio State and DePaul—and Pitt. The committee decided to give the Dukes the first opportunity to accept it because, as Swartz stated, "I felt that since Duquesne's record was better than Pitt, the Dukes should get the bid."[1]

Along with Westminster, Duquesne decided to spurn the NCAA bid in favor of the National Invitation Tournament (NIT), which at the time was considered just as prestigious. Duquesne publicity director Jack Davis explained, "It was the choice of Coach Davies and the team."[2] With the Dukes deciding to go to Madison Square Garden for the NIT, the Panthers were given the bid to the NCAA tournament to face coach Bill Lange and the Southern Conference champion North Carolina Tar Heels, who were led by center George Glamack, a great player despite the fact he was hampered with severe vision issues.

While they would eventually become one of the legendary teams in the country, the Tar Heels were not quite at that level yet. They were still successful, capturing seven conference titles in 18 years, but in 1941 they were competing in just their first NCAA tournament. While fans were expecting an exciting matchup in this quarterfinal, what they got was a sluggish battle that would be remembered as the lowest-scoring game in NCAA tournament history. The sputtering offenses came as quite a surprise, especially since North Carolina was one of the better offensive teams in the country at the time, averaging 49.9 points per game.

Pitt broke out to an early lead but was inept offensively in the first 20 minutes, only managing to muster 8 points. After Kocheran opened the scoring with two free throws, he scored a basket on a long pass, then Milanovich hit a foul shot, and the Panthers were ahead 6–5. It wasn't a lead they held for long, as Bob Rose and Glamack quickly scored to put North Carolina on top 9–6, eventually going into the locker room ahead only 12–8.

With their season on the line and only 20 minutes left to turn things around, Pitt came out aggressively in the second half. The Panthers clamped down against Glamack, while Straloski and Clair Malarkey, who was a key player off the bench for Carlson during the season, began to take control of the game. Straloski hit two quick baskets from long range early in the second half, including one from near midcourt, to lead a 9–0 surge that resulted in a 17–12 Pitt advantage.

Glamack finally scored to make it 17–14, but the two heroes, Straloski and Malarkey, countered with baskets of their own to give the Panthers their biggest lead of the game, 21–14. Glamack would hit a long shot from the corner, and Paul Severin hit a long one of his own to cut it once again to three at 21–18. The Pitt defense would dominate the rest of the game as the Panthers would emerge victorious in this ugly contest, 26–20, to move on to a spot in the semifinals against a team they had beaten earlier in the season, Wisconsin.

While they were celebrating the victory, they did so knowing their leading scorer was hurt late in the game and may not be able to play against Wisconsin. Straloski had been involved in a couple of incidents during the season when he was injured, the most famous of which in a win over West Virginia when he first was sent to the court in an aggressive manner by the Mountaineers Rudy Baric while driving to the basket. Later in the game while he was trying to toss the ball to the referee, he accidently hit WVU's Scotty Hamilton in the head with it when the two were diving for a loose ball. Moments later Hamilton punched Straloski in the face, once again knocking him to the floor. In this quarterfinal contest, the team captain hurt his eye in a collision late in the game and was taken off the court and into the locker room. While he did eventually play against Wisconsin, scoring a game-high 12 points to lead Pitt to a 4-point halftime lead, they would lose to the eventual national champions, 36–30. Despite the disappointing defeat, this team will be remembered for doing something no other Panthers team ever did: reaching the Final Four.

Pittsburgh

Player	Fg	Ft	Pts
Straloski	3	0	6
Kocheran	2	2	6
Port	0	3	3
Klein	0	0	0
Paffrath	0	0	0
Milanovich	1	2	4
Malarkey	3	1	7
Totals	9	8	26

North Carolina

Player	Fg	Ft	Pts
Rose	1	0	2
Paine	0	0	0
Severin	1	1	3
Glamack	4	1	9
Pessar	1	0	2
Howard	1	0	2
Gersten	0	0	0
Suggs	1	0	2
Totals	9	2	20

Team	1st	2nd	Final
Pittsburgh	8	18	26
North Carolina	12	8	20

PITT PANTHERS 33, SOUTH CAROLINA GAMECOCKS 9
DECEMBER 29, 1980
MEN'S DIVISION I NCAA FOOTBALL

The Real Heisman Trophy Winner

For most of its history there has seemed to be an unwritten rule that the Heisman Trophy was only meant for offensive players. Defensive players would have the opportunity for their own trophies, but when it came to the most illustrious one, their odds of winning it were just about zero. Michigan's Charles Woodson would become the first defensive player to win the award in 1997, 17 years after another player became the first to be seriously considered. While George Rogers of South Carolina led the nation in rushing with 1,781 yards, and freshman running back Herschel Walker was in the process of leading the University of Georgia to the national championship, there was a defensive player from the University of Pittsburgh who was getting attention like no other defensive player before. His name was name Hugh Green.

Considered one of the greatest defensive players in the annals of college football, Green had been a three-time consensus All-American at defensive end and had his number retired by the university before his college career had been completed. Even with credentials that seemingly outshined any other player in the nation that season, Green finished second in the voting, 267 points behind Rogers, the eventual winner. That disappointment coupled with the 10–1 Panthers getting shut out of the major bowl selections left both Green and his teammates upset. While there was frustration in being left out of the spotlight bowl games, at least the Panthers could take solace in knowing that according to several computer polls, such as the one conducted by the *New York Times,* they were the best team in the country. The good news is that Pitt wasn't shut out of the postseason completely. The Panthers earned an invitation to the Gator Bowl against South Carolina, where Green would go head-to-head against Rogers with a chance to show the college football world who, in fact, the best player was.

Hugh Green was one of the greatest defensive players in college football history. A three-time first-team All-American who had his number retired by the school before he finished his senior season, Green finished second to George Rogers of South Carolina in the 1980 Heisman Trophy race. He had the chance to show who was best head-to-head in the 1980 Gator Bowl as Pitt defeated the Gamecocks 37–9. (Courtesy of the University of Pittsburgh Athletics)

To say Hugh Green was a force in college football would have been an incredible understatement. In 2006, collegefootballnews.com named him as the fifth-best collegiate player of all time. Seven years earlier ESPN ranked him as the 14th greatest player in NCAA history. Green was included in the *Sporting News*'s All-Time All-American team as selected in 1983, and *Sports Illustrated*'s included him in the All-Century team in 1999. To put it simply, he was the greatest defensive force, bar none, during his time on the college football gridiron and a legitimate contender to win the Heisman Trophy.

Later on when asked if he had expected to make history by winning the Heisman, Green responded, "Yes, very much so, because of the year we had the previous season. We had started campaigning in the summer leading up into it. During that period of time in college football, the focus had shifted more toward defense. The dominant players coming out back then were all defensive players—guys like Kenny Easley and Ronnie Lott. So those kinds of players were getting a lot of attention. But there were some timing issues that year for us that affected things. We played Penn State after the Heisman vote was due and that was one of the large problems I had to overcome."[1]

As it turned out, the preference for offensive players winning the award, coupled with the fact that Green had one game left to play before it was given, proved to be the deciding factors in him finishing a close second in the voting. Green did capture the Walter Camp Award, the Lombardi Trophy, the Maxwell Award, the Sporting News Player of the Year, and both the United Press International Player of the Year and its Lineman of the Year awards.

While Green's personal goal of winning the Heisman wasn't achieved, the team was 10–1 and ranked third in the nation. Because several of the major bowls had conference affiliations (Pitt was an independent team at the time) and because the directors of the bowl games decided on other attractive matchups, the third-ranked team in the nation was left out of the New Year's Day bowl mix. Despite the snub, the Panthers still had an opportunity to win the national championship if Notre Dame defeated Georgia in the Sugar Bowl and Oklahoma beat Florida State in the Orange Bowl. And then, of course, the Panthers defeated the 18th-ranked South Carolina Gamecocks in the Gator Bowl.

It was a disappointing bowl and an unsatisfactory opponent for a team so highly rated, but it would give the country the chance to see the nation's two top players on the field together. Pittsburgh coach Jackie Sherrill tried to put the best light on the situation, stating, "The options just didn't go our way (getting a major bowl bid). I told them (the team) what was going on and they were just happy about going to a bowl game."[2]

Disappointed in the situation, the Panthers would take it out on Rogers and the Gamecocks in a big way. The Panthers won the coin toss and, rather than get the ball first, they defiantly decided to kick off and let the Heisman Trophy winner start the game with the football. Any chance Rogers had to show the college football nation he deserved the award over Green ended early. He gained 5 yards on the first play and then was leveled by future pro football Hall of Famer Ricky Jackson and fumbled. Pitt recovered at the South Carolina 29.

Even without starting halfback Joe McCall, who was suspended for the game, the Panthers quickly scored, even after a Rick Trocano-to-Randy McMillan touchdown pass was called back on a penalty. Trocano scored on a 1-yard run to put Pitt ahead, 7–0.

The Gamecocks moved the ball in the next series before defensive tackle Greg Meisner ended it by crushing Rogers for a 3-yard loss on third down, forcing a punt. Pitt would began the rout at that point. A 36-yard David Trout field goal was followed by a Willie Collier touchdown reception from freshman Dan Marino to give the Panthers a decisive 17–3 lead at the half. If

Better known for the tremendous job he did as a college football analyst on ESPN, Mark May was one of the greatest offensive linemen in Pitt history. He would win the 1980 Outland Trophy Award as the country's best lineman and has the distinction of having his number retired by the university. (Courtesy of the University of Pittsburgh Athletics)

the Gamecocks harbored any thoughts of a comeback, the impenetrable Pitt defense ended those hopes in the third.

But first the Pitt offense added to the lead. McMillan, who ran for 59 yards on 13 carries while catching two passes for 46 more, started the first drive of the second half with runs of 14 and 7 yards that led to a Trout 25-yard field goal and a 20–3 advantage. Steve Fedell immediately picked off a pass that gave the Panthers the ball at the South Carolina 41. Trocano led them downfield, and McMillan ended the drive with a 3-yard scoring jaunt to increase the lead to 24.

A less-than-stellar Gamecocks punt put Pitt in scoring position again at the South Carolina 35-yard line. After Trocano lost 7 yards on the first play, he found McMillan with a screen pass, and the fullback did the rest—running 42 yards into the end zone to put the Panthers ahead decisively, 34–3, as the third quarter came to an end.

Rogers had arguably his worst game of the season, gaining 113 yards, far below his season average, on 27 carries with two fumbles. The fabulous Pitt defense felt they had hit him so much that he just didn't want the ball anymore. Fedell, who picked off two passes, said, "He's a great football player but they gave him the ball too much. We put some good shots on him in the second half and after that he didn't seem to want to run the ball anymore. He was tired."[3]

Pitt ended up winning 37–9, but there was still debate over who really deserved college football's greatest individual award. Defensive middle guard Jerry Boyarsky stated, "I don't want to take anything away from Hugh Green, but that man (Rogers) deserved the Heisman."[4] But there were many who didn't agree with him. Pitt's defense in 1980 was certainly one of the best in college football history, but it was their Hall of Fame defensive end in Green that quite a few folks felt was the true Heisman Trophy winner.

Team	1	2	3	4	Final
Pittsburgh	10	7	17	3	37
South Carolina	3	0	0	6	9

Team	Play	Score
Pitt	Trocano 1-Yd Run (Trout Kick)	7–0
Pitt	Trout 36-Yd Field Goal	10–0
SC	Leopard 39-Yd Field Goal	10–3
Pitt	Collier 3-Yd Pass From Marino (Trout Kick)	17–3
Pitt	Trout 26-Yd Field Goal	20–3
Pitt	McMillan 3-Yd Run (Trout Kick)	27–3
Pitt	McMillan 42-Yd Pass From Trocano (Trout Kick)	34–3
Pitt	Trout 29-Yd Field Goal	37–3
SC	Gillespie 14-Yd Pass From Beckham (Kick Failed)	37–9

Rushing—Pitt

Player	Att	Yds	Ave	Td
McMillan	13	59	4.5	1
Hawkins	9	50	5.6	0
Trocano	8	41	5.1	1
DiBartola	3	12	4.0	0
Thomas	2	5	2.5	0
Jones	1	3	3.0	0
Marino	1	2	2.0	0
Daniels	3	-7	-2.3	0

Rushing—SC

Player	Att	Yds	Ave	Td
Rogers	27	113	4.2	0
Wright	4	23	5.8	0
Harper	4	-7	-1.8	0
Reeves	3	-2	-0.7	0
Beckham	2	-11	-5.5	0

Receiving—Pitt

Player	Rec	Yds	Ave	Td
Collier	5	57	11.8	1
Pryor	4	36	9.0	0
Collins	3	50	16.7	0
McMillan	2	46	23.0	1
Dombrowski	2	30	15.0	0
Hawkins	1	14	14.0	0

Receiving—SC

Player	Rec	Yds	Ave	Td
Scott	7	109	15.6	0
Gillespie	2	32	16.0	1
Cornett	1	14	14.0	0
Gettel	1	13	13.0	0

Passing—Pitt

Player	Comp	Att	Pct	Yds	Td	Int
Trocano	10	21	47.6	155	1	2
Marino	7	13	53.8	78	1	0
Daniels	0	1	00.0	0	0	1

Passing—SC

Player	Comp	Att	Pct	Yds	Td	Int
Harper	7	16	43.8	116	0	1
Beckham	4	10	40.0	52	1	1
Reeves	0	1	00.0	0	0	1

PITT PANTHERS 33, KANSAS JAYHAWKS 19
DECEMBER 26, 1975
MEN'S DIVISION I NCAA FOOTBALL

Setting the Table

In the history of the University of Pittsburgh's football program, there is perhaps no more joyous memory than the surprising national championship the team won in 1976. While some may credit the one-sided victory at Notre Dame as the spark that led to the undefeated season, the true inspiration may have occurred nine months earlier—on the day after Christmas 1975, when the young Panthers squad gave a preview of what was to come.

The third season of head coach Johnny Majors's rebuilding process in 1975 had been a unique one indeed. Majors, the former Heisman Trophy contender who finished second to Notre Dame's Paul Hornung in 1956, must have felt his team was not improving as fast as it should after a disappointing beginning of the season.

Majors had won six and seven games in his first two seasons, whereas the program had won only four times in the two years before his arrival. While it appeared as if the Panthers may not have moved forward—standing at 6–3 with two games left against nationally ranked Notre Dame and Penn State—he had done many other things to get the program moving in a positive direction. He revived the interest among the boosters, as the Golden Panthers club saw its membership increase by 700 percent, jumping from 300 members to over 2,000. Season ticket sales had also doubled in the same time period. Majors had recruited an impressive array of young talent that was spearheaded by a dynamic junior tailback from Hopewell, Pennsylvania, named Tony Dorsett. Dorsett had already eclipsed the 1,000-yard plateau in each of his first two seasons—the first two times it had been done in the program's history.

Even though the enthusiasm for this team was higher than it had been in over a decade, the results in 1975 had been mixed indeed. The Panthers had

The statue of the Panther stands on the spot where Pitt Stadium used to be, right next to the Peterson Events Center. Below the statue is engraved the retired numbers of the great Pitt players who led their teams to the many victories included in this book. (Courtesy of the author)

handily defeated the teams that it looked like they should beat, but when it came to their tougher competitors, they lost decisively: to Oklahoma, 46–10; to Navy, 17–0; and to archrival West Virginia, 17–14.

As the Panthers prepared to face Notre Dame in the second-to-last game, most expected more of the same. But Pitt showed they had the potential to be a national power, upsetting the ninth-ranked Irish, 34–20, on the strength of Dorsett's school-record 303 yards rushing. The next week the Panthers faced their nemesis, Penn State, a team who not only was ranked 10th in the country but who hadn't lost to Pitt since 1965. In fact, only once during that stretch had Pitt come within three touchdowns of Penn State. But in 1975, again showing the overall improvement of the program, the Panthers lost a close one, 7–6. Pitt had shown the college football world that they could play with anyone.

With the confidence they'd gained in their final two contests, the 7–4 Panthers accepted a bid to the Sun Bowl to face off against coach Bud Moore and the tough Kansas Jayhawks, who also finished 7–4. The Jayhawks were ranked as high as

17th in early November after defeating second-ranked Oklahoma, which had crushed Pitt earlier in the season. Kansas was led by the finest running quarterback in the nation in Nolan Cromwell, who had amassed 1,223 rushing yards that season. Moore's potent running attack also featured the mercurial LaVerne Smith. Smith, who became the fourth-round pick of the Steelers following his senior season in 1976, finished the year with 982 yards. It would be the third successive difficult opponent for Majors and his Panthers, but that gave them an opportunity to show just how explosive their offense could be.

The "veer" offense was brought to Pitt by Majors and had been run effectively throughout his tenure there. It's an option offense that was developed by the University of Houston's Bill Yeoman in the mid-1960s. When run properly, the quarterback reads the defense before pitching to one of the following backs; if done improperly, it can lead to extensive turnovers. On this day, it would be run to perfection.

It was a cold yet sunny day in El Paso, Texas, with temperatures in the mid-40s. What eventually would become a one-sided affair began as a contest in which Kansas looked every bit like the team who defeated Oklahoma a month before. After Pitt missed a 57-yard field goal, the Jayhawks quickly moved the ball to the Panthers' 16, where they faced fourth-and-inches and decided to go for it. Future All-American defensive tackle Al Romano beat the odds by making a spectacular play for Pitt, pushing the center into Cromwell on a sneak up the middle for a loss that ended the drive and turned the ball back over to Pitt.

Majors had to make a key decision at quarterback going into the game: whether to start the effective runner Robert Haygood, who was injured in the loss to Navy and hadn't played since, or Matt Cavanaugh, the better passer who had performed well in the final four contests of the season. The eventual Hall of Fame coach decided to go with Haygood, whom he felt was the better of the two in practice the week before the game. Stating he would have no issue replacing Haygood with Cavanaugh if he were not effective, Haygood gave him no reason to do so as he ran the veer to perfection.

Soon after taking over on downs, Haygood flipped the football to running back Elliott Walker, who broke through two tackles and rambled 60 yards for a touchdown that gave the Panthers an early 7–0 advantage. "One big block came from Robert Hutton," Walker said, "and I made the move off that. The another came from John Hanhauser and on that one I knew I was gone."[1]

It was a play that gave Haygood some much-needed confidence. "I felt rusty the first couple plays," he said, "then I started to get the feel of things."[2]

The Panthers quickly increased their lead as Dorsett scored twice, once from 8 yards and later from 2. They missed the extra point after the first and were unsuccessful on a 2-point conversion on the next one, but the Panthers went into halftime with a surprising 19–0 lead.

Kansas struck back in the third quarter, cutting the Pitt advantage to 12 when Smith split through the Panthers' defense for a 55-yard touchdown run. With the momentum on the Jayhawks' side, Haygood and Pitt quickly took it back. In the fourth quarter, Walker scored from 2 yards out. Then Haygood found freshman receiver Gordon Jones with a 7-yard completion for another Pitt touchdown, giving the Panthers a dominant 33–13 advantage as Smith scored on a 17-yard run between the two Panthers scores.

Reserve Kansas quarterback Scott McMichael would hit running back Skip Sharp with a meaningless 38-yard touchdown toss late in the game to make the score look closer, but Pitt had thoroughly dominated. Three players ripped through the tough Kansas defense for over 100 yards rushing: Dorsett (142), Walker (123), and Sun Bowl MVP Haygood (108). The trio combined to give the Panthers an impressive 373 yards rushing on the day.

While proud of the performance, Majors knew there would be lofty expectations ahead for a Panthers team who had won just the school's first bowl game since 1937. "We'll be rated high for 1976," he said, "and there's not much I can do about it."[3]

Of course, the high expectations came to fruition and the story played out better than any Pitt fan could have imagined, as the Panthers won the national championship a year later. And while there were many key moments throughout that championship season, it all began nine months earlier with an impressive win over Kansas.

Team	1	2	3	4	Final
Pittsburgh	7	12	0	14	33
Kansas	0	0	7	12	19

Team	Play	Score
Pitt	Walker 60-Yd Run (Long Kick)	7–0
Pitt	Dorsett 8-Yd Run (Kick Failed)	13–0
Pitt	Dorsett 2-Yd Run (Pass Failed)	19–0
Kansas	Smith 55-Yd Run (Swift Kick)	19–7
Pitt	Walker 2-Yd Run (Long Kick)	26–7
Kansas	Smith 17-Yd Run (Kick Failed)	26–13
Pitt	Jones 7-Yd Pass From Haygood (Long Kick)	33–13
Kansas	Sharp 38-Yd Pass From McMichael (Run Failed)	33–19

Rushing—Pitt

Player	Att	Yds	Ave	Td
Dorsett	17	142	8.3	2
Walker	11	123	11.2	2
Haygood	14	108	7.7	0

Rushing—Kansas

Player	Att	Yds	Ave	Td
Smith	16	118	7.4	2
Crowell	24	99	4.1	0
Banks	13	64	4.9	0

Receiving—Pitt

Player	Rec	Yds	Ave	Td
Jones	4	26	6.5	1
Corbett	3	25	8.3	0
Clark	1	9	9.0	0

Receiving—Kansas

Player	Rec	Yds	Ave	Td
Sharp	1	38	38.0	1
Fender	1	16	16.0	0
McCamy	1	14	14.0	0

Passing—Pitt

Player	Comp	Att	Pct	Yds	Td	Int
Haygood	8	11	72.7	60	1	0
Cavanaugh	0	1	00.0	0	0	1

Passing—Kansas

Player	Comp	Att	Pct	Yds	Td	Int
Cromwell	0	6	00.0	0	0	1
McMichael	4	8	50.0	76	1	0

DUQUESNE DUKES 79, ST. BONAVENTURE BONNIES 74
MARCH 1, 1961
MEN'S NCAA BASKETBALL

Redemption

Things looked good for the St. Bonaventure Bonnies men's basketball team in the winter of 1961. They stood at 21–2, were ranked second in the nation, and had already accepted a bid to play in the NCAA tournament. For the Duquesne University Dukes, things were going a little differently. This once proud program had fallen on hard times. It had been only six years since they were one of the premier programs in the country, winning the school's lone basketball national championship in the 1955 National Invitation Tournament (NIT). Six years later, coach Red Manning and his Dukes were coming off an 8–15 campaign in 1959–60 and stood at only 11–7 as they hosted the Bonnies, a team who had beaten Duquesne comfortably earlier in the season 89–78. Rather than a coronation for St. Bonaventure, the rematch would prove to be one of redemption for the underdogs. It not only gave them one of biggest regular-season victories in the school's history but provided them a springboard back into the national college basketball limelight a year later.

For years, Duquesne had been on the precipice of winning a national championship, only to fall short of the goal with one disappointing loss after another. Finally, in 1955 they won their long-awaited title with a victory over Dayton in the NIT championship game. While many thought there were more championships just around the corner, that was the end of the line. The administration, with its championship in hand, began to take money away from the program. Within two years, the team had fallen to 10–12, and their phenomenal coach, Dudey Moore, had left the school to accept the job as head coach of LaSalle.

Duquesne named assistant John "Red" Manning as his successor, but the team continued to struggle over the next two and a half seasons. While he would go on to greater glory on the Bluff, winning 247 games, Manning was a young, inexperienced coach still learning his way. By all accounts, Manning had a no-nonsense approach, and his players understood the he wanted things done his way. But it was a young team who had a poor season the year before, and after a 7–1 start to this campaign, the Dukes had lost six of their previous 10 games.

Coach Edward Donovan's Bonnies were moving in the other direction. Led by senior Tom Stith, who had been named first-team all-American by the Associated Press prior to the game, St. Bonaventure had lost only twice, including a 2-point defeat to top-ranked Ohio State. The Bonnies had been ranked second in the country since beating the Dukes on January 7, and not many in the sellout crowd of 5,439 who filed into Pitt's Fitzgerald Field House—which Duquesne also called home—expected much of a contest.

Despite the fact that few held out hopes of an upset, it was the largest crowd to date to watch the Dukes play at this facility. Manning didn't have a deep bench and would have to rely on his starting quintet. Seniors Ned Twyman (the brother of Naismith Basketball Hall of Famer Jack Twyman) and Bob "Slobbo" Slobodnik were playing the last home game of their college careers and made sure it was a memorable one.

Twyman couldn't miss early on, connecting on his first four shots as the teams went back and forth. After the score was tied at 8, the Bonnies began to play more aggressive defensive, causing three quick turnovers, each resulting in a St. Bonaventure layup. The anticipated blowout seemed to be coming to fruition. The Bonnies built a 23–11 lead at the midpoint of the first half, but at that point the underdogs began to play inspired basketball. The Dukes fought back, outscoring the Bonnies 19–10 in the final 10 minutes of the half to turn what was becoming a one-sided affair into a tight 33–30 contest at the half.

Donovan hoped that the Dukes' starting five would be worn down in the final 20 minutes of regulation after fighting back so hard. But this wasn't the case, as Duquesne continued to play tough. The Bonnies managed to hang onto their lead for the first 8 minutes of the second half, but when Twyman drove the length of the court for a layup, and the Dukes had finally tied the contest at 48 apiece.

The teams continued this intense battle, with St. Bonaventure creeping to a slim advantage, only to have Duquesne fight back to tie it three times. Unable to surge in front for most of the half, the Dukes finally took the lead with 3:01 left when Slobodnik hit two free throws. He then hit a jump shot to put them up 63–60.

The Field House was loud and enthusiastic as it appeared the men from the Bluff were going to pull off a monumental upset. But then Stith took over, scoring twice to put St. Bonaventure back ahead 64–63 with a little over a minute left. After connecting on a foul shot, the Bonnies held a 2-point lead, but with 20 seconds remaining, Slobodnik netted another clutch shot to tie the score once again. Donovan called timeout and instructed his team to hold the ball for the last shot. Bob McCully eventually got the basketball down low for a dunk that appeared to be the winning shot. But the crowd went from disappointed to exaltated when the basket was ruled to have come after the final buzzer, and the two teams headed for overtime.

McCully started the overtime period by missing two free throws, but Stith would score on his next two shots to counteract baskets by Slobodnik and Clyde Arnold and keep the score tied, 69–69. It was at that point, after 42.5 minutes of play, that Duquesne finally took control.

Arnold, who had played the last 9 minutes of regulation with four fouls, hit a shot and was fouled. He completed the 3-point play with a free throw, and then Twyman, who finished with a game-high 31 points, scored on two consecutive shots before Slobodnik finished the overtime onslaught with a bucket of his own. The jubilant fans, which included their former coach Moore, began chanting "WE BEAT THE BONNIES" over the final 2 minutes of overtime. When the dust settled, the Dukes had themselves a 79–74 victory.

To celebrate, university president Henry J. McAnulty canceled classes and gave the students the next day off. It was arguably the greatest regular-season victory in the school's history, and not only gave the Bonnies some retribution for the disappointing seasons they had endured over the past few years but seemed to inspire them to provide more satisfying days like this one.

Duquesne went on to win their final three games of the season to finish 15–7. It was a prelude to the next campaign in which the Dukes were back among the best in the East with a 22–7 mark that included a return to the NIT, where they would reach the semifinals. It was a success that partially came from the confidence the team gained with this impressive victory.

St. Bonaventure

Player	Fg	Ft	Pts
Crawford	13	3	29
Stith	8	3	19
McCully	3	3	9
Martin	5	0	10
Jirele	2	1	5
Hannon	1	0	2
Totals	32	10	74

Duquesne

Player	Fg	Ft	Pts
Twyman	14	3	31
Arnold	7	2	16
Slobodnik	6	3	15
Stromple	1	1	3
Benec	6	2	14
Totals	34	11	79

Team	1st	2nd	OT	Final
St. Bonaventure	33	32	9	74
Duquesne	30	35	14	79

#27

CARNEGIE TECH TARTANS 20, PITT PANTHERS 10
NOVEMBER 5, 1938
MEN'S NCAA FOOTBALL

Now We Believe

For fans and alumni of Carnegie Tech, it was hard to believe their team looked so successful early on. The 1938 squad was playing outstanding football, posting a 4–1 mark as they entered their yearly battle with their rivals from the University of Pittsburgh. The Tartans had already played a formidable schedule to this point, but no one would blame the Tartans' fans for not believing they could defeat Pitt; most of the decade, the Tartans were the worst of Pittsburgh's three major college football schools (Pitt, Duquesne, and Carnegie Tech). But by the time this game was over, it would be clear that this edition of the Tartans was special indeed.

Under coach Walter Steffen, Carnegie Tech was at their best while the program played at the major college football level, beating Notre Dame on three occasions. When he retired following the 1932 campaign, Steffen turned over the reins of the program to his former player, arguably the greatest ever to don a Tartans uniform, Howard Harpster. Harpster enjoyed little success in his new endeavor, compiling a 12–19–3 mark in four seasons at his alma mater. The administration then decided to hire a protégé of Pitt's legendary coach John "Jock" Sutherland, William Kern, in 1937.

Kern had been a tremendous football player for Pitt, being named a first-team All-American tackle in 1927 and moving on to a two-year career in the National Football League with the Green Bay Packers. In 1936 he returned to his alma mater as an assistant for Sutherland during the school's seventh national championship season. After the campaign, he was named as Harpster's successor at Carnegie Tech. The team continued their downtrend with a 2–5–1 mark in his first season that included a 25–14 loss to the Panthers.

The following year, the Tartans started out with two one-sided victories against Davis & Elkins and Wittenberg to match their 1937 victory total. But a matchup against nationally ranked Holy Cross stood on the horizon as the first test of Kern's club in 1938. Tech held strong and handed the Crusaders what would be their lone loss of the season, 7–6.

With confidence now in hand, the Tartans would face Notre Dame next and were in the midst of a tough scoreless battle in the fourth quarter when a mistake by the referee cost them the game. The Tartans were at their own 46-yard line when referee John Gettchel informed Tech quarterback Paul Friedlander it was third down. Friedlander ran a conservative play that fell short of a first down when Gettchel figured out he had made a mistake and it actually had been fourth down, not third. Instead of punting and putting Notre Dame in poor field position, the ball was turned over to the Fighting Irish, who went down the field for the only score of the day in a 7–0 victory. Kern, who would have punted had they not been told it was third down, was livid, as were his players. After rebounding to defeat Akron the next week, 27–13, the Tartans went into their annual game against Pitt, wondering if they would be able to take the next step into the national spotlight against a team they hadn't defeated in 14 years.

The Panthers came into this contest as the two-time defending national champions and were No. 1 in the nation following a 24–13 victory against ninth-ranked Fordham. Pitt was undefeated after six contests, outscoring their opposition by a 158–32 margin and was expecting to easily defeat the 16th-ranked Tartans as they had so many times in the past.

Pitt Stadium was full for this contest as 61,000 looked on for what appeared to be a long day for Tech after the Panthers' Curly Stebbins took the opening kickoff for the touchdown. Stebbins darted through the Carnegie Tech defenders, aided by a magnificent block by the Panthers' Heisman Trophy candidate, Marshall Goldberg, that took out two Tartans. It was a great moment for Goldberg, who spent most of the week ill in the hospital before insisting to Sutherland that he would play. The hero of Pitt's Rose Bowl victory the previous year, Bill Daddio, knocked in the extra point and Pitt was up 7–0.

In the previous decade, Carnegie Tech most likely would have faltered at this point, allowing the Panthers an easy victory, but two drives later they showed this was a different team. After punting back to the Panthers following their futile first drive of the contest, Tech got the ball back in great field position at the Pitt 48 following a Merlyn Condit 21-yard punt return. Running back George Muha rambled around right end for 11 yards and a couple plays later

Pitt coach Jock Sutherland (*left*) talks to his star running back Marshall Goldberg (*right*). Goldberg had been in the hospital the week before the Carnegie Tech game but made sure he was on the field on Saturday for the game. (Courtesy of the University of Pittsburgh Athletics)

was on the receiving end of a Condit 25-yard pass for a touchdown. With Ray Carnelly converting on the extra point, it was 7–7.

With Goldberg now on the bench for the remainder of the game after Sutherland decided he was not healthy enough to continue, the Panthers and their faithful were concerned. Daddio helped dispel those concerns late in the first quarter after Pitt drove from its own 35 to the Tartans' 6. He converted on a 12-yard field goal to put the Panthers up once again, 10–7. It would be their last lead of the day.

The Pitt defense held firm until late in the first half, as the Panthers squandered a chance to take control of the contest. First they drove to the Tartans' 13 before turning the ball over on downs. Then Pitt quarterback Ben Kish tossed an interception to set up Carnegie Tech at the Panthers' 33. With time running out in the half, Carnelly tossed a desperation third-down pass toward Karl Striegel in the end zone. Pitt's John Chickerneo jumped up and knocked the pass down, but instead of hitting the ground, the football bounced into the hands of Striegel for the touchdown that put the underdogs ahead, 14–10.

Many in the sellout crowd expected Pitt to come back in the final 30 minutes, but they would soon find out the Panthers no longer were the best team in the city. Carnegie Tech got the first opportunity in the third quarter, driving to the Pitt 16 on the strength of a Muha 41-yard run. When the drive stalled, the Tartans lined up for a field goal but pulled off a surprise. Carnelly took the snap and threw the ball short of his target, Muha, to keep the game at 14–10.

Time and time again the Tartans would drive while the Panthers' offense was proving ineffective. But the Pitt defense toughened up as Tech would threaten to score, keeping the game at 14–10. As dominant as Tech was, it was still only a 4-point game as time was winding down. Finally, midway through the fourth quarter, Larry Peace returned a short Pitt punt to the Panthers' 21-yard line. Five plays later, Muha bolted over right tackle into the end zone from the 1 to give the Tartans what turned out to be an insurmountable 20–10 lead.

Pitt was unable to mount a comeback, and the Tartans closed out their unbelievable 20–10 victory. It was a win that made everyone, from the coach down to the fans, believe that this truly was a remarkable season. Tech went on to finish 7–1, capturing the Lambert Trophy—symbolic of the best team in the East—and wound up ranked sixth in the country. The Tartans accepted a bid to play top-ranked TCU in the Sugar Bowl, where Tech gave the Horned Frogs all they could handle before eventually falling, 15–7.

Despite the loss, it was a magnificent season—the last Carnegie Tech enjoyed at the major college football level. And a big part of it was the Tartans' memorable, long-awaited victory over their archrivals.

Team	1	2	3	4	Final
Carnegie Tech	7	7	0	6	20
Pittsburgh	7	3	0	0	10

Team	Play	Score
Pitt	Stebbins 97-Yd Kickoff Return (Daddio Kick)	0–7
Tech	Carnelly 25-Yd Pass From Condit (Carnelly Kick)	7–7
Pitt	Daddio 12-Yd Field Goal	7–10
Tech	Striegel 33-Yard Pass From Carnelly Kick)	14–10
Tech	Muha 1-Yd Run (Kick Failed)	20–10

Stat	Tech	Pittsburgh
First Downs	13	9
Rushing Yards	196	135
Passing Yds	69	51
Comp-Att-Int	3–10–3	3–16–4
Total Yards	265	186
Punt Average	393	31
Fumbles Lost	1	2
Penalty Yards	10	5

PITT PANTHERS 60, XAVIER MUSKETEERS 55
MARCH 26, 2009
MEN'S BASKETBALL

Sweet Sixteen Celebration

In the eight seasons after coach Ben Howland revived the University of Pittsburgh basketball program, it had been a bittersweet repetitive cycle for the Panthers: play hard, have regular-season success, stumble, and lose in the Sweet Sixteen round. In Howland's final three seasons on the Pitt bench, the team was 76–25, losing to Mississippi State in the NIT second round while dropping consecutive Sweet Sixteen NCAA contests to Kent State and Marquette. When his star pupil, Jamie Dixon, took over as head coach when Howland took over at UCLA, the seasons had a similar feel. In his first five years, Dixon posted a 131–39 record but had less-than-stellar results in the NCAA tournament: a first-round loss, two second-round losses, and two more Sweet Sixteen defeats. It was tough for Pitt fans to remain positive about the program, knowing the trend of phenomenal regular seasons ending with difficult losses in the postseason.

As the 2008–09 campaign unfolded, the team seemed to be playing at a higher level. The Panthers achieved a No. 1 ranking in the Associated Press poll for the first time in school history and were 28–3 entering the Big East tournament. After reaching the Big East finals in seven of the previous eight tournaments, Pitt lost to their bitter rivals from West Virginia in their opening game. Then, after receiving a No. 1 seed in the NCAA tournament, the Panthers struggled against heavy underdog East Tennessee State before winning 72–62 in the first round. They weren't much better defeating eighth-seeded Oklahoma State 84–76 in the second round—the game was tied at 74 with just over 2 minutes left before guard Levance Field scored 5 consecutive points to help secure the Pitt win. It set the Panthers up with a Sweet Sixteen match against the fourth-seeded Xavier Musketeers. Despite the Panthers being the higher seed, Pitt fans were nervous, remembering the disappointment from the previous few years. And when the Musketeers came out strong, it appeared as if another Sweet Sixteen letdown was about to occur.

After the Panthers' Jermaine Dixon hit a shot to tie the score at 27 with 3:12 left in the half, Xavier began to take control. The Musketeers' Derrick Brown, who would finish the contest with 14 points, hit a 3-point shot on the next possession as Xavier scored 10 of the final 12 points in the half to send the teams in the locker room with the underdogs comfortably ahead, 37–29.

If Pitt was going to avoid another third-round embarrassment, they would have to get their talented offense moving more efficiently. Out of all the teams in the new winning era at the school, this one was perhaps the most talented. Three of their starters made various All-American squads as Fields was on the *Sports Illustrated* third-team squad, Sam Young was on *SI*'s second team and on the Wooden first-team, while local star DeJuan Blair became the school's first consensus first-team All-American since Don Hennon in 1958.

As the second half began, the Panthers were determined. The first team to garner a No. 1 seed in the tournament in school history continued their struggles early in the second half, and then a 9–0 run put Pitt ahead, 38–37, with 14:33 remaining in the contest.

Xavier head coach and former Pitt guard Sean Miller calmed his team down, and the contest turned into a close, hard-fought affair. Xavier pulled to a 45–42 advantage with 8:29 minutes remaining; then the Panthers' defense clamped down. Pitt outscored the Musketeers, 10–2, in the following 4 minutes to go up by 5 point following a layup by Fields. Xavier forward B. J. Raymond had been struggling most of the game, but with Pitt ahead 52–47, Raymond hit a clutch 3-point field goal, followed by two free throws that evened the game at 52. With only 1:52 left, Xavier took a 2-point advantage on a Dante Jackson jumper. It looked like Pitt was about to experience another tournament nightmare—until Levance Fields came to the forefront.

With 56 seconds left, Field knocked down his second three-pointer of the game, putting the Panthers up 55–54. After Miller took a timeout, Fields stole the ball and went in for a layup that gave Pitt a 57–54 advantage. A few seconds later, Young, who had a game-high 19 points for Pitt, netted two free throws to put the finishing touches on a 60–55 victory.

Dixon was proud of his team, particularly of his senior point guard's clutch play in the game's final moments. "They pushed us around in the first half, but we responded in the second half like we usually do," Dixon said. "Like I've said before, I never get tired of seeing Levance take big shots. He's made them year after year."[1]

The Panthers couldn't enjoy this huge moment for long, suffering a tough loss in the Elite Eight when they were upset by Villanova 78–76. While the loss was tough to take, the victory over Xavier was huge for the program. After so many disappointments, the Panthers finally had a Sweet Sixteen trip to remember.

Pittsburgh

Player	Fg (3pt)	Ft	Pts
Blair	5	0	10
Biggs	0	0	0
Young	7(1)	4	19
Fields	5(2)	2	14
Dixon	2	0	4
Brown	2(1)	2	7
McGhee	0	0	0
Gibbs	0	0	0
Wanamaker	1	4	6
Totals	22(4)	12	60

Xavier

Player	Fg (3pt)	Ft	Pts
Brown	6(2)	0	14
Anderson	2	2	6
Raymond	6(1)	2	15
Love	0	1	1
Jackson	4(1)	1	9
Mclean	1	0	2
Frease	1	2	4
Holloway	0	1	1
Redford	1(1)	0	3
Totals	21(5)	8	55

Team	1st	2nd	Final
Pittsburgh	29	31	60
Xavier	37	18	55

#25

CALIFORNIA (PA) VULCANS 86, CALIFORNIA BAPTIST LANCERS 69
MARCH 27, 2015
WOMEN'S DIVISION II NCAA BASKETBALL

Number 44

From all accounts, No. 44 for the California University of Pennsylvania's women's basketball team, Shanice Clark, was a great teammate and an outstanding human being. She was a six-foot reserve senior forward from Toronto who had transferred to Cal from Santa Fe College in Gainesville, Florida, and was sitting out her first season as a redshirt. Things were going well for the Vulcans, who had aspirations of winning the program's second national championship.

Then, early in the morning of January 18, Clark was found unresponsive in her bed. Attempts to revive her failed, and she was pronounced dead a short time later. Originally thought to have choked on her gum while sleeping, it was later revealed that the senior had succumbed to a sickle cell trait that can, at times, lead to sudden death. The team was devastated and proceeded to dedicate the rest of the campaign to her memory.

The Vulcans had stumbled a few times early in the season, and after postponing the game at Gannon following the tragedy, they fell against the Lady Knights four days later, 71–63, dropping to 14–3 and tumbling out of the top 25. Cal salvaged their season by winning nine of the next 10 games, losing only at home to Gannon once again.

Cal would open the Pennsylvania State Athletic Conference (PSAC) tournament by facing the team who defeated them twice in the season. On their third attempt, the Vulcans finally found a way to beat Gannon in the quarterfinals and raced to the conference title.

The Division II NCAA tournament would be a bit more difficult. The Vulcans struggled against PSAC foes West Liberty and Bloomsburg in the second round and Sweet Sixteen but found a way to defeat each. The Bloomsburg

Devastated by the loss of teammate Shanice Clark, the players on the California University of Pennsylvania Vulcans women's basketball team would drape her jersey on a chair in her honor. After defeating California Baptist to win the national championship, they all put up four fingers in honor of her No. 44. (Courtesy of the California University of Pennsylvania Athletics)

game was a particularly close call, as Cal fell behind by four with 2:24 left in overtime before outscoring Bloomsburg 9–2 to end the game.

Now ranked 14th, the Vulcans knocked off Nova Southeastern to reach the Final Four and then took Emporia State by 5 points in the national semifinal. It had been an emotional run to the first final for the school since 2004, when Cal won the program's first national title. Win or lose, the Vulcans would play this title game with Clark in mind, and at the end they would each hold up four fingers, as they had since her death, to represent the No. 44 that their fallen teammate wore so proudly.

Freshman forward Shatara Parsons acknowledged losing their teammate was the inspiration that propelled the team to this point. "Since January 18, you can basically tell losing Shanice was the extra mile to get us where we are today," she said. "Before, it was just for a championship and ring."[1] She added, "We all sat down and wrote our goals on the board, and we all agreed that this was our year, despite everything we went through. We continued to work for what she wanted us to get, which was a championship and a ring."[2] That was the

One of the greatest players ever to don a basketball uniform at the California University of Pennsylvania is guard Miki Glenn. The All-American was a pivotal part of the team's second national championship run in 2015 as a sophomore. She saved her best for last, scoring 31 points in the final against California Baptist. (Courtesy of the California University of Pennsylvania Athletics)

emotion the Vulcans would draw on as they faced a tough California Baptist squad at Sioux Falls, South Dakota, in the final.

Things didn't look good early on, as California Baptist moved out to a quick 11–2 advantage. But the Vulcans scored the game's next 21 points to move ahead, 23–11.

Try as they might, California Baptist had no answer for Cal, who continued their onslaught throughout the first half, with the Vulcans going to the locker room firmly in front, 48–28. While they played almost perfect in the first half, it would be tough to maintain that level of intensity. The Lancers made that clear as they began the second half playing aggressively, outscoring the Vulcans 21–9 to cut the lead to single digits at 57–49. Vulcans coach Jess Strom called a timeout at the 12:35 mark to make sure this once certain victory didn't completely evaporate.

The Vulcans increased their defensive intensity, shutting down the Lancers over the next 2 minutes while scoring 6 points to increase the lead back to 14. California Baptist would never reduce the deficit to single digits again. Cal sophomore guard Miki Glenn was at her finest, netting 16 points over the final 8 minutes to finish the contest with 31—hitting 10 of 17 shots from the floor and a perfect 10-for-10 from the free throw line. Senior forward Kaitlynn Fratz, who was named the tournament's most valuable player, scored 15 while Emma Mahady and Seairra Barrett contributed 19 and 12, respectively, in the 86–69 rout.

The 17-point margin of victory was the highest in a women's Division II final in nine seasons and gave Cal the program's second national championship in 11 years to the day. As fabulous as it was to achieve such heights, it was a bittersweet moment. As the game ended, each player held up four fingers in honor of Shanice Clark—the inspiration that helped drive their memorable run to a championship.

California (PA)

Player	Fg (3pt)	Ft	Pts
Glenn	10(1)	10	31
Mahady	8(2)	1	19
Fratz	7	1	15
Kukolj	2	2	6
Doran	1(1)	0	3
Barrett	6	0	12
Dixon	0	0	0
Martin	0	0	0
Totals	34(4)	14	86

California Baptist

Player	Fg (3pt)	Ft	Pts
Burnside	11	5	27
Diaz	8(2)	0	18
Nelson	7(1)	0	15
Mihalko	2	4	8
Cambronero	0	1	1
Asher	0	0	0
Brown	0	0	0
Totals	28(3)	10	69

Team	1st	2nd	Final
California (PA)	48	38	86
California Baptist	28	41	69

#24

CARNEGIE TECH TARTANS 27, NOTRE DAME FIGHTING IRISH 7
NOVEMBER 17, 1928
MEN'S NCAA FOOTBALL

Knute's Albatross

There are things that defy logic in sports—such as when one team is seemingly inferior to another yet seems to find a way to emerge victorious.

When it comes to ranking Notre Dame's greatest coaches, the conversation begins and ends with one man: Knute Rockne. As great as Rockne was, he continually had problems defeating a school that, by all appearances, the Irish should have easily handled. That underdog team pulled off one of the great upsets in college football history against the Irish in 1926, then ending their 23-year home undefeated streak two years later. That underdog team was the Carnegie Tech Tartans, who would became an albatross to Rockne.

Unlike two years earlier, when Notre Dame had national championship aspirations, the Irish had struggled in 1928. They stood at a relatively modest 5–2 as they entered their matchup with Carnegie Tech. But Notre Dame did carry the momentum of a great upset in its previous contest, a 12–6 victory over the powerful Army Black Knights. It was a contest that is famed in college football lore for the "Win One for the Gipper" speech Rockne gave at halftime, inspiring his players with the story of the death of their tremendous teammate George Gipp.

However, the Tartans were enjoying one of the finest campaigns in school history. They were undefeated after six contests, outscoring their opponents, 174–20, and picking up victories over Georgetown and their Oakland neighbors, the University of Pittsburgh.

The two teams would battle at Cartier Field, the home of the Irish since 1900. Having the need for a new, larger stadium as the Irish football program grew, a graduate of the school bought 10 acres of land and donated lumber for additional stands. The stadium's new capacity then reached 27,000. Cartier

Field had become one of the toughest places to play in the sport, as the home team had not lost a game there since 1906. While Carnegie Tech was having a better season than Notre Dame, once you combined the momentum of the Irish victory over Army, the fact that Rockne was looking for revenge for the 1926 upset, and with the tremendous advantage Cartier Field gave them, the Fighting Irish were the clear favorites. But the Tartans would nullify early on any advantage Notre Dame may have had.

It was a dark, rainy day, but a standing room only crowd of more than 30,000 jammed into Cartier Field to see if the Irish could capitalize on the momentum from the Army defeat. It began to appear early on that they could not. All-American quarterback Howard Harpster, one of the greatest ever to don a Tartans uniform, stunned the Irish defense on the second play from scrimmage by hitting Ted Rosenzweig with a pass down to the Notre Dame 12. C. J. Letzelter took the handoff on the next play, ripping over right tackle and into the end zone for a touchdown. Harpster's extra point attempt was blocked, but Tech had the early lead, 6–0.

Any hope that the home team could quickly tie this contest ended on the next drive. Taking over on his 20, John Niemiec fired a pass, but Carnegie Tech's Dutch Eyth slipped in front of it, picking it off at the Notre Dame 34. Led by a 10-yard dash by Rosenzweig, Tech pushed it through the tough Fighting Irish defense, and Harpster completed a seven-play drive with a 1-yard scoring plunge. The extra point made it 13–0, as the home team found themselves in the unusual position of trailing by double digits at home.

As effective as the Tartans' offense was, the defense was equally adept, frustrating Rockne's troops in the first quarter. As the quarter was coming to an end, Letzelter ran it 25 yards more to the Notre Dame 30, and on the first play of second quarter, Rosenzweig all but put the game away when he took a pitch around right end and finished the drive with a 30-yard touchdown run. Harpster's extra point made it 20–0. With Tech playing one of the finest games in program history, coupled with the fact it would be difficult to mount a comeback in the rain, the game was seemingly over. But with Rockne on the sideline, nothing was out of the realm.

Late in the first half, Notre Dame started moving the ball on the Carnegie Tech defense, taking it down to the Tartans' 4-yard line. But the Tartans kept the Irish out of the end zone, taking over on downs and running out the clock as the teams went into the locker room with Tech still holding a decisive 20-point lead.

There was no "win one for the Gipp" speech in the locker this week, but the Irish nonetheless came out inspired, hoping they could continue to move the ball on the Tartans. While they did score early in the half, it had nothing to do with the Notre Dame offense. Carnegie Tech had the ball to begin the half, and Harpster promptly fumbled. Notre Dame's Larry "Moon" Mullins picked up the fumble at the Tech 10 and ran it in for the score to cut the lead to 20–7.

With momentum in hand, Notre Dame hoped to capitalize on the break and get back in the game. But the Tartans' defense wouldn't allow that, holding the Irish in check for the rest of the third quarter. With time running down in the fourth, Harpster began the drive that put the game away, returning a punt to the Notre Dame 48. Tech drove to the 16, where Harpster hit Letzelter with a short pass, and Letzelter took the ball the rest of the way to restore the Tartans' 20-point lead at 27–7.

Notre Dame moved the ball to the Tartans' 1-yard line on the next drive, but an interception in the end zone by John Karcis, who eventually would play in the NFL and be elected to the Beaver County Sports Hall of Fame, ended the scoring drive. Carnegie Tech had handed Notre Dame their first loss at Cartier Field since 1905. The 27 points scored against the Irish also matched the most ever allowed by a Knute Rockne team, tying it with the same total Army scored in 1925.

There was talk that the upset win over Notre Dame and the Tartans' undefeated record would help propel them to the national championship. All they had to do was defeat New York University in the finale. But Tech couldn't follow up their magnificent victory over Notre Dame and fell to NYU, 27–13.

Despite the disappointing loss to end the season, the victory the week before still represents one of the highest points in the program's history. Beating Rockne was near impossible; doing it twice in a row was truly remarkable. No matter what achievements the Tartans' program has garnered over the years, being the albatross around Knute Rockne's neck was their greatest.

Team	1	2	3	4	Final
Carnegie Tech	13	7	0	7	27
Notre Dame	0	0	7	0	7

Team	Play	Score
Tech	Letzelter 12-Yd Run (Kick Failed)	6–0
Tech	Harpster 12-Yd Run (Harpster Kick)	13–0
Tech	Rosenzweig 30-Yd Run (Harpster Kick)	20–0
ND	Mullins 10-Yd Fumble Return (Carriedo Kick)	20–7
Tech	Letzelter 16-Yd Pass From Harpster (Harpster Kick)	27–7

#23

PITT PANTHERS 36, WEST VIRGINIA MOUNTAINEERS 35
OCTOBER 17, 1970
MEN'S NCAA FOOTBALL

A Comeback of Epic Proportions

It was a dark time for the University of Pittsburgh football program as it entered the 1970s. Wins were few and far between, and only the occasional outstanding performance would be remembered. During the decade's first Backyard Brawl between Pittsburgh and West Virginia, one of those memorable performances—a comeback of epic proportions—made quarterback Dave Havern a revered figure in Pitt football lore. It was also an afternoon that would stay with Hall of Fame coach Bobby Bowden, as losing such a big lead taught a lesson that he and his opponents would never forget.

In 1963 the Panthers surprisingly finished 9–1, losing only to the 10th-ranked Navy Midshipmen, who eventually finished second, 24–12. Pitt finished the season ranked fourth and while a return to the glory days was hoped for, it turned out to be a quick downward trend, never seen before in the history of Pitt football and beginning a run in 1966 that saw them finish 1–9 for three consecutive seasons.

Chancellor Wesley Posvar and his new athletic director, Caz Myslinski, needed a new coach to turn around the fortunes of the Panthers. But the job was not as esteemed as it used be, reflected by one prominent head coach who agreed to take the job but then backed out only a few days later. A couple more strong candidates were considered, only to turn Pitt down. Finally, the administration turned to a former player, one who had great success as a head coach (albeit at the NAIA level) and had won a national championship in 1966. His name was Carl DePasqua, and he brought a long-overdue winning attitude to the program, telling the players when he first addressed them, "We are going to win. I've been with winners. My staff has been with winners. We all know what it takes to win. And that's precisely what we're going to do here."[1]

It was his exuberance that guided the Panthers to more victories in his first campaign in 1969 (four) than they had managed the previous three combined. There was an enthusiasm among fans that hadn't been seen in years. The following year's media guide proudly declared, "The Pitt Panther Is Back."[2]

Linebacker Ralph Cindrich, who would become a renowned sports agent, led the charge defensively while Dave Havern, a quarterback from nearby McKees Rocks, would run DePasqua's offense. Havern, nicknamed "Mighty Mouse" due to his slight build for a major college quarterback, actually had Pitt football coursing through his blood—his grandmother was a cousin of legendary Panthers coach Jock Sutherland.

Sutherland would have been proud. Havern burst onto the scene his sophomore season in 1968, throwing for 1,810 yards while setting school records by completing 29 passes in a game, attempting 51 in a contest, and completing 287 for the season. After sitting out his junior year in 1969 with mononucleosis, he returned for the 1970 campaign but had lost his job to John Hogan. After Hogan was injured following the second game of the season, Havern came back and led the previously moribund Panthers' offense to wins against Baylor and Kent State. With Havern playing well and Cindrich leading the tough Pitt defense, the Panthers sprinted to a 3–1 record and prepared to welcome their nearby rivals from Morgantown, West Virginia, for the annual Backyard Brawl.

Led by Bobby Bowden, a head coach who would go on to be one of the greatest in the game's history, the Mountaineers came into this contest with high hopes. They began the season ranked 20th and rose to 11th after four consecutive victories before an upset loss to Duke dropped them out of the poll altogether. They traveled to Pittsburgh with hopes of resuming their winning ways, and as the contest began, that's exactly what appeared to be happening.

The Panthers were down four starters to injury before the game, including three on defense, and it showed early on. West Virginia dominated Pitt on both sides of the ball in the first half. The Mountaineers were running at will against what appeared to be an outmanned Pitt defense, with each West Virginia score coming after a long offensive drive. WVU running back Ed Williams scored three touchdowns to give the Mountaineers a 21–0 lead. After the Panthers came back with a 78-yard drive that culminated with a Dennis Ferris 1-yard touchdown run and a Havern two-point conversion that cut the lead to 21–8, WVU tacked on two more touchdowns: a Bob Gresham 2-yard run and a 35-yard pass from quarterback Mike Sherwood to Jim Braxton. As the final seconds of the half ticked down, West Virginia had what appeared to be an insurmountable 35–8 advantage.

Bowden's team was dominant in every sense of the word, reflected by

Gresham topping the 100-yard plateau in rushing by the end of the second quarter. The WVU offense was doing anything it wanted to, and with DePasqua running a ball control offense, the Panthers would have to be perfect in the second half to have a chance. The odds looked even longer when Cindrich and defensive back Charlie Hall left the contest in the first half with injuries.

With the comfortable lead, Bowden switched his offense to a power inside running attack to run the clock down and presumably to try to prevent embarrassing his opponent. DePasqua stuck to his ball control offense, but a funny thing began to happen. The thin Panthers' defense began to bottle up West Virginia as the Mountaineers tried to run inside, and DePasqua's running attack found holes in the WVU front line it hadn't before.

Many of the 50,000 who had entered Pitt Stadium at the outset were gone by the half, including Havern's father, who rushed back in when he found out what was transpiring. The Pitt offense began some long drives of its own. After WVU gained 248 yards on the ground and 103 through the air in the first half, Pitt dominated the Mountaineers, holding them to just 62 total yards in the final 30 minutes. Havern, however, led Pitt on drives of 58 and 68 yards, with Ferris and Dave Garnett scoring on short touchdown runs. Two-point conversion passes from Havern to tight end Joel Klimek reduced the once seemingly insurmountable lead to a more manageable 35–24 as the third quarter was coming to an end. Early in the fourth, Pitt fullback Tony Esposito ended a 70-yard drive, bolting into the end zone from the 1 yard line to cut the lead to a mere 5 points after the quarterback missed on another 2-point pass. The now impenetrable Panthers' defense stopped West Virginia again and forced another punt. Then Pitt took over at their own 30 with a little over 9 minutes remaining. Havern then led the Panthers on one of the greatest drives in the history of Pitt football.

The Panthers were pushing the exhausted Mountaineers' defense down the field, calling rushing plays on 16 out of first 17 plays. They found themselves at the WVU 5 with a minute to play. As the West Virginia front line geared up for what it assumed would be yet another rushing attempt, Havern pulled the ball back on a play-action pass and flipped the ball to an open Bill Pilconis in the end zone, putting Pitt ahead, 36–35.

While another 2-point conversion would have forced West Virginia to score a touchdown to win the game rather than kick a field goal, DePasqua decided to kick the extra point, later explaining he thought Pitt's defense could hold the West Virginia offense again. The kick was no good, and the Panthers found themselves up by just a point with time running out.

The Mountaineers finally got their offense going, driving to the Panthers' 39 with only 19 seconds remaining. On the next play, Sherwood hit Chris

Potts over the middle, and for a split second, it appeared there was nothing but open field ahead of him. But Pitt linebacker George Feher, who had come into the game for Cindrich, remembered the scouting report on West Virginia. He knew that when the wide receiver he was covering didn't cross the line of scrimmage, the play was going over the middle. Reacting to the play he knew was coming, Feher belted Potts, who fumbled the ball. Pitt defensive tackle John Stevens dove on it to secure the Panthers' remarkable victory.

Bowden's decision to switch to a conservative offensive formation turned out to be a mistake, one he would never make again in his career. Afterward, the legendary coach said, "I will tell you what, I learned something. You never had me sitting on the ball again, did you? I'd get accused of running up the score. Well, you're darn right." He added, "I would have liked to have died. It was the only time (his wife) Anne ever cried."[3]

Havern called the contest "my Andy Warhol moment,"[4] wondering many times what would have happened if Pitt had lost. "One of the things I've thought about," he said years later, "is that I hope that game hasn't defined me as a person, hasn't defined my life. I've thought sometimes, 'Would I have the same contacts in life? Would the same girl still have married me? Would my buddies still be my buddies?' You know, realistically, I don't know. I think I'd still be the same person, but it is something to think about."[5]

Pitt won, temporarily putting them into the top 20. The Panthers went as high as 15th after defeating Miami (Florida) the next week. But becoming a truly successful college football program was still a few years away, as the Panthers lost their final four games of the season, followed by 3–8 and 1–10 campaigns the next two years that would ultimately bring the DePasqua era to an end. Regardless of the way the season ended, it will always be remembered for this phenomenal comeback of epic proportions.

Team	1st	2nd	3rd	4th	Final
West Virginia	14	21	0	0	35
Pittsburgh	0	8	16	12	36

Team	Play	Score
WVU	Williams 2-Yd Run (Samuelson Kick)	7–0
WVU	Williams 3-Yd Run (Samuelson Kick)	14–0
WVU	Williams 8-Yd Run (Samuelson Kick)	21–0
Pitt	Ferris 1-Yd Run (Run Good)	21–8
WVU	Gresham 1-Yd-Run (Samuelson Kick)	28–8
WVU	Braxton 33-Yd Pass From Sherwood (Samuelson Kick)	35–8
Pitt	Ferris 2-Yd Run (Pass Good)	35–16
Pitt	Garnett 5-Yd Run (Pass Good)	35–24
Pitt	Esposito 1-Yd Run (Pass Failed)	35–30
Pitt	Pilconis 5-Yd Pass From Havern (Kick Failed)	35–36

Rushing—WVU

Player	Att	Yds	Ave	Td
Gresham	15	149	9.9	1
Ed Williams	20	118	5.9	3
Tom Williams	2	7	3.5	0

Rushing—Pitt

Player	Att	Yds	Ave	Td
Esposito	16	44	2.8	1
Ferris	39	144	3.7	2
Havern	8	-20	-2.5	0
Sgrignoll	2	9	4.5	0
Garnett	14	81	5.8	1
Moss	1	3	3.0	0
Hasbach	1	0	0.0	0

Receiving—WVU

Player	Rec	Yds	Ave	Td
Ed Williams	1	33	33.0	0
Potts	3	31	10.3	0
Porter	2	18	9.0	0
Braxton	2	44	22.0	1

Receiving—Pitt

Player	Rec	Yds	Ave	Td
Esposito	3	44	14.7	0
Ferris	2	12	6.0	0
Pilconis	5	61	12.2	1
Glinden	1	21	21.0	0

Passing—WVU

Player	Comp	Att	Pct	Yds	Td	Int
Sherwood	9	16	56.3	139	1	0
Braxton	0	1	00.0	0	0	0

Passing—Pitt

Player	Comp	Att	Pct	Yds	Td	Int
Havern	11	16	68.8	138	1	0

PITT PANTHERS 24, PENN STATE NITTANY LIONS 7
NOVEMBER 26, 1976
MEN'S DIVISION I NCAA FOOTBALL

A New Experience

When he decided to retire following the 1965 campaign, Rip Engle had been an exceptional coach at Penn State University for 16 seasons. As he stepped down, he persuaded a 39-year-old assistant by the name of Joe Paterno to take over the program. It would be a decision that quickly changed the fortunes of Nittany Lions football, as Paterno quickly turned the program into a national power. What he also did was take the bitterly fought rivalry between the University of Pittsburgh and Penn State University and turn it into a one-sided affair. For nine seasons, Pitt came no closer than 20 points of the Lions. The next year, the Panthers proved to be a formidable foe, but their kicker Carson Long had his worst game in his career, with two missed fourth-quarter field goals, three overall in the game, and a failed extra point attempt as Penn State prevailed 7–6.

Losing had become a regular occurrence in the rivalry for Pitt, one that would finally change in 1976 when the two squads met at Three Rivers Stadium in Pittsburgh. The Panthers came in as the No. 1 team in the nation and would finally find a way to beat Joe Paterno.

While his reputation would eventually be tarnished in the wake of the Jerry Sandusky scandal shortly before Paterno passed away in 2012, Joe Paterno was bigger than the game for the better part of five decades. When he took over for Engle in 1966, the Panthers had a solid lead in the Penn State series with a 35–27–3 mark. But between 1966 and 1974, the Lions outscored Pitt 381–129—an average score of 42–14—and Paterno took pride in being able to beat his rival so convincingly.

Despite the fact that Long, who would go on to break the NCAA career scoring record for kickers, had a difficult game in the Panthers' close loss to Penn State the year before, that game was somewhat of a positive for the program. It finally gave the Panthers confidence that they could not only play with the Nittany Lions but become a national power themselves.

Pitt had a dominant defense, led by All-American middle guard Al Romano, but it was their "veer" offense that really made this team dangerous. The Panthers had lost two quarterbacks to injury during the season, with Robert Haygood lost for the season in the second game against Georgia Tech and then Matt Cavanaugh going down a few weeks later versus Louisville with a fractured fibula. Pitt was able to overcome such adversity because they had one of the greatest running backs ever to grace the gridiron in Tony Dorsett.

Dorsett was at his best his senior season, breaking Archie Griffin's all-time NCAA career rushing record against Navy on October 23. Led by Dorsett's magnificent season, the Panthers were in a position to win the national championship. They finally ascended to the top position in both major polls after they handily defeated Army on November 6 while Purdue upset the top-ranked Michigan Wolverines. Pitt defeated the Mountaineers of West Virginia the next week to improve to 10–0 and set up what appeared to be the most important matchup in the history of the interstate rivalry—at least from the Panthers' perspective.

At the outset of 1976, Penn State was not having a typical Paterno season. After beating Stanford in the opener, the Nittany Lions lost three consecutive games to Ohio State, Iowa, and Kentucky. With his team at 1–3, Paterno helped the Lions turn the campaign around, and they came into this contest on a six-game winning streak.

As the first half began to unfold in front of a sellout crowd of 50,360, it was apparent to all that Penn State was a dangerous opponent on this unseasonably warm, wet evening. With the way the Panthers had struggled in the series over the past decade, many Pitt faithful feared another disastrous loss that would derail their national championship hopes.

Penn State quarterback Chuck Fusina fueled those fears early when he found Bob Torrey with a short pass in the flat and Torrey took the ball through the tough Panthers' defense for a 21-yard scoring play that gave Penn State a surprising 7–0 lead. The Nittany Lions held onto it through the first quarter, and even though Pitt was able to tie the score by the end of the half when Dorsett rambled for a 6-yard score, the Nittany Lions were playing tough defense, holding the eventual Heisman Trophy winner to only 58 yards, which put him on pace to a 116-yard game, far under his 177-yard-per-game average.

Pitt coach Johnny Majors had done a superb job resurrecting what had been a poor football program. With the ultimate prize of a national title potentially slipping through his hands, he came up with arguably two of his best strategic maneuvers in his career at Pitt. The first was setting an unbalanced offensive line that would turn out to be very effective. The second maneuver was even more surprising: taking the greatest halfback in the game and lining him up at fullback, which had Dorsett hitting the line much quicker than the Lions could react to. Both moves made Majors look like a genius. "We used it maybe ten plays this season," the Pitt coach said of the unbalanced line. "We worked on it periodically."[1]

The Lions hung tough for most of the third quarter, but as the period was winding down, it was apparent the Pitt offense was about to break through. A poor Lions punt put the Panthers at midfield, where Dorsett finally broke through. He powered up the middle for 10 yards on two carries before going up the middle on the third play for perhaps the most important play of the evening. This time he broke free and was able to show off his blazing speed for a 40-yard run to the end zone that put the Panthers ahead 14–7.

With Majors's new strategies, Dorsett was finding space much easier than he had in the first half. Early in the fourth quarter, he went through the Lions' defense for a 10-yard run that made him the first running back in college football history to eclipse 6,000 yards in his career. Elliott finished that drive with a 12-yard touchdown run to put the Panthers ahead by 14 points. After the issues Carson Long had the year before, perhaps the most fitting way to end the scoring was on a 47-yard field goal that put the finishing touches on a convincing 24-7 win.

The Panthers' defense had thoroughly confused Fusina after his first-quarter success, intercepting him four times in the game. Defensive back Bob Jury snagged two to extend his nation-leading total to nine. On offense, Dorsett was spectacular in the second half, finishing with 224 total yards after Majors made the shift.

Facing defeat for the first time in his career against his rivals, Paterno knew he had no answer for the adjustments made by Majors at the half. "I didn't think I'd see him (Dorsett) at fullback," Paterno said. "We saw it before, but we weren't quite good enough to handle it."[2] While he admitted it was a great maneuver, he didn't want to give Dorsett too much credit for the victory. "Dorsett didn't beat us," Paterno said. "The whole team did. Ah, heck, I don't know what happened."[3]

What happened is Paterno was finally outcoached by a Panthers head coach who not only gave Pitt the new experience of beating a Paterno team but put the Panthers one step closer to the national championship they would capture a little over a month later.

Team	1st	2nd	3rd	4th	Final
Penn State	7	0	0	0	7
Pittsburgh	0	7	7	10	24

Team	Play	Score
PSU	Torrey 21-Yd Pass From Fusina (Capozolli Kick)	7–0
Pitt	Dorsett 6-Yd Run (Long Kick)	7–7
Pitt	Dorsett 40-Yd Run (Long Kick)	7–14
Pitt	Walker 12-Yd Run (Long Kick)	7–21
Pitt	Long 47-Yd Field Goal	7–24

Rushing—PSU

Player	Att	Yds	Ave	Td
Geise	13	60	8.6	0
Torrey	7	30	4.3	0
Guman	10	33	3.3	0
Fusina	6	-48	-8.0	0
Suhey	4	24	6.0	0
Hostetler	1	7	7.0	0

Rushing—Pitt

Player	Att	Yds	Ave	Td
Dorsett	38	224	5.9	2
Hutton	7	29	4.1	0
Walker	5	19	3.8	1
Cavanaugh	15	6	0.4	0

Receiving—PSU

Player	Rec	Yds	Ave	Td
Shuler	2	16	8.0	0
Torrey	2	26	13.0	1
Geise	1	3	3.0	0
Mauti	1	27	27.0	0
Fitzkee	1	25	25.0	0
Donovan	1	23	23.0	0
Cefalo	1	15	15.0	0

Receiving—Pitt

Player	Rec	Yds	Ave	Td
Jones	4	111	27.8	0
Corbett	3	20	6.7	0
Taylor	1	10	10.0	0

Passing—PSU

Player	Comp	Att	Pct	Yds	Td	Int
Fusina	8	16	50.0	120	1	3
Donovan	0	1	00.0	0	0	0
Hostetler	1	2	50.0	15	0	1

Passing—Pitt

Player	Comp	Att	Pct	Yds	Td	Int
Cavanaugh	8	16	50.0	141	0	2
Swider	0	1	00.0	0	0	0

#21

DUQUESNE DUKES 67, LA SALLE EXPLORERS 65
DECEMBER 31, 1954
MEN'S NCAA BASKETBALL

Ringing in the New Year

There's a tradition in New York City's Times Square that began in 1907. Adolph Ochs, the owner of the *New York Times,* decided to organize the first—and now famed—New Year's Eve celebration. In college basketball during the 1950s, there was another New York City tradition the same time of year called the Holiday Festival, in which some of the country's best teams would descend on Madison Square Garden to play one another. Begun in 1952, it was the country's premier in-season tournament and a good indicator of who the best team in the nation was at that point of the season.

In the 1955 Holiday Festival, Duquesne would take on the defending national champion LaSalle Explorers in the finals of that famed tournament on New Year's Eve. It was the perfect way for the Dukes, who had been among the nation's elite for the better part of two decades, to ring in the New Year of what would be the best campaign in the program's history.

But LaSalle had also built a special program. The Explorers had achieved greatness under coach Ken Loeffler, who led the school to the NIT title in 1951–52 before capturing their only NCAA championship with a 92–76 victory over Bradley two years later.

As impressive as LaSalle's run was, having a player like Tom Gola on your roster made winning championships much easier. A four-time All-American, Gola eventually had his number retired by the school, was elected to the Naismith Hall of Fame, and had the arena that the Explorers currently play in named after him.

After Gola left LaSalle, he would help the Philadelphia Warriors to an NBA title in his rookie season, was elected to the Pennsylvania House of Representatives in

Probably the greatest player ever to wear a Duquesne uniform was Dick Ricketts (No. 12). While he eventually went on to a professional career in baseball with the St. Louis Cardinals, Ricketts ended his career on the Bluff as the school's all-time scoring leader (1,953) and rebounding leader (1,359), two records he still holds. (Courtesy of Duquesne University Athletics)

1966, coached his alma mater to a 23–1 mark in 1969, and became a Philadelphia city controller after he left coaching.

The Explorers were ranked third in the country after dispatching eight of its first 10 opponents. Duquesne, however, had moved up to eighth in the polls and was riding a four-game winning streak.

The Dukes' Dick Ricketts and Sihugo Green each had their chance to shine in the tournament, both setting the festival's all-time single-game scoring record, but other opponents had some success in slowing down the Dukes' offense with a solid zone defense, the same that LaSalle played so effectively. Loeffler would employ an aggressive zone, just like the Flyers had, with the hope that the Explorers could send the Dukes back to the Bluff with their second loss.

Ricketts and Gola were the top two scorers in the tourney after two games with 63 and 60 total points, respectively (with Green just behind at 58), and promised to put on quite a show, which would be televised live in Pittsburgh on WENS-TV. What should have been an intriguing matchup of two top 10 teams was not embraced by New York basketball fans, mostly because there were no local teams to root for, as only 12,135 people (far fewer than had been on hand for the earlier games) showed up on this New Year's Eve matchup.

Those who did show up saw a tense, classic contest, with LaSalle taking leads during the first 5 minutes and the Dukes battling back each time to tie

Sihugo Green, driving to the basket in the picture, was one of the greatest players ever to wear a Duquesne uniform. Green went on to be named to two consensus All-American squads in 1955 and 1956 and was at his best in the 1955 NIT finals, where he scored a game-high 33 points in the Dukes' win. (Courtesy of Duquesne University Athletics)

the game. As the first half was unfolding, Gola led LaSalle to a 19–14 lead, but the Dukes battled back once again tying the contest at 21 with 7 minutes left.

Even though Moore's squad was fighting hard, the Dukes' season appeared to take a drastic turn when Ricketts went down after twisting his ankle. But the Dukes' center stayed in the game and, even though he was hurting, helped Duquesne to a 32–27 halftime advantage.

Early in the second half, Ricketts and Green, who each led the Dukes in the contest with 23 points apiece, pushed the Dukes to a 40–33 lead before the Explorers battled back, taking the lead for the first time since the 7-minute mark of the first half at 41–40. Jim Fallon gave Moore's squad the advantage once again with a jump shot, but LaSalle then netted 4 straight points, making the score 45–42.

The Dukes showed their toughness, despite a string of setbacks: their star center was not healthy; they played with a short bench, as they would most of this season because Tom Peszko was ruled academically ineligible; and Lou Iezzi was out for the season with an illness. They scored 12 straight points to sprint to a 9-point lead. But LaSalle wouldn't be outdone, responding with a 12–2 run of its own that put the Explorers up 57–56 with 6 minutes remaining.

Not intimidated by the LaSalle run, the Dukes responded. Guard Mickey Winograd scored his only bucket of the game to give the Dukes a 58–57 advantage they would not relinquish. Gola could not be stopped, scoring the final 10 points for LaSalle, but unfortunately for the Explorers no one else was able to contribute. With the Dukes up by just 2 points with under a minute left, Green hit two clutch free throws that stretched the lead to 67–63. Gola tossed in a shot as the buzzer went off to make the final 67–65. Gola finished the contest with 30 points and was named the tournament MVP, but the Dukes were able to celebrate something more important: a second consecutive Holiday Festival championship.

Impressed, both United Press International and the Associated Press would vault Moore's team to second in the nation behind the Wildcats of Kentucky, giving Duquesne what it had hoped for when it came to the Garden a few days earlier: respect as national championship contenders and a truly special way to ring in the new year.

Duquesne

Player	Fg	Ft	Pts
Green	7	9	23
Da. Ricketts	2	3	7
Di. Ricketts	8	7	23
Fallon	4	0	8
Winograd	1	4	6
Totals	22	23	67

Lasalle

Player	Fg	Ft	Pts
Singley	1	0	2
Greenberg	4	0	8
Gola	9	12	30
O'Malley	2	0	4
Lewis	6	5	17
Blatcher	2	0	4
Gomez	0	0	0
Totals	24	17	65

Team	1st	2nd	Final
Lasalle	27	38	65
Duquesne	32	35	67

#20

PITT PANTHERS 24, MIAMI (FL) HURRICANES 14
NOVEMBER 24, 2017
MEN'S DIVISION I NCAA FOOTBALL

Pickett's Charge

Pickett's Charge during the Battle of Gettysburg in 1863 is remembered as perhaps one of the most ill-conceived military strategies in the history of American warfare. But for fans of the University of Pittsburgh's football program, the term is remembered in a vastly different manner. To them, "Pickett's Charge" happened 154 years later. It was the day freshman quarterback Ken Pickett finally got the chance to start a game and lead Pitt to a convincing victory over second-ranked Miami, the third time in 10 years that a Pitt team would defeat the second-ranked team in the country, beating Clemson the year before and a memorable win against West Virginia in 2007.

Coming into this ballgame, the two formerly nationally prominent programs were going in different directions. After a run in the early twenty-first century during which Miami won a national championship while finishing second twice, the program began to lose luster. The Hurricanes struggled in the decade that followed, being ranked in the final top 25 poll only once between 2006 and 2015. After the much-heralded Al Golden era ended in disappointment, the administration at Miami turned to Mark Richt, a coach who was relieved of his job at Georgia, despite the fact he was 145–51 with the Bulldogs, including a 10–5 record in bowl games.

As it turned out Georgia's disappointment was the Hurricanes' gain. Miami gave Richt a second chance as he began a resurgence at the school they enthusiastically refer to as the U. In 2016 they finished 9–4 with a spot in the final top 25 poll for the first time since 2009. A year later they were doing much better than that. Coming into the final regular-season game of 2017, they stood undefeated with a perfect 10–0 mark. After a series of close victories against Atlantic Coast Conference (ACC) opponents, the Hurricanes started to believe that they were

Freshman quarterback Ken Pickett, in the No. 8 jersey, had a very long season while waiting for an opportunity to play for Pitt. Finally, on the last game of the year against second-ranked Miami (Florida), he got his chance to start leading the Panthers to a surprising 24–14 upset. (Courtesy of the University of Pittsburgh Athletics)

one of the best teams in the land after decisively beating the two toughest teams they would face in the regular season, Virginia Tech and Notre Dame.

All of a sudden they were the talk of the college football world. They rose to No. 2 in the country. Their defense had been incredible at forcing turnovers, and the "turnover chain" (a neck chain awarded to a Miami player who forced a turnover) was becoming a national phenomenon. With a win against Pitt at Heinz Field on the day after Thanksgiving, as well as a victory in the ACC championship versus Clemson, a playoff spot was theirs for the taking.

Pitt, however, was taking an unexpected fall under third-year coach Pat Narduzzi. The Panthers stood at 4–7 and had struggled offensively through a yearlong quarterback controversy during which none of the options had much success. First-stringer Max Browne was not mobile and struggled behind an offensive line that was having issues protecting him. Browne was injured against Syracuse, while redshirt sophomore Ben DiNucci, a local high school hero, took over. DiNucci was mobile but not an effective passer. Narduzzi controversially burned freshman Kenny Pickett's red shirt against Syracuse on the final play, after DiNucci was hurt late in the game. But the freshman never was put in the lineup for the games afterward and stood on the sidelines as DiNucci had problems leading the Panthers to victory.

With a red shirt no longer an option, many wondered when Pickett would get his chance. It finally came against Virginia Tech, when he entered the contest in the first quarter following a DiNucci interception. He threw for 242 yards, including a 74-yard pass to Jester Weah with under a minute left that put Pitt at the Hokies' 1-yard line. But the Panthers were unable to complete the drive and fell to the heavily favored Hokies, 20–14. Despite the loss, Narduzzi was impressed and called on the freshman to make his first start against the nation's second-ranked team the following week.

Pickett started quickly, rambling for a 9-yard gain on the first play of the game, but then, after the first Panthers drive stalled at their own 42, he would direct Pitt into an early lead. The Panthers' defense showed it could be formidable, forcing Miami to punt from its own 10 on the next series. Pickett once again ran on the first play of the following Pitt drive for a substantial gain, this one for 11 yards, and three plays later, Alex Kessman kicked a 46-yard field goal to give Pitt an early 3–0 advantage.

A Panthers fumble a few minutes later gave Miami great field position in Pitt territory, but once again the Panthers' defense came through, forcing another punt. But it wouldn't be long until the Hurricanes' offense finally started moving.

Midway through the second quarter, Miami quarterback Malik Rosier found Ahmmon Richards with a 23-yard scoring toss to complete a nine-play, 80-yard drive that gave Miami a 7–3 lead. When Pitt tight end Chris Clark fumbled after catching a Pickett pass on the next series and Miami recovered, it looked like the Hurricanes were gearing up for a big win.

As the year had gone on, the Pitt defense had substantially improved, and they were at their best this afternoon. The Panthers forced another punt as the visitors were unable to capitalize on the great field position. With just under 5 minutes left in the half, the young Pitt quarterback calmly led them down the field on an 11-play drive. He completed four passes and converted on three third-down situations, the last being a third-and-goal from the 6, where Pickett scrambled after not being able to find a receiver. He was hit at the 1 but forced his way into the end zone to give the Panthers back the lead with only 35 seconds left. Miami ran out the clock and the home team went into the locker room with a 4-point lead.

As good as the Panthers' defense was in the first half, it was even more dominant in the second. The Panthers limited the undefeated visitors to 21 yards on their first three series before the Panthers regained possession at their own 35 with 6:06 left in the third. After the Panthers moved the ball deep into

Hurricanes territory with passes to Weah (29 yards) and Aaron Mathews (9), running back Quadree Ollison took over, running for 22 yards on three plays, which put the ball at the Miami 3. Two plays later, he caught a 5-yard shovel pass for a touchdown that gave Pitt a stunning 17–7 lead.

While moving more effectively in the fourth quarter, the Hurricanes still couldn't finish their drives, punting three more times to Pitt as time was running out. With 8:56 remaining, they pinned the underdogs deep in their own territory at the Pitt 10. If the Hurricanes were going to come back, they would have to quickly force a punt.

Miami's defense had been the driving force of this remarkable team in 2017, but when they needed to get a stop, they couldn't get one. Ollison continued his great second half with a 13-yard run on the first play of the drive; then three plays later Miami's final chance literally slipped through their hands. On a third-and-9, the young Pitt quarterback rolled out and saw a wide-open Henderson. He threw a line drive pass without seeing the defender in front of his receiver, defensive back Trejan Bandy. The ball went through Bandy's hands, tipped up in the air, and Henderson pulled it in for the 19-yard gain and a first down.

The Panthers continued to push through the vaunted Hurricanes' defense, but with 3:03 remaining they were seemingly stopped on the Hurricanes' 22, where they faced fourth-and-6. Narduzzi had a decision to make: try to get a first down and run the clock or attempt a field goal that could potentially give them a 13-point lead. Not wanting to risk a blocked kick, the Pitt coach decided to run the ball on fourth down. What followed was one of the greatest plays in the program's history.

Pickett faked the handoff and rolled to his left. The Miami defense was completely fooled by the play fake as Pickett ran around the end untouched and dove into the end zone for a stunning touchdown making it 24–7 with 2:54 remaining. But with the game seemingly out of hand, the Hurricanes quickly scored 38 seconds later and then recovered the onside kick.

The fans at Heinz were stunned and bracing for a worst-case scenario. Facing third-and-3 at their own 41, the Hurricanes were looking to get in field goal position. Rosier dropped back to pass, but blitzing Pitt defensive back Avonte Maddox knocked the ball out of his hands. The Panthers' Dewayne Hendrix pounced in it to clinch the victory, which ended Miami's dreams of a national championship. For the second time in two years and the third in 10, Pitt defeated the second-ranked team in the nation—this time thanks to Pickett's charge.

Team	1st	2nd	3rd	4th	Final
Miami	0	7	0	7	14
Pittsburgh	3	7	7	7	24

Team	Play	Score
Pitt	Kessman 46-Yd Field Goal	0–3
Miami	Richards 23-Yd Pass From Rosier (Badgley Kick)	7–3
Pitt	Pickett 6-Yd Run (Kessman Kick)	7–10
Pitt	Ollison 5-Yd Pass From Pickett (Kessman Kick)	7–17
Pitt	Pickett 22-Yd Run (Kessman Kick)	7–24
Miami	Berrios 39-Yd Pass From Rosier (Badgley Kick)	14–24

Rushing—Miami

Player	Att	Yds	Ave	Td
Rosier	12	31	2.6	0
Horner	7	12	1.7	0
Dallas	3	4	1.3	0
Shirreffs	1	-2	-2.0	0

Rushing—Pittsburgh

Player	Att	Yds	Ave	Td
Ollison	14	62	4.4	0
Pickett	13	60	4.6	2
Hall	10	30	3.0	0
Henderson	4	23	5.8	0
Team	4	-23	-5.8	0

Receiving—Miami

Player	Rec	Yds	Ave	Td
Berrios	4	61	15.3	1
Richards	3	47	15.7	1
Herndon IV	3	41	13.7	0
Harris	3	29	9.7	0
Irvin II	1	7	7.0	0
Horner	1	2	2.0	0

Receiving—Pittsburgh

Player	Rec	Yds	Ave	Td
Weah	6	80	13.3	0
Henderson	3	36	12.0	0
Clark	2	25	12.5	0
Araujo-Lopes	2	21	10.5	0
Ollison	3	17	5.7	1
Mathews	1	9	9.0	0
Hall	1	5	5.0	0

Passing—Miami

Player	Comp	Att	Pct	Yds	Td	Int
Rosier	15	34	44.1	187	2	0
Shirreffs	0	2	00.0	0	0	0

Passing—Pittsburgh

Player	Comp	Att	Pct	Yds	Td	Int
Pickett	18	29	62.1	193	1	0

DUQUESNE DUKES 7, PITT PANTHERS 0
OCTOBER 17, 1936
MEN'S NCAA FOOTBALL

A New Sheriff in Town

For the majority of the Jock Sutherland era, the University of Pittsburgh was the dominant college football program in town. Carnegie Tech (now Carnegie Mellon University) and Duquesne University had their moments, but Pitt had become one of the best programs in the nation and usually won decisively against its Forbes Avenue neighbors. On a rainy fall afternoon at Pitt Stadium in 1936, that would change, as Duquesne showed the favored Panthers that they could play at their level.

Sutherland had been an All-American at Pitt, winning two national championships. He was also a graduate of the school of dentistry with a professorship in teaching bridge and crown. After his collegiate career ended, he played a season of professional ball for the Massillon Tigers before taking a position as head coach at Lafayette College, where he won a share of the national championship in 1921.

After the legendary Pop Warner left the University of Pittsburgh before the 1924 campaign, the school called on its former All-American to lead the program. Not only was Sutherland as successful as Warner, but he took the school to the next level. He won three national championships going into the 1936 campaign, a season in which he had one of his most talented teams, led by Marshall Goldberg, Ave Daniell, and Bobby LaRue. The Panthers had been perfect defensively after three games in 1936, outscoring their opponents by a 93–0 margin. They also were as dominant defensively against their city rivals, never allowing the Dukes to score in the three contests they had played against them to that point.

Up on the Bluff, the Dukes had been building toward being competitive in major college football, hiring Notre Dame legend Elmer Layden in 1927. After

Having some fun as they prepare for another contest are members of the 1936 national champion University of Pittsburgh Panthers football team. One of the stars of the squad was Ave Daniell (*second from left*). A tackle at the school, Daniell was named a consensus All-American in 1936. (Courtesy of the University of Pittsburgh Athletics)

Layden brought them to 10–1 in 1933 and earned a spot in the Festival of Palms game, he left to take over as head coach at his alma mater. The Dukes had gone through two coaches in two seasons following Layden's departure, when the school hired another Fighting Irish alum, John "Clipper" Smith. Smith was a consensus All-American under Knute Rockne and began his coaching career at North Carolina State in 1931, where he was an unspectacular 10–12–5 in three seasons.

Smith came to Duquesne in 1935, taking a job as a line coach with the Dukes. The next year he was promoted to head coach following the departure of Christy Flanagan. The Dukes also stood at 3–0 before this intercity matchup, outscoring Waynesburg, Rice, and Geneva 61–0 in the process. Their level of opponents hadn't been as impressive as Pitt's, so the Panthers went into this contest as a prohibitive favorite, despite the matching records.

It was a rainy, dreary day at Pitt Stadium, as only 25,000 fans decided to take in what would be a classic contest. Both teams had difficulty maneuvering through the sloppy field until late in the first period, when Pitt took over at their own 48 after a poor Dukes punt. Goldberg ripped through the Duquesne line for 25 yards in two runs that put the Panthers at the 22. The Panthers took it down to the 13 where they faced a fourth-and-1, and Sutherland decided to go for the first down. He sent his Heisman Trophy hopeful, Goldberg, up the middle as the Duquesne defense rose to the occasion, stopping Goldberg in his tracks to take the ball back on downs.

Early in the second quarter, George Matsik replaced Beto Vairo at halfback for the Dukes. The substitution seemed minor at the time, but after Duquesne took over possession at their 22 following a Pitt punt, the move became significant. The leader of the Duquesne offense, quarterback Boyd Brumbaugh, gained 7 yards on two carries to set up a third-and-3 from the Dukes' 29. On the next play, Matsik took a handoff over left tackle and broke through the tough Panthers' defensive line. As a convoy of blockers joined him, no Pitt defender could catch the Ambridge, Pennsylvania, native. Matsik not only ended the scoreless streak against Pitt, but on a day in which the playing conditions were less than stellar, he gave the Panthers and their fans something to worry about. Unfortunately for Matsik, he broke his finger not long after the touchdown, sidelining him for the rest of the game, but his run is remembered in the annals of Duquesne football history as one of the program's greatest moments.

With the conditions and weather on his side, Smith turned to his defense to keep the Panthers off the board the rest of the game. But this was a great Pitt team, and that feat would be easier said than done. The Panthers had a great chance midway in the third when Brumbaugh was forced to punt from deep in his end zone. Pitt got the ball at the Dukes' 37, but a fumble by LaRue after securing the punt gave the ball back to Duquesne. As the third quarter was coming to an end, the Panthers were only 30 yards away from tying the score. But Brumbaugh picked off an errant Frank Patrick toss at the Duquesne 5 and returned it 51 yards to the Panthers' 44.

Losing Matsik and Vairo, who was hurt trying to tackle LaRue in the third quarter and had to be carried off the field, left the Dukes thin on defense, and Pitt kept trying to take advantage with time running out. Taking over on their own 20 early in the final quarter, the Panthers began to rip through the Dukes' defensive line. A 16-yard run by Patrick was followed soon after by a 26-yard Goldberg dash to the Duquesne 29. Goldberg then tried to find LaRue with a pass, but Frank Zoppetti stepped in front of it for an interception that stopped another Pitt drive.

Pitt would have a few more chances in the final minutes, but the now confident Dukes' defense easily stopped the Panthers each time. Finally, the Dukes were able to run out the clock and secured the incredible upset.

The Duquesne student body joyously ran onto the field and mobbed Smith and the players as they tried to return to the locker room. Sutherland, thinking his national championship quest was now over, was pelted by wet newspapers and bottles thrown by frustrated fans.

But the Panthers went undefeated the rest of the way, winning five contests, three against top 10 teams, including the fifth-ranked Washington Huskies in the Rose Bowl, 21–0. They eventually did win the national championship that season, Sutherland's fourth, while the Dukes would go into a slump following the Pitt victory. They lost to West Virginia Wesleyan and Detroit before rebounding at 8–2, a season that included an Orange Bowl victory against Mississippi State and their first Associated Press national ranking at 14th.

Despite the great ending for the University of Pittsburgh, it was this loss that showed Duquesne was a formidable foe. Within three years, the Dukes would become the best football program in Pittsburgh, surpassing both Pitt and Carnegie Tech. It was this win that proved to their rivals that there was truly a new sheriff in Pittsburgh college football.

Team	1st	2nd	3rd	4th	Final
Duquesne	0	7	0	0	7
Pittsburgh	0	0	0	0	0

Team	Play	Score
Duquesne	Matsik 71-Yd Run (Brumbaugh Kick)	7–0

Stat	Duquesne	Pittsburgh
First Downs	3	7
Rushing Yards	134	150
Passing Yds	75	50
Comp-Att-Int	0–1–0	4–15–3
Total Yards	209	200
Punt Average	41	37
Fumbles Lost	3	2
Penalty Yards	70	35

#18

PITT PANTHERS 31, NOTRE DAME FIGHTING IRISH 10
SEPTEMBER 11, 1976
MEN'S DIVISION I NCAA FOOTBALL

Changing of the Guard

As the University of Pittsburgh football team was coming off a three-game stretch to end the 1975 campaign—in which it defeated nationally ranked Notre Dame, lost by one point to a perennial top 10 program in Penn State, and thrashed Kansas in the Sun Bowl—hopes among the Panthers faithful were high that they were about to become a national power in 1976. While most good programs start off the season with a couple of easy games to make sure they have ironed out any issues before they begin their more difficult contests, Pitt did not choose that path. If the Panthers truly were to see the resurrection of Pitt as a national power, they would do so going on the road to play an opening game against a program that had been one for most of the twentieth century: the Notre Dame Fighting Irish.

Under coach Ara Parseghian, between 1964 and 1974, Notre Dame excelled. The Irish finished in the top 15 in each of his 11 seasons, capturing national championships in 1966 and 1973. Most humbling for the University of Pittsburgh was the Parseghian-led teams defeating the Panthers in each of his 11 campaigns, including a 31–10 triumph in Tony Dorsett's freshman season of 1973.

After Parseghian retired following 1974, Notre Dame chose former Green Bay Packers head coach Dan Devine to lead the program. His first year was a huge disappointment, as the Irish finished outside the top 20 for the first time since Parseghian took over. They even lost to Pitt 34–20 as Dorsett humiliated their defense for a school-record 303 yards rushing. In 1976 Devine seemed to have a more talented team, and better times were expected for the Irish. They would not have to wait long to seek redemption for the embarrassment against the Panthers the year before. In fact, many expected that the Notre Dame-Pitt rivalry would return to what it had been for most of the post–Jock

Sutherland era: an easy victory for the Fighting Irish. And the first drive of the game seemed to back up that theory.

Along with future Hall of Famer Joe Montana, Rick Slager had been in an offseason battle for the Notre Dame starting quarterback slot, but Slager captured the spot right before the season began. It looked like it was the right decision by Devine, as Slager drove the team downfield 86 yards on their first possession of the season. He eventually found tight end Ken McAfee with a pass in the left flat, and McAfee sprinted the rest of the way for a 25-yard score, giving Notre Dame the early lead 7–0. Pitt defensive back Jeff Delaney was upset giving up such an early touchdown. "We didn't read it right," he later said. "We were watching crossing routes but forgot to cover up on the outside."[1] The Notre Dame fans were already thinking revenge was only a couple hours away, but they would be forced to change their outlook only a few minutes later.

The pain of seeing Dorsett running all over the once proud Notre Dame defense was still fresh in the minds of the sellout crowd of 59,035. Just to make sure the fans didn't forget, Dorsett took his first handoff of the game and rambled 61 yards. The Heisman Trophy winner would finish the drive with a 5-yard touchdown run that tied the score at 7.

While Pitt easily moved downfield on their first possession, the Panthers would have difficulty against the tough Irish defense for the rest of the day. But the Panthers' defense made amends for their poor performance on their first series of the game and dominated Slager and the Notre Dame offense for the duration. With the score still tied going into the second quarter, the Fighting Irish quarterback got a firsthand look at how good the Panthers' defensive backfield was.

Looking for a short completion, Slager instead saw a short pass intercepted by Pitt's Leroy Felder, who took the ball from the Notre Dame 27 down to the 2. Two plays later, quarterback Bobby Haygood bolted in from the 1 to give Pitt the lead. Delaney then picked off another Slager pass at the 33 just a minute later. Dorsett continued to easily mow through the defensive line, running 21 yards on two carries to set up another Haygood 1-yard touchdown run, and all of a sudden the Panthers were up 21–7.

Each team had an opportunity to score late in the first half. Notre Dame missed a chance after recovering a fumbled punt return by Gordon Jones at the Panthers' 23, but kicker Dave Reeve missed a 43-yard field goal. Pitt then could have scored a touchdown, but Dorsett fumbled the ball though the end zone as he was about to cross the goal line. A Reeve 53-yard field goal for Notre Dame in between the two chances were the final points of the half as the Panthers went into the locker room with a 21–10 advantage.

Trying to get back in the game, the Irish moved to the Panthers' 37 on their first drive of the second half, where 1,000-yard rusher Al Hunter fumbled the ball. Pitt's Arnie Weatherington recovered, but the Panthers were unable to move the ball. The Pitt offense was sputtering, so coach Johnny Majors inserted Matt Cavanaugh (who would go on to star for Pitt after Haygood was lost for the season against Georgia Tech the next week). Cavanaugh finally got the offense going again, leading the Panthers on a drive that ended with a Carson Long 34-yard field goal that restored their 14-point lead.

Soon after a poor Notre Dame punt, the Panthers took over on the Irish 36. The formidable Notre Dame defensive line of Willie Fry, Ross Browner, and Bob Golic appeared to stop Dorsett at the line on the next play, but somehow the All-American squirted through and ran for 28 yards to the Notre Dame 8. Cavanaugh ran it in for the touchdown on the next play to round out the scoring as Pitt held on for the convincing 31–10 victory.

At the end of the day, Notre Dame gained no revenge on the Panthers, nor did their defense show they could stop Tony Dorsett, as he ran for 181 yards on the day. It brought his career total against Notre Dame to a remarkable 754 yards on 96 carries.

Scheduling such a tough opener was a gutsy maneuver, but it turned out to be the perfect first game for the Panthers—one that announced to the college football world they had arrived as a serious contender for the national championship.

Team	1st	2nd	3rd	4th	Final
Pittsburgh	7	14	0	10	31
Notre Dame	7	3	0	0	10

Team	Play	Score
ND	McAfee 25-Yd Pass From Slager (Reeve Kick)	0–7
Pitt	Dorsett 5-Yd Run (Long Kick)	7–7
Pitt	Haygood 1-Yd Run (Long Kick)	14–7
Pitt	Haygood 1-Yd Run (Long Kick)	21–7
ND	Reeve 53-Yd Field Goal	21–10
Pitt	Long 34-Yd Field Goal	24–10
Pitt	Cavanaugh 8-Yd Run (Long Kick)	31–10

Rushing—Pitt

Player	Att	Yds	Ave	Td
Dorsett	22	181	8.2	1
E. Walker	4	8	2.0	0
Hutton	7	11	1.6	0
Haygood	10	-17	-1.7	2
Cavanaugh	7	4	0.6	1
Sindewald	3	4	1.3	0

Rushing—ND

Player	Att	Yds	Ave	Td
Heavens	24	93	3.9	0
Hunter	13	39	3.0	0
Slager	10	-26	-2.6	0
McLane	1	1	1.0	0
Forystek	2	-1	-0.5	0

Receiving—Pitt

Player	Rec	Yds	Ave	Td
Corbett	4	72	18.0	0
Jones	1	11	11.0	0
Reutershan	1	4	4.0	0

Receiving—ND

Player	Rec	Yds	Ave	Td
McAfee	4	70	17.5	1
Hunter	1	16	16.0	0
Heavens	1	10	10.0	0
Kelleher	2	25	12.5	0
Domin	1	14	14.0	0
Orsini	1	38	38.0	0
Eurick	1	11	11.0	0

Passing—Pitt

Player	Comp	Att	Pct	Yds	Td	Int
Haygood	5	9	55.6	83	0	0
Cavanaugh	1	4	25.0	4	0	0

Passing—ND

Player	Comp	Att	Pct	Yds	Td	Int
Slager	6	22	27.3	85	1	2
Forystek	5	16	31.3	99	0	2

#17

PITT PANTHERS 13, WEST VIRGINIA MOUNTAINEERS 9
DECEMBER 1, 2007
MEN'S DIVISION I NCAA FOOTBALL

Crushed Hopes

It was a tough season for Pitt Panthers on the gridiron in 2007. After winning their first two games of the season, albeit against less-than-stellar competition in Eastern Michigan and Grambling, they only won two of their next nine contests and stood at 4–7 as they went to Morgantown, West Virginia, to face the second-ranked West Virginia University Mountaineers. It seemed like it would be little more than an easy exercise for the home team.

With a victory against their struggling rivals in the Backyard Brawl, the Mountaineers would punch their ticket to the national championship game. It was a golden opportunity not only for the program to win its first football national championship but for the Big East conference itself after being constantly criticized by the media for its substandard level of play. On paper, it appeared it would be a one-sided affair. But, as the saying goes, that's why they don't play games on paper. The Panthers did something special that crushed the hopes of their bitter rivals in one of the most stunning upsets in college football history.

Dave Wannstedt was a celebrated former Panthers player who had been called back to try to turn around the fortunes of his alma mater following the departure of Walt Harris in 2004. Much was expected of the former Chicago Bears and Miami Dolphins head coach, but his first two seasons had been mired in mediocrity. After going 11–12, his third season in 2007 had been a disaster. Tyler Palko, who finished his career with the third-most passing yardage in school history, was gone at quarterback, and his incumbent, Bill Stull, had been injured. Pat Bostick, a former prized prospect who had not lived up to expectations, had taken over the controls of the offense. LeSean McCoy had emerged as one of the premier running backs in the country while the defense had performed well. But other than a 24–17 victory over the University of Cincinnati, at the time

146

the 23rd-ranked team in the country, it had been a poor 4–7 campaign to this point for the Panthers. There were even some influential calls by the alumni to end the Wannstedt era at Pitt. But the administration believed in him and gave him a three-year extension the day before the game.

However, West Virginia was at their zenith. Coach Rich Rodriguez had installed an innovative and highly successful spread offense at WVU led by quarterback Pat White. The Mountaineers had emerged victorious in 10 of their 11 contests at that point, losing only to 18th-ranked South Florida early in the season. As the Backyard Brawl was approaching, WVU was coming off a very impressive 66–21 victory against the 20th-ranked Connecticut Huskies, and oddsmakers had made the Mountaineers a 28.5-point favorite against their archrivals in the regular-season finale.

The Panthers' odds were long indeed, but college football had seen a very weird year that included a memorable Appalachian State upset over Michigan, Alabama losing to Louisiana-Monroe, and USC dropping a contest to 41-point underdog Stanford—a record at the time for an upset against the biggest point spread in college football history.

As the game began, the excited crowd at Mountaineer Field became exuberant as Pat Bostick tossed an interception into the hands of West Virginia's Antonio Lewis, who returned the ball 48 yards to the Pitt 27. The young Panthers' defense, which would play one of the greatest defensive games in school history, began by stopping the potent WVU offense at the 2, setting up what appeared to be an easy field goal by the sure-footed Pat McAfee. Surprisingly, McAfee missed, and the game remained scoreless.

Pitt's offense was inept early on and gave the ball back to the Mountaineers late in the first quarter in great field position. Once again, West Virginia drove the ball deep into Pitt territory, led by a 21-yard scramble by White. The Mountaineers reached the Pitt 15, where the bend-but-don't-break Panthers stopped them. McAfee lined up once again for a short field goal, this one from 32 yards, but he missed once more. The first quarter ended with the game still scoreless.

Pitt eventually got their offense rolling, moving into WVU territory, where Bostick tossed another interception, this one by Vaughn Rivers. The turnover inspired the Mountaineers' offense, who went on a 14-play 74-yard drive, culminating with a 6-yard Jarrett Brown touchdown run to give them a 7–0 lead. The touchdown relieved the West Virginia faithful for the moment, but soon the fans had something else to be concerned about, as White dislocated his thumb on the drive.

The Panthers finally got on the board as time ran out in the half. Thanks to a 15-yard personal foul penalty by the WVU defense, Pitt put themselves in position for a half-ending 48-yard field goal by Connor Lee to give the Panthers momentum going into the locker room, down just 7–3 to the heavily favored Mountaineers.

West Virginia had a chance to regain the momentum as it took the kickoff to open the second half. Rivers made a phenomenal return to the WVU 48 but fumbled the ball on the hit and the Panthers pounced on it, giving them their best field position of the game. McCoy was finding cracks in the tough WVU line as the Panthers methodically moved downfield. Eventually Bostick pushed it into the end zone from 1 yard out to give Pitt its first lead of the game 10–7.

The fans at Mountaineer Field were stunned, and as the Panthers' defense continued to play well, hopes for a national championship began to get cloudy. The Panthers were now controlling the game and put themselves in position to increase their lead, but Lee missed a 35-yard field goal as time was running out in the third quarter to keep their advantage at three.

With the Pitt offense controlling the ball in the second half, West Virginia only managed two Mountaineers possessions that netted 6 yards. But as the fourth quarter began, WVU still only trailed by a field goal. Before the Mountaineers could get anything going, Pitt's Tommy Duhart sacked Brown at the Mountaineers' 17, forcing a fumble, which the Panthers recovered. Pitt moved to the 1, but rather than risk no points if they went for it on fourth down, Wannstedt opted to send Lee out for a short field goal that made it 13–7. The score now forced West Virginia to try to score a touchdown against the suddenly impenetrable Panthers' defense.

While West Virginia couldn't trust their offense to move the ball, they could rely on their return game, which had been solid all evening. The speedy Noel Devine returned the ensuing kickoff 48 yards to the Panthers' 33, but West Virginia could only move 9 yards and were unable to take advantage of the fortuitous field position. The Mountaineers turned the ball back over to the Panthers on downs at the Pitt 24.

After a Pitt punt, WVU took over with only 2:50 remaining in regulation. White was back in the game and completed a 20-yard pass to Darius Reynaud to the Panthers' 33. The Mountaineers would move to the 28, but Pitt held firm, and the Mountaineers once again gave it back to the Panthers' offense on downs following a White incompletion with 1:34 left.

Pitt melted away the final seconds, and on the last play of the game, not wanting to risk a punt block, punter Dave Brytus ran out of the end zone for an intentional safety to make the final 13–9. Wannstedt, who was on crutches for the game following Achilles tendon surgery, was ecstatic. But Rodriguez and the rest of Mountaineer Nation were devastated at seeing their national championship hopes disappear. Following the contest, McAfee, who grew up near Pittsburgh in Plum, Pennsylvania, had his car vandalized and received death threats by some irrational WVU fans for missing what they felt were easy field goals.

LeSean McCoy rushed for 148 yards to lead the Pitt offense, and a monumental Panthers defensive effort held one of the most potent offenses in the country to a mere 183 total yards that would bring joy to Panthers' fans and misery to West Virginia fans for years to come. Bostick remembered the ride home. "Getting out of there, it was like a ghost town," he said. "It was a pretty depressing scene, I guess, from a West Virginia fan's perspective, and I understand why. It was empty, and you could've probably heard a pin drop outside the confines of our buses."[1]

It was a painful loss for WVU, losing out on a rare opportunity to play for the national championship. Crushed hopes that seemed to hurt the Mountaineers' players and fans alike as the years go on, just as they did on that memorable evening.

Team	1st	2nd	3rd	4th	Final
Pittsburgh	0	3	7	3	13
West Virginia	0	7	0	2	9

Team	Play	Score
WVU	Brown 6-Yd Run (McAfee Kick)	0–7
Pitt	Lee 48-Yd Field Goal	3–7
Pitt	Bostick 1-Yd Run (Lee Kick)	10–7
Pitt	Lee 18-Yd Field Goal	13–7
WVU	Punter Brytus Runs Out Of End Zone For Safety	13–9

Rushing—Pitt

Player	Att	Yds	Ave	Td
McCoy	38	148	3.9	0
Stephens-Howling	6	15	2.5	0
Collins	4	11	2.8	0
Murray	1	3	3.0	0
Bostick	2	-4	-2.0	1

Rushing—WVU

Player	Att	Yds	Ave	Td
White	14	41	2.9	0
Brown	9	28	3.1	1
Schmitt	2	13	6.5	0
Slaton	9	11	1.2	0
Devine	7	11	1.6	0

Receiving—Pitt

Player	Rec	Yds	Ave	Td
Turner	3	29	9.7	0
Strong	2	25	12.5	0
McCoy	1	10	10.0	0
Porter	2	2	1.0	0
Stephens-Howling	2	1	0.5	0

Receiving—WVU

Player	Rec	Yds	Ave	Td
Reynaud	3	46	15.3	0
Slaton	1	9	9.0	0
Lyons	1	9	9.0	0
Jalloh	2	6	3.0	0
Gonzales	1	5	5.0	0
Sanders	1	4	4.0	0

Passing—Pitt

Player	Comp	Att	Pct	Yds	Td	Int
Bostick	10	19	52.6	67	0	2

Passing—WVU

Player	Comp	Att	Pct	Yds	Td	Int
White	5	10	50.0	50	0	0
Brown	4	6	66.7	29	0	0

PITT PANTHERS 22, PENN STATE NITTANY LIONS 21
DECEMBER 7, 1963
MEN'S NCAA FOOTBALL

A Tragic Victory

It was a game no one wanted to play, even though it was a continuation of one of the country's greatest rivalries and was amid a phenomenal season that put the University of Pittsburgh football program back into the national spotlight.

But the tragic death of President John Fitzgerald Kennedy made thoughts of a potential prime bowl matchup against their bitter rivals a moot point for the Panthers as the nation mourned its fallen leader. In light of Kennedy's death on November 22, the game was rescheduled from its original date of November 23 to two weeks later on December 7. While it turned out to be arguably the greatest game in the history of this heated rivalry, it was played in the shadows of a horrific moment in American history.

Before the events of that fateful day in Dallas, it had been a magnificent season for Pitt football. Years before, John Michelosen had been the single wing quarterback for legendary coach Jock Sutherland's power Panthers squads between 1935 and 1937, winning the national championship in his final two seasons. After graduating, Michelosen was hired by his mentor as an assistant at Pitt before becoming the youngest head coach ever to begin a season in the modern era of the National Football League, a record he held until Lane Kiffin broke it in 2007. Michelosen took the job for the Pittsburgh Steelers in 1948 following the death of Sutherland, who had taken over the Steelers two years earlier and led them to the only postseason playoff contest the team would play in the franchise's first 40 seasons.

Michelosen could not continue the success with the Steelers that Sutherland had begun and was relieved of his duties following the 1951 campaign. Four years later he would be called back to Pitt to assume the head coaching position of his alma mater, taking over a program that had struggled since Sutherland left in 1938. The team immediately began to thrive under his tutelage, going to the Sugar Bowl in 1955 before earning a trip to the Gator Bowl a year later.

As good as the beginning of his tenure was, it paled in comparison to 1963. Pitt had fallen into mediocrity following its Gator Bowl loss to Georgia Tech in 1956 and was coming off a 5–5 campaign in 1962. When it came to the Penn State rivalry, the Panthers hadn't beaten the Nittany Lions since a 22–7 victory in 1959.

There wasn't much to suggest that the 1963 edition of the Panthers would be any better. It was a group of local kids from western Pennsylvania who would form an amazing bond that inspired them to do things not many imagined they could. Michelosen was banking on an effective group of sophomores led by quarterback Kenny Lucas, who was the favorite to start coming out of spring practice, as well as halfbacks Eric Crabtree and Dale Lucas. As it turned out, a group of experienced upperclassmen would carry them instead.

Incumbent starting quarterback Fred Mazurek, who was an effective runner but wasn't able to show off his passing skills the year before because of a broken finger, and fullback Rick Leeson, who was hoping to become the first Pitt fullback since the great Marshall Goldberg to eclipse 1,000 yards in his career, were pivotal parts of the offense this season. This talented team also included future NFL coach Marty Schottenheimer and All-Americans Paul Martha, who would go on to become CEO of the Pittsburgh Penguins, and Ernie Borghetti, the father of famed University of Pittsburgh executive associate athletic director E. J. Borghetti.

The Panthers began the year with a 20–0 shutout at UCLA and with only one blemish on their schedule—a 24–12 loss to Roger Staubach and the 10th-ranked Navy Midshipmen—they went into their matchup against Penn State with a 7–1 mark. They had a shot at a major bowl if they defeated both the Nittany Lions and the Miami (Florida) Hurricanes in their final two games.

As the two rivals were going through their final preparations for the contest, the news broke that President Kennedy had been killed. As a devastated nation mourned, it was announced the following day that all college football games would be postponed.

The Panthers resumed their season the next week, defeating the Hurricanes 31–20 to improve their mark to 8–1. But because of the rescheduling of the Penn State game, it appeared that Pitt's hopes for a bid to the Cotton or Orange Bowl were now gone; the committees for both games didn't want to extend a bid and take the chance the Panthers may lose to Penn State. With the hopes of a potential national championship now gone, Pitt still had the opportunity to make a statement with a win, but the Nittany Lions were not going to make it easy for them.

A large crowd of 52,349 was on hand on this sunny afternoon. In the box score at least, Pitt dominated the contest, outgaining the Lions in total yardage 421–279, including a 310–128 advantage on the ground. But turnovers and a blocked punt threatened to turn this contest from a coronation for the Panthers into one of the most devastating upsets in school history.

A good amount of Penn State's yardage came on the second play of the contest when Lions quarterback Pete Liske flipped a screen pass to Don Caum. Schottenheimer was caught out of position, and Caum broke through the Pitt secondary and didn't stop until he hit the Panthers' 11 to cap an exciting 68-yard play. A 15-yard personal foul penalty would back the Nittany Lions up, and Ron Coates's 29-yard field goal attempt fell short to keep the game scoreless.

While the Lions blew a great early opportunity, they took advantage of their second scoring chance. After an unsuccessful opening drive by the Panthers, Tom Black's punt from the 17 was blocked. A couple plays later from the 9, Liske faked a handoff and then threw the ball into the hands of Gary Klingensmith. The play once again fooled Schottenheimer, and he cut inside too quickly. Klingensmith went around him into the end zone as the Lions were up 7–0. While Schottenheimer was devastated at giving up two big plays, the linebacker would thank his defensive coach, Carl DePasqua, for sticking with him, and Schottenheimer rebounded to play a magnificent game.

Pitt eventually got back into the game following a poor Penn State punt that set the Panthers up at their own 46. Mazurek, who had broken Warren Heller's 32-year-old all-purpose yard record for a career the week before, hit on passes of 16 and 12 yards to Bill Howley, taking Pitt to the 2-yard line as time ran out in the first quarter. Two plays into the second, Martha bolted into the end zone from the 1 to cut the Lions' lead to a single point. But Penn State kept the lead when Mazurek rolled out but was stopped short of the end zone on the ensuing 2-point conversion attempt.

After a Panthers interception by Glen Lehner, Mazurek fumbled the ball, giving it back to Penn State at the Pitt 34. Klingensmith led a charge downfield with a 14-yard run that set up a 9-yard scoring toss to Gerry Sandusky, giving the Nittany Lions a 14–6 lead. But Pitt once again would bounce back and cut into the Lions' advantage. Mazurek led the Panthers on an 80-yard drive on the strength of a 34-yard pass to Leeson and 16-yard tosses to Martha and Al Grigaliunas. After a face mask penalty on Penn State put the ball at the 1, Leeson went over for the touchdown. Mazurek once again missed the 2-point attempt, this time on an incomplete rollout pass, as the teams went into the locker room at the half with the Lions up by 2 points.

In the third quarter, Lucas got his chance to play after Mazurek was injured following a 42-yard run. The sophomore completed two passes for 21 yards before an 11-yard sack forced the Panthers to settle for a 35-yard Leeson field goal that gave them their first lead of the day at 15–14. But their advantage was short-lived as Liske took Penn State on a 75-yard drive on the next series. A 30-yard run by Chris Weber and an acrobatic 10-yard, third-down scoring catch by Caum once again put Penn State ahead, 21–15, as the quarter was coming to an end.

Down by six and their great season now in peril, Pitt took over at their own 23. Lucas found Crabtree with a 26-yard completion to the Penn State 45; then Mazurek returned for the beginning of the final quarter. But the Panthers had trouble moving the ball and faced fourth-and-1 at the 41. Michelosen decided to go for it, and his injured quarterback rolled out and ran for 2 yards and a crucial first down.

The drive continued as Bill Bodie caught an 11-yard pass and then Mazurek ran to the 21. Running back John Telesky took it 4 yards to the 17 when Mazurek dropped back to pass. He rolled to his right but found no one open. Seeing open space in front of him, he took off for the end zone and scored to tie the game. Leeson kicked the extra point to put the Panthers back ahead 22–21 early in the fourth quarter.

Statistically, Pitt had been the superior team all afternoon, but the underdog Lions just wouldn't go away. With one chance left, Penn State began the final drive of the game. After Schottenheimer missed an opportunity for interception, which would have ended the visitor's chances, Mazurek was penalized for pass interference that gave Penn State the ball at the Pitt 43. Klingensmith then ran 18 yards to the Pitt 25 and, after the Lions gained 5 more yards, the drive stalled at the 20, giving the Nittany Lions a shot at the game-winning field goal. With tension filling the stadium, Coates lined up for the 37-yard attempt with only 1:29 remaining, but the kick sailed wide, and the Panthers held on for a thrilling victory.

After the game, the team was offered a spot in the Sun Bowl, but since it wasn't the game Pitt wanted, they declined. Martha explained later, "We wanted to play Navy again. In those days, and I shouldn't say this, the bowl games weren't that big; they weren't like they are now. We knew how good we were, we knew who we had beaten that year, and we just wanted to play one more team again, and that was Navy."[1]

So without a bowl game, the Panthers wound up finishing with a No. 3 national ranking after a 9–1 season that ended with a memorable victory over a bitter rival, albeit played under tragic circumstances.

Team	1st	2nd	3rd	4th	Final
Penn State	7	7	7	0	21
Pittsburgh	0	12	3	7	22

Team	Play	Score
PSU	Klingensmith 9-Yd Run (Coates Kick)	7–0
Pitt	Martha 1-Yd Run (Run Failed)	7–6
PSU	Sandusky 9-Yd Pass From Liske (Coates Kick)	14–6
Pitt	Leeson 1-Yd Run (Pass Failed)	14–12
Pitt	Leeson 35-Yd Field Goal	14–15
PSU	Caum 10-Yd Pass From Liske (Coates Kick)	21–15
Pitt	Mazurek 17-Yd run (Leeson Kick)	21–22

Rushing—PSU

Player	Att	Yds	Ave	Td
Klingensmith	14	47	3.3	1
Stuckrath	5	26	5.2	0
Vargo	1	4	4.0	0
Weber	7	38	5.4	0
Liske	2	-4	-2.0	0
Huber	1	1	1.0	0
Powell	1	-6	-6.0	0

Rushing—Pitt

Player	Att	Yds	Ave	Td
Leeson	15	70	4.7	1
Martha	6	21	3.5	1
Bodie	4	16	4.0	0
Mazurek	23	142	6.2	1
Crabtree	1	2	2.0	0
Telesky	9	38	4.2	0
Roeder	3	5	1.7	0
Lucas	1	-11	-11.0	0
Blick	1	-7	-7.0	0

Receiving—PSU

Player	Rec	Yds	Ave	Td
Caum	4	99	24.8	1
Anderson	2	14	7.0	0
Sandusky	1	9	9.0	1
Klingensmith	3	38	12.7	0
Vargo	1	13	13.0	0

Receiving—Pitt

Player	Rec	Yds	Ave	Td
Howley	2	28	14.0	0
Leeson	1	34	34.0	0
Grigaliunas	2	33	16.5	0
Martha	1	2	2.0	0
Kuzneski	1	11	11.0	0
Crabtree	2	26	13.0	0
Bodie	1	11	11.0	0

Passing—PSU

Player	Comp	Att	Pct	Yds	Td	Int
Liske	11	23	47.8	173	2	1

Passing—Pitt

Player	Comp	Att	Pct	Yds	Td	Int
Mazurek	7	15	46.6	108	0	0
Leeson	0	1	00.0	0	0	0
Lucas	3	4	75.0	37	0	1

#15

PITT PANTHERS 43, CLEMSON TIGERS 42
NOVEMBER 12, 2016
MEN'S DIVISION I NCAA FOOTBALL

The Blemish

Going into Clemson's Memorial Stadium seemed like a fool's errand for the University of Pittsburgh football team. At 5–4, the 2016 Panthers had enjoyed some success, but now they'd face an undefeated Clemson Tigers squad in their home stadium. Plus, the Tigers had plenty to play for, since they were pushing toward one of four playoff spots for the national championship. Winning this game appeared to be a task that was beyond this Panthers squad.

While Clemson had a couple of close brushes with defeat—a 24–17 come-from-behind overtime victory over North Carolina State and a narrow 42–36 win over fifth-ranked Louisville—there was no reason to think this game with Pitt would be close. The Panthers' offense was having a fabulous season under second-year head coach Pat Narduzzi, but their defense, particularly their pass defense, was among the worst in the nation, allowing 333 yards per game and a 63.8 completion percentage. With Clemson's record-setting quarterback Deshaun Watson and wide receiver Mike Williams each having phenomenal years going against the porous Panthers' defense, the Pitt offense appeared as if it was going to be in a high-scoring game. To pull off the upset, it was going to take almost a perfect game plan by Panthers offensive coordinator Matt Canada. After the first scoring drive of the game, it was apparent he had such a plan.

Following the opening kickoff, Pitt quickly drove into scoring position thanks to a 44-yard completion from quarterback Nate Peterman to wide receiver Jaymar Parrish. Before the game was 2 minutes old, Peterman connected with fullback George Ashton for a 15-yard touchdown that gave the visitors an early 7–0 advantage.

James Conner inspired fans around the nation with his memorable battle against cancer before the 2016 campaign. His story became even more incredible with his return in 2016 as the school's second all-time leading rusher with 3,733 yards. Conner had a phenomenal season, including a terrific game in the 43–42 upset of second-ranked Clemson. (Courtesy of the University of Pittsburgh Athletics)

When Clemson took the next drive deep into Pitt territory, Watson was picked off in the end zone by defensive back Ryan Lewis, giving the Panthers the ball back at their own 25. They were quickly stopped and the Tigers soon tied the score as the Pitt pass defense, as suspected, proved to be no match for the Clemson offense.

Knowing they needed a near-flawless performance to win, the Panthers quickly responded when the inspirational James Conner, who came back this year after missing most of 2015 with his much-publicized battle against cancer, pulled in a pass from Peterman and rambled 46 yards for the go-ahead score that gave Pitt a 14–7 lead.

The rest of the first quarter settled into a back-and-forth affair, with the Tigers scoring twice to take their first lead of the game. Then Pitt tight end Scott Orndoff snagged in a toss from Peterman and outran the Clemson secondary for a 55-yard touchdown. But Pitt kicker Chris Blewitt missed the extra point, which kept Pitt behind by one.

Even though they had difficulty stopping Watson, the Panthers were able to intercept him at key times, including an Avonte Maddox interception at the Panthers' 14, which set up a 10-play, 86-yard drive. It started with a 26-yard run up the middle by Conner before he took the ball for a 27-yard ramble to the Clemson 7. Three plays later, Ashton caught a 1-yard scoring toss for a 27–21 Pitt lead.

With 2:23 left in the half, Pitt hoped they could stop the Tigers and hold on to the lead at the intermission. But the Tigers wouldn't cooperate, as Watson efficiently guided them 75 yards for a touchdown and a 28–27 advantage at the half.

Many times in a game like this, the heavy favorite makes adjustments at halftime and convincingly pulls away from the underdog in the second half. Following an early Pitt fumble by Peterman, which gave the Tigers the ball at the Panthers' 47, it looked like that was exactly what was about to happen. Watson, who would set a school record with 580 yards passing in the game, completed passes of 25 and 27 yards—the latter for a touchdown that extended the Clemson lead to eight.

With the game looking as if it were about to get out of hand, the Pitt offense took control. Aided by pass-interference and personal-foul penalties against the home team, the Panthers cruised down the field, and Orndoff caught his second scoring toss of the game to pull Pitt back to within 1 point. After Watson once again directed the Tigers to a touchdown and a 42–34 lead late in the third quarter, a strange thing happened. It was as if the Panthers' defense simply had enough of being embarrassed and played more effectively in the final quarter.

As Clemson drove to the Pitt 3 with 5:42 left in the game, middle linebacker Saleem Brightwell picked off Watson in the end zone and returned the football 70 yards to the Tigers' 30. Four plays later, Conner ripped through the Clemson defense for a 20-yard touchdown run to make the score 42–40. The Panthers failed on a 2-point conversion that could have tied the game but soon got the ball back after stopping the Tigers' Wayne Gallman on a fourth-and-1 at the Pitt 35 with 58 seconds remaining. The failed play impressed Clemson coach Dabo Sweeney. "We had a chance to put the game away and they stopped us," he said. "We had been making those kinds of plays this year."[1]

Pitt had under a minute to get into field goal range. Peterman, who would pass for 308 yards and five touchdowns for the game, quickly knifed through the Clemson defense with a 9-yard run and two passes to Orndoff, taking them to the Clemson 30. After two more incomplete passes, Narduzzie called on Blewitt, giving him a hug and a kiss on the cheek as he sent him out to try to make history.

With 6 seconds left, Blewitt kicked the ball through the uprights, giving the program one of the greatest upsets in its long history. Conner, who ran for 132 yards and caught three passes for 57 more, felt some sympathy for Clemson, who appeared to have squandered their national title chances. "Hey, sorry to do that," he said to reporters afterward, "but we wanted this one bad. We'll remember this one forever."[2]

But the loss actually didn't take Clemson out of the running. The Tigers recovered to win the ACC championship and received a spot in the playoffs, where they defeated Ohio State and then Alabama for the national championship.

Clemson's title only made Pitt's upset win even sweeter, as the Panthers put the lone blemish on the record of the 2016 national champions.

Team	1st	2nd	3rd	4th	Final
Pittsburgh	14	13	7	9	43
Clemson	14	14	14	0	42

Team	Play	Score
Pitt	Ashton 15-Yd Pass From Peterman (Blewitt Kick)	7–0
Clemson	Gallman 1-Yd Run (Huegel Kick)	7–7
Pitt	Conner 46-Yd Pass Fro M Peterman (Blewitt Kick)	14–7
Clemson	Gallman 1-Yd Run (Huegel Kick)	14–14
Clemson	Williams 15-Yd Pass From Watson (Huegel Kick)	14–21
Pitt	Orndoff 55-Yd Pass From Peterman (Kick Missed)	20–21
Pitt	Ashton 1-Yd Pass From Peterman (Blewitt Kick)	27–21
Clemson	Scott 13-Yd Pass From Watson (Huegel Kick)	27–28
Clemson	Cain 27-Yd Pass From Watson (Huegel Kick)	27–35
Pitt	Orndoff 7-Yd Pass From Peterman (Blewitt Kick)	34–35
Clemson	Gallman 1-Yd Run (Huegel Kick)	34–42
Pitt	Conner 20-Yd Run (2-Pt Conversion No Good)	40–42
Pitt	Blewitt 48-Yd Field Goal	43–42

Rushing—Pitt

Player	Att	Yds	Ave	Td
Conner	20	132	6.6	1
Peterman	6	18	3.0	0
Hall	3	9	3.0	0
Ford	1	1	1.0	0
French	1	0	0.0	0
Henderson	2	-4	-2.0	0

Rushing—Clemson

Player	Att	Yds	Ave	Td
Gallman	18	36	2.0	3
Watson	5	8	1.6	0
Fuller	2	6	3.0	0

Receiving—Pitt

Player	Rec	Yds	Ave	Td
Orndoff	9	128	14.2	2
Conner	3	57	19.0	1
Parrish	1	44	44.0	0
Weah	2	38	19.0	0
Ashton	4	29	7.3	2
Ford	2	14	7.0	0
Mathews	1	-2	-2.0	0

Receiving—Clemson

Player	Rec	Yds	Ave	Td
Williams	15	202	13.5	1
Scott	13	125	9.6	1
Leggett	6	95	15.8	0
Renfrow	7	77	11.0	0
Cain	3	45	15.0	1
McCloud	4	26	6.5	0
Gallman	4	10	2.5	0

Passing—Pitt

Player	Comp	Att	Pct	Yds	Td	Int
Peterman	22	37	59.5	303	5	0
Team	0	1	00.0	0	0	0

Passing—Clemson

Player	Comp	Att	Pct	Yds	Td	Int
Watson	52	70	74.3	580	3	3

#14

The Storck Delivers

We've all heard the stories of storks delivering babies. While those tales are pure fantasy, when the fans of the California University of Pennsylvania's women's basketball team ask where national championships come from, they all say the same thing: the Storck delivers them.

While she hit unquestionably the biggest shot in the history of the program, Meghan Storck came into the 2003–04 season with a burden on her shoulders. The previous year, the program began its ascent into the elite level of Division II women's basketball by qualifying for the NCAA tournament for the second time. The Vulcans fought their way to the national semifinals, where they found themselves in a narrow contest with Northern Kentucky. Storck, who would finish her career with the third-most three-point field goals in program history, missed an open 3-point shot with under a minute left that might have turned the contest in the Vulcans' favor. They eventually lost, 45–43, and the young freshman was anxious to atone for her miss. She would get that opportunity a year later as Cal was about to complete the quest they had started the previous season.

The team had been good for the most part since they began playing NCAA basketball in 1981, but for coach Darcie Vincent, good wasn't enough. She excelled at Duquesne University as a player, where she finished her career in 1992 as the school's all-time leading scorer. Also an Academic All-American, she was the first woman ever selected to the Duquesne Sports Hall of Fame and began her coaching career at a rival Pennsylvania State Athletic Conference (PSAC) school, Slippery Rock. She took them to new heights, going 23–7 in 1999–2000 while capturing the school's only NCAA regional title.

The next season, Vincent took over for Tom Kendall at Cal, taking the Vulcans to their first PSAC title game and then winning the conference a year later,

162

There was no more prolific passer in the history of women's basketball with the California University of Pennsylvania Vulcans than Meghan Storck. Her 767 assists are not only a school record but the highest total in the Pennsylvania State Athletic Conference history. Even though she would have been renowned for that alone, it was her clutch three-point shot in the 2004 national championship that helped give Cal its first title that she is most remembered for. (Courtesy of the California University of Pennsylvania Athletics)

when they reached the Division II Final Four and eventually lost to Northern Kentucky. But the team was young and bounced back from that disappointment to finish 35–1 the following year, capturing their second consecutive PSAC crown and NCAA eastern regional championship. This time in the Final Four, the Vulcans won their semifinal matchup, advancing to the national finals where they would face Drury University.

But the Vulcans' trip to the national championship final was not an easy one. They'd faced South Dakota State and Merrimack in the regional final and Final Four contests, and early on both contests looked like routs. The Vulcans ran up significant leads of 16 and 21 points, respectively, in each affair, but both their opponents cut the lead to a mere six points in each game. Against Drury it would happen again.

The Vulcans raced out to a 41–33 halftime advantage, but Vincent knew this was a tough Drury team who wouldn't be beaten easily. Cal stayed focused in the second half. Led by Sarah McKinney, who led all scorers with 26 points, the Vulcans continued to control the game, running up their advantage to 15 points to 59–44. It began to look like Cal was going to cruise to an easy victory and their first national championship. But for the third straight game, the Vulcans allowed a seemingly beaten opponent back in the game.

Led by a 3-point basket by Magan Brunson and a 3-point play following a bucket and a foul shot by Amy Belew, Drury quickly reduced the lead to 9 points. California began to struggle, and the Panthers continued to cut into their advantage. Cal scored on six of their next seven possessions, finally taking the lead at 63–61 when Jill Curry hit two free throws with 7:07 remaining. The once one-sided affair had now turned into a fierce battle as the teams went back and forth over the next 5 minutes, with the Panthers holding onto a 72–71 lead with under a minute to play. In a strikingly similar scenario to the year before, the opportunity for redemption would come for Storck.

On Cal's next possession, Storck found herself wide open with the basketball. "I don't really know what was going through my mind at that time," she said. "It was a scramble and I just looked and saw I was open. . . . I just had to shoot."[1] It was a shot that would carve out Storck's legacy at the school. If it were off the mark, she would be remembered for missing the two biggest shots of her career and not for how successful her time with the Vulcans was. This time, she would not miss. The ball went through the rim to give Cal a 74–72 lead with 30 seconds remaining.

On the final possession, Drury's Kara Rutledge missed a chance to win the game with 3 seconds remaining as her 23-foot 3-point shot fell short. The Vulcans added a free throw in the final seconds as they held on to win the national championship, 75–72. For seniors like Becky Siemback, it was a surreal moment. "There are three people in Division II right now, three women, that can say they're ending their career with a national championship," she said. "It's just like a storybook ending for me. Its everything I've ever dreamed of, everything I've ever wanted."[2]

It was a sentiment that every player on the team was feeling, especially Storck. Her shot, the most memorable in Vulcans history, was a pivotal part of what turned out to be a school Hall of Fame career when she was given Cal's most prestigious honor two years later. On that spring night in 2004, the Storck truly did deliver.

California (PA)

Player	Fg (3pt)	Ft	Pts
Dillon	5 (2)	0	12
Siemback	2	1	5
Storck	6(2)	2	16
Philyaw	5	2	12
McKinney	11	4	26
Gottuso	0	0	0
Nukks	0	4	4
Clark	0	0	0
Totals	29 (4)	13	75

Drury

Player	Fg (3pt)	Ft	Pts
Curry	4	6	14
Newton	6	5	17
Hunt	4(2)	0	10
Regier	2(1)	0	5
Rutledge	5(2)	3	15
Stratton	0	0	0
Creed	0	0	0
Brunson	2(2)	0	6
Belew	1	3	5
Totals	24 (7)	17	72

Team	1st	2nd	Final
California (PA)	41	34	75
Drury	33	39	72

#13

PITT PANTHERS 34, NOTRE DAME FIGHTING IRISH 20
NOVEMBER 15, 1975
MEN'S DIVISION I NCAA FOOTBALL

303

To sports fans, iconic numbers mean everything. In Pittsburgh, when you mention the number 3,000 to baseball fans, thoughts automatically go to Roberto Clemente's final hit total. The number 100 makes NBA fans think of Wilt Chamberlain and his magnificent single-game effort in which he scored 100 points, a record that most likely will never be beaten.

In Pitt football, the number 303 is perhaps the most memorable of all. It reminds Panthers fans of that remarkable afternoon when the school's lone Heisman Trophy winner, Tony Dorsett, set a rushing mark that has not only stood the test of time but has marked the day when his up-and-coming young team finally secured a victory over a nationally prominent program, giving the Panthers the confidence they'd need for their national championship run the next season.

When coach Johnny Majors came from Iowa State to try to resurrect a decaying football program at Pitt, he knew he needed good players quickly. One of the first he found was Dorsett, a small halfback from Hopewell High School, right outside of Pittsburgh. The speedy Dorsett caught the eye of assistant coach Jackie Sherrill, who helped recruit the star, believing Dorsett was the right guy to lead Pitt's new offense. He used a unique strategy to recruit him: Sherrill went after his close friend at Hopewell, linebacker Ed Wilamowski. "Ed was white and Tony was black, and at every school they visited, they were separated (in the college dorms)," Sherrill said. "I don't know if I was smarter than the others, but I didn't separate them. I knew Tony was very, very close to Ed. We kept them together."[1] Dorsett would acknowledge later that Sherrill's strategy was one of the main reasons he came. Months later, when Majors finally had

The greatest running back ever to grace the gridiron at the University of Pittsburgh is Tony Dorsett. The only Heisman Trophy winner in school history, Dorsett set many school and NCAA records. Perhaps his most impressive is the 303 yards he ran for against Notre Dame in 1975. The school record still stands today. (Courtesy of the University of Pittsburgh Athletics)

a chance to see Dorsett play in the state's annual high school all-star game, the Big 33 Football Classic, he knew he had his star running back.

In his first few years, the Aliquippa native did not disappoint his new coach. Dorsett finished second in the nation in rushing in 1973 with 1,586 yards, becoming the first freshman to be named as a first-team All-American in 29 years. Dorsett had rewritten the Panthers' record book in one season, breaking Toby Uansa's single-season Pitt rushing record while becoming the first Panthers player ever to go over 1,000 yards in a season. He also broke the NCAA record for rushing yards in a game by a freshman with 265 against Northwestern. Dorsett followed it up with a somewhat disappointing sophomore season, although he still broke the 1,000-yard plateau. He continued to excel during a solid junior season, but it would take a dramatic turn against the Fighting Irish.

Dorsett had enjoyed success against Notre Dame. He rushed for more yards his first game against the Irish (209) than any running back had ever gained against a Notre Dame team. It was a record that would last only two years.

The Fighting Irish were coming into this game needing a convincing win. They were 7–2, having lost to Michigan State and third-ranked USC, but had found their way into the top 10, ranked ninth, after convincing victories against Navy and Georgia Tech. They knew if they had any chance of securing a major bowl bid, they needed to pick up another impressive win at Pitt Stadium. Because they had beaten the Panthers in every season since 1963, the Irish were confident this matchup would be no different.

For Pitt, it was a chance to finally take their rebuilding efforts to the next level. Johnny Majors and his staff had done a magnificent job getting the Panthers to this point. After beginning the season ranked in the top 20, disappointing losses to Navy and West Virginia and a 46–10 thrashing by top-ranked Oklahoma had the Panthers sitting at 6–3. With another game remaining against 10th-ranked Penn State, a loss to Notre Dame and a second straight season without a true marquee victory would give them the feeling that they had made little progress.

A sellout crowd of 56,480 filed into Pitt Stadium, and the fans were quickly given a preview of the incredible show they were about to witness. Earlier in the season against Army, Dorsett had broken his own single-game Pitt mark for rushing yards with 268. After Pitt took the opening kickoff, he showed that record might be in jeopardy by sprinting for 57 yards to the Notre Dame 3. Quarterback Matt Cavanaugh stiff-armed an Irish defender on the next play as he ran for a touchdown and a quick 7–0 Pitt lead only 57 seconds into the game.

Notre Dame quickly came back with a scoring drive of its own, ending when Dave Reeve knocked through a 48-yard field goal to cut the lead to 4 points. On the ensuing kickoff, Pitt wide receiver Gordon Jones fumbled the ball at the 5, and the Irish recovered. A couple plays later, quarterback Rick Slager took it in from a yard out as Notre Dame went in front 10–7. In recent seasons, this was the point in a game against a tougher opponent when Pitt would usually come apart. The next series proved to be an important one, as the team finally began to show that they were evolving from an up-and-coming program to one who could contend among the nation's elite.

From his own 29, Cavanaugh tossed a pitch to Dorsett, who broke through the line and sprinted to the Irish 29. At that point, Jones atoned for his fumble with an incredible block, taking out two Notre Dame defenders and clearing the path for the Hopewell alum to reach the end zone and restore Pitt's lead at 14–10. After Reeve and the Panthers' Carson Long exchanged field goals, Dorsett came to the forefront again, this time as a receiver. Following a Notre Dame fumble, the home team moved to the Irish 49. Cavanaugh then tossed a pass to his All-American running back across the middle near midfield. Aided by another phenomenal block by Jones, Dorsett slipped behind the linebackers and raced into the end zone for the score that extended Pitt's lead to 24–13.

The Panthers took that lead into the half, and Dorsett had accumulated 161 yards rushing at that point. On three plays, including his touchdown reception, he had amassed 177 yards in setting up all three Panthers scores. As it turned out, it was only the beginning. Legendary Pitt announcer Bill Hillgrove recalled running into a frustrated Notre Dame athletic director Moose Krause at halftime. "I was coming down the steps at that rickety, old press box at Pitt Stadium," he said, "and Moose Krause was saying, 'We didn't make any adjustments (to stop Dorsett).' I felt like saying, 'Moose, what are you going to adjust to?'"[2]

Long tacked on a 30-yard field goal in the third after a Jones 78-yard punt return before Slager led Notre Dame on their best drive of the day. He topped off a 77-yard drive with a spectacular 10-yard touchdown pass to tight end Ken McAfee, who leaped for the ball at the 5 before taking it into the end zone to cut Pitt's lead to 27–20 with a quarter left to play.

With the lead in danger, Cavanaugh began the season's most important drive at his own 20-yard line. He didn't do anything complicated to take Pitt down the field; he just handed off to one of the greatest running backs in the history of college football. Dorsett ran for 52 of the 80 yards on three carries, and Cavanaugh put an end to Notre Dame's dreams of a comeback and a major bowl appearance by pushing the ball over from the 1 late in the game to restore the Panthers two-touchdown lead 34–20.

The victory appeared assured at that point, but there was still one big moment left. With under a minute left to play, Dorsett eclipsed the 300-yard plateau rushing—303 to be exact—setting a record by an Irish opponent that has never been beaten as well as a school record that also currently remains. The Panthers and their fans were thrilled with what was the biggest victory in the Majors era at this point and the subsequent Sun Bowl bid that came with it.

For the skinny kid who was always at his best against Notre Dame, he would go on to achieve everything a football player could hope for. He became the first player to win a national championship in college, to win a Super Bowl title in the NFL, and then to be elected to both the College and Pro Football Halls of Fame.

For all the plaudits he would eventually receive, it was this day against Notre Dame that sealed his legend both as a Pitt Panthers player and in the history of college football.

Team	1st	2nd	3rd	4th	Final
Notre Dame	10	3	7	0	20
Pittsburgh	14	10	3	7	34

Team	Play	Score
Pitt	Cavanaugh 3-Yd Run (Long Kick)	0–7
ND	Reeve 48-Yd Field Goal	3–7
ND	Slager 1-Yd Run (Reeve Kick)	10–7
Pitt	Dorsett 71-Yd Run (Long Kick)	10–14
ND	Reeve 47-Yd Field Goal	13–14
Pitt	Long 42-Yd Field Goal	13–17
Pitt	Dorsett 49-Yd Pass From Cavanaugh (Long Kick)	13–24
Pitt	Long 30-Yd Field Goal	13–27
ND	McAfee 10-Yd Pass From Slager (Reeve Kick)	20–27
Pitt	Cavanaugh 1-Yd Run (Long Kick)	20–34

Rushing—ND

Player	Att	Yds	Ave	Td
Eurick	10	38	3.8	0
Heavens	17	80	4.7	0
Browner	5	15	3.0	0
McLane	9	33	3.7	0
Slager	8	-1	-0.1	1
Weller	1	-4	-4.0	0

Rushing—Pitt

Player	Att	Yds	Ave	Td
Dorsett	23	303	13.2	1
Cavanaugh	12	10	0.8	2
Walker	11	74	6.7	0
Hutton	4	24	6.0	0

Receiving—ND

Player	Rec	Yds	Ave	Td
McLane	4	20	5.0	0
Browner	1	4	4.0	0
McAfee	3	26	8.7	1
Schmitz	1	9	9.0	0
Heavens	2	26	13.0	0
Kelleher	5	65	13.0	0
Eurick	1	8	8.0	0

Receiving—Pitt

Player	Rec	Yds	Ave	Td
Corbett	1	11	11.0	0
Jones	1	12	12.0	0
Dorsett	3	71	23.7	1

Passing—ND

Player	Comp	Att	Pct	Yds	Td	Int
Slager	17	32	53.1	158	1	0

Passing—Pitt

Player	Comp	Att	Pct	Yds	Td	Int
Cavanaugh	5	14	35.7	94	1	1

#12

Double Duty

In today's college basketball, the NCAA tournament means everything. It's the event that all programs set as their goal for each season. If a well-known, big-budget program is selected to play in the National Invitation Tournament, it generally means that it has fallen short of its aspirations.

In the 1940s and 1950s, things were different. Back then, the NCAA tournament was a restrictive one, limiting bids to only one school per conference. The NIT had no such restrictions and was more prominent than the NCAA tournament. Teams that won either tournament had a legitimate claim to the national championship—it was March Madness indeed. Until the 1950s, when the NCAA outlawed a school accepting both an NCAA and NIT bid, teams could accept invitations to both. In 1940 the first two teams to take on the challenge of playing in both were the University of Colorado and the Duquesne University Dukes.

Coach Charles "Chick" Davies had taken over the Duquesne program in 1924 and had turned it into one of the best in the nation. Born in nearby New Castle, Davies had endured a less-than-stellar season on the Bluff with a 6–11 mark before improving to 14–4 a season later in 1938–39. This version of the Dukes started out with three dominant victories before falling to Indiana University, 51–49, at the arena located underneath Pitt Stadium. They then came back to defeat a strong Colorado club in overtime six days later. The victory spurred Duquesne to a phenomenal campaign.

The Dukes went on to win their final 14 regular-season contests, finishing the campaign 17–1, which garnered them the first postseason bid in the history of the program—a trip to Madison Square Garden in New York City to play in the NIT. After beating hometown St. John's and then Oklahoma A&M

(now Oklahoma State), the Dukes would play a rematch with Colorado in the finals. Unfortunately for Duquesne, the Buffaloes gained revenge with an easy 51–40 victory for the title.

Disappointed as they were, Davies and his squad got an opportunity not only for redemption but for a chance at history when they received a bid to play in the NCAA basketball championship tournament. While Davies was skeptical of making the season even longer, he gave the players the responsibility of making the decision. They were unanimous in their choice to accept the bid. The coach had his doubts, though, and thought the long season had taken its toll on the Dukes by the NIT final. "Colorado has a great team," he said, "but it still would have been anyone's game if our boys had been at peak position."[1]

Davies nonetheless had to get ready for an NCAA quarterfinal matchup against the Western Kentucky State Teachers College (now Western Kentucky University). Duquesne was the prohibitive favorite over Coach Ed "High-Diddle" Diddle's Hilltoppers squad in front of a capacity 7,500 fans at the Butler Fieldhouse. While his team was the favorite, the coach knew that the 24–5 Western Kentucky club was a dangerous opponent for Duquesne, especially if his team were as tired as Davies thought they were.

Known for waving a red towel on the sidelines (the same red towel that is currently part of the Western Kentucky logo), Diddle was a legend at the school, eventually winning 759 games and 32 conference titles over 42 seasons. He would also be elected to the Basketball Hall of Fame and have the school's arena named after him. He was at his best this season, directing a potent team led by center Carlyle Towery and the fine playmaker Howard "Tip" Downing from Butler, Pennsylvania.

While the game was tied at 6 early on, it was because Duquesne was missing several easy opportunities rather than Western Kentucky playing on their level. Finally, the Dukes started hitting their shots and took a 12–6 lead. But not long afterward, Davies's men resumed their poor shooting, missing six consecutive layups as they scored only 2 more points the rest of the first half. The Dukes held a precarious 14–12 advantage at the intermission.

In the second half, Davies hoped his club would take control of a game that he felt they should be winning handily. The problem was that Duquesne stars Moe Becker and Paul Widowitz, along with Rudy Debnar, were in early foul trouble, which forced the team into a more cautious style. Becker had also injured his ankle in the NIT and was playing a reduced a role off the bench.

The Dukes' struggles continued in the second half, as Western Kentucky scored the first 7 points after the break, turning a 2-point deficit into a 5-point lead. The Dukes' Bill Lacy came to the rescue, leading a Duquesne resurgence as the men from the Bluff scored 11 of the next 16 points to finally wrestle the lead back at 25–24 with only 10 minutes left in regulation.

The Dukes' defense kept Western Kentucky's offense at bay, but their trouble shooting extended to the foul line. Duquesne made only four of 12 free throws for the day, which kept the game close. Though struggling, the Dukes clung to a 1-point lead with time running out. But the Dukes still had problems. Becker reaggravated his ankle and was pulled from the game. Then Lacy missed two foul shots, and the Hilltoppers grabbed the rebound and quickly sped down the court, frantically looking for the game-winning shot. They took six shots on the possession, but none of them connected, and the Dukes hung on for the exciting 30–29 victory that sent them to the national semifinal for the lone time in school history.

Ironically, it was Colorado that didn't have the stamina to survive in the NCAAs as they lost their first game to Southern California. Davies and his crew had just enough to survive and advance. While they lost their next contest in a rematch with Indiana, 39–30, this Dukes team will always be renowned in Duquesne history not only as having its lone national semifinal appearance but for being among the first in college basketball history (along with Colorado) to play in two postseason tournaments in the same year.

Duquesne

Player	Fg	Ft	Pts
Kasperic	1	0	2
Milkovich	2	2	6
Lacy	4	0	8
Widowitz	2	1	5
Debnar	3	1	7
Becker	1	0	2
Totals	13	4	30

Western Kentucky

Player	Fg	Ft	Pts
Ball	1	2	4
Fulks	0	0	0
Towery	6	1	13
Walter	4	4	12
H. Downey	0	0	0
A. Downey	0	0	0
Shelton	0	0	0
Totals	11	7	29

Team	1st	2nd	Final
Duquesne	14	16	30
Western Kentucky	12	17	29

#11

Vengeance Is Ours

There always seems to be one club that can give a team all they can handle, not only finding a way to beat their opponent every time but ripping their heart out in the process. In the Jock Sutherland era at the University of Pittsburgh, the gridiron Panthers were one of the greatest programs in the country, losing only 20 times in 15 seasons while winning shares of five national championships. As good as they were, there was one team who managed not only to consistently beat them but to embarrass them in the process: the University of Southern California.

Hall of Fame coach Howard Jones came to USC a year after Jock Sutherland began his legendary Pitt tenure, and he led the Trojans to four national titles. Twice he had the chance to face the University of Pittsburgh in his backyard with an opportunity to gain national supremacy, and twice Jones came out victorious. In 1930 the two squads met in Pasadena on New Year's Day for a Rose Bowl clash. USC rolled out to a 33–0 lead en route to a 47–14 win. Three years later in the 1933 Rose Bowl, Sutherland thought if the team left Pittsburgh earlier and practiced in Tucson for a few days, they would be fresher and more focused. But the results were much of the same: the Panthers were thoroughly humiliated by Jones and his USC squad, 35–0.

In 1934 the two national powers were scheduled for a third matchup, this time during the regular season at Pitt Stadium. Would the Panthers be able to overcome the nightmare of the previous USC games and finally defeat their West Coast rivals? Or did USC enjoy such a mental edge over Pitt that no matter where they played, they would emerge with a comfortable victory?

It was the Panthers' third game of the season after defeating Washington & Jefferson and then West Virginia by a combined 53–12 score. USC equally

In the late 1920s and 1930s, one of the premier coaches in the country was Dr. John "Jock" Sutherland. An All-American player in 1917, Sutherland returned to his alma mater in 1924. In 15 seasons he was an incredible 111–20–12 while winning five national championships. Later on, Sutherland also had the honor of being the only Steelers coach before Chuck Noll to lead the franchise to a postseason playoff game. (Courtesy of the University of Pittsburgh Athletics)

dominated their first three opponents, outscoring them 66–14, but in the Trojans' fourth home contest in the Los Angeles Memorial Coliseum, they were upset by Washington State, 19–0. This loss provided fans and experts alike another question: Was this a sign that the Trojans were about to falter, or was Pitt the opponent they needed to get back on track?

There were other signs USC was falling apart, as reports coming out of Los Angeles claimed the popular Trojans players were becoming victims to the Hollywood atmosphere that surrounded them. The school newspaper, the *Daily Trojan,* stated, "The team had little to say on the charges they were largely a group of Hollywood-struck boys who were as toys in the clutches of the film queens and movie magnets."[1] The charges irritated Jones and his players. The coach pushed his players to the brink in preparation for the Pitt game, stopping in Kansas City to put them through an incredibly difficult practice, hoping to get them focused once again. If the Trojans hoped hard work was all they needed to refocus, they were mistaken.

The Panthers came out inspired and dominated the contest early on in front of 55,000 excited Pitt fans. With the ball at their own 20 on the first possession, the Trojans' Bill Howard fumbled and the Panthers' Mike Nicksic recovered

Greensburg's Jesse Quatse was one of the greatest tackles in Pitt history, garnering the honor of being named consensus All-American for the Panthers in 1931. (Courtesy of the University of Pittsburgh Athletics)

it. After two USC offside penalties and a Nicksic 9-yard run, fullback Izzy Weinstock gave Pitt the first lead they ever had against the Trojans with a 1-yard touchdown burst up the middle.

In the second quarter, the Panthers continued their surprising dominance with a quick drive that saw Heinie Weisenbaugh ramble for a 31-yard gain and then complete a pass to Verne Baxter to the Trojans' 25. Two plays later, Weisenbaugh completed the one-man drive with a 22-yard touchdown run that gave Pitt a 13-point advantage.

Pitt again drove deep into Trojans territory, but the USC defense stiffened and stopped the Panthers on downs. It was at that point that USC finally got back in the game, thanks to a 40-yard completion from Irvine Warburton to Calvin Clemens, putting the ball on the Panthers' 10. Two plays later, the two connected again, this time for an 8-yard scoring toss as the teams went into the locker room at the half with USC down by only a touchdown at 13–6.

Would the thoughts of Rose Bowls past enter the minds of the Pitt players and their coaches in the second half? It was a reasonable question to ask after the Trojans made what had appeared to be turning into a rout much closer. USC dominated the third period, repeatedly driving into Panthers territory before the Pitt defense would stiffen up and stop the Trojans. One play that made a big difference in the third quarter was when Baxter stopped Haskell Wotkyns on a key third down, tossing him for an 8-yard loss. Following the dramatic play, Wotkyns booted a miserable 11-yard punt that gave the Panthers great field position just inside the 50. Baxter wasn't finished, pulling in a long pass on the next play, then diving over the goal line for a 20–6 lead.

USC kept driving in the fourth quarter but couldn't manage any points as the Panthers hung on for a win that not only gave Jones his first back-to-back losses in 10 years at the school but also gave Pitt the vengeance it had been looking for. And by season's end, this victory would prove to be the catalyst for a share of Pitt's sixth national championship.

Team	1st	2nd	3rd	4th	Final
USC	0	6	0	0	6
Pittsburgh	7	6	7	0	21

Team	Play	Score
Pitt	Weinstock 1-Yd Run (Weinstock Kick)	0–7
Pitt	Weisenbaugh 22-Yd Run (Kick Failed)	0–13
USC	Clemens 8-Yd Pass From Warburton (Kick Failed)	6–13
Pitt	Baxter Touchdown Catch (Weinstock Kick)	6–20

#10

DUQUESNE DUKES 13, MISSISSIPPI STATE BULLDOGS 12
JANUARY 1, 1937
MEN'S NCAA FOOTBALL

Hefferle's Folly

There was a time in college football history when you needed only to travel 2.7 miles down Forbes Avenue in Pittsburgh to see two of the sport's most powerful programs. In the 1930s you had the University of Pittsburgh Panthers—winner of four national championships during the decade—and the Duquesne Dukes—who, under Elmer Layden and John "Clipper" Smith, were quickly becoming a program that was at the level of great teams like Pitt.

January 1, 1937, was the pinnacle of college football in the city's history, a day when both programs were at their apex. Pitt was playing for a piece of the national championship against the University of Washington in the Rose Bowl, while the Dukes were taking on the Mississippi State Bulldogs in Miami for the third annual Orange Bowl. As it turned out, it became the single greatest day ever for college football in the Steel City.

While Pitt's part of this phenomenal day will be chronicled later in this book, Duquesne's momentum began with a great finish the year before. After a 1–3 start in 1935, the Dukes won their last five games, including shutouts against Carnegie Tech, Oklahoma A&M (now Oklahoma State), and West Virginia. In the offseason, Duquesne coach Christy Flanagan resigned his post to enter his father's oil shipping business in Texas. The administration looked toward another disciple of Knute Rockne to continue the success that the Dukes enjoyed under their last three Irish alum head coaches in Layden, Joe Bach, and Flanagan. John "Clipper" Smith had head coaching experience at Trinity College, Newark Academy, and North Carolina State and got off to a great start on the Bluff, shutting out Waynesburg, Rice, and Geneva in his first three games on the Dukes sideline. Fans weren't expecting a fourth straight

Center Mike Basrak has the distinction of becoming the first All-American football player in the program's history. Basrak was at his best when his team needed him, playing a phenomenal contest in the 1937 Orange Bowl where he was named MVP. (Courtesy of Duquesne University Athletics)

win as the Dukes were next slated to face one of the nation's best programs in Pitt. But Duquesne upset Pitt 7–0 on a rainy afternoon at Pitt Stadium.

While some felt the big win could have been a catalyst for an undefeated season, the Dukes fell to West Virginia Wesleyan and Detroit the next two weeks before finishing the year with shutouts over Washington (Missouri), Carnegie Tech, and Marquette to complete the campaign with a 7–2 record, a 14 ranking in the Associated Press poll, and a bid to the Orange Bowl.

It marked the second postseason bid in school history, the first coming in 1933 when Layden led them to a win over Miami in the precursor to the Orange Bowl, the Festival of Palms. This time, the Dukes faced a much tougher opponent in Mississippi State.

The Bulldogs were led by coach Ralph Sasse, who had a successful run at West Point before moving on to Starkville, where he guided Mississippi State to the Orange Bowl in his second season. Playing in the tough Southeastern Conference, the Bulldogs had a successful 7–2–1 mark coming into the contest against the Dukes, losing only to Alabama and seventh-ranked LSU while fighting to a scoreless tie against Texas Christian. While going into the bowl game as an underdog, Mississippi State's prognosis seemed to improve when it was announced that Duquesne quarterback Boyd Brumbaugh may not be able to play.

Brumbaugh had been the sparkplug of the Dukes' offense all season, but he had a bad case of tonsillitis in the week preceding the game and hadn't been able to practice. He was on the bench when the game began as Sasse's troops took full advantage to pull out to a quick lead.

With Duquesne looking to shut down the Mississippi State rushing game, focusing on stopping running back Ike Pickle, the Bulldogs came out with an aggressive passing offense that confused the Dukes' defense early on. Quarterback Charles "Pee Wee" Armstrong moved the Bulldogs from their own 20 to the Duquesne 8-yard line. From there, Pickle ripped around left end into the end zone to give Mississippi State an early 6–0 lead, an advantage that stayed when Duquesne blocked the extra point.

At that point, Smith realized his offense wouldn't be able to win this game without his quarterback and inserted the ill Brumbaugh into the contest. At first it made little difference, as the Dukes were unable to move the ball and gave it back to the Bulldogs, who quickly doubled their lead. Armstrong found Fred Walters with a short pass to the Dukes' 35-yard line, and Walters darted the rest of the way for a touchdown, making the score 12–0 after Mississippi State missed another extra point, a mistake that proved pivotal by game's end.

Down by two scores in the 80-degree Miami heat and playing a quarterback who had been sick all week, the situation looked dire for Clipper Smith and his team, but Brumbaugh turned things around and would be spectacular for the rest of the day. He drove the Dukes 62 yards to the Bulldogs' 1, where the State defense toughened up and forced Duquesne into a fourth-and-inches play. Brumbaugh bolted into the end zone and then made the only extra point of the day to bring his team to within 5 points at 12–7, a score that held until late in the fourth quarter. The Dukes were fortunate to still be in the game at that point, since Mississippi State had outplayed them throughout most of the second half. The Bulldogs missed an opportunity to put the game away early in the fourth quarter when they turned the ball over to the Dukes on downs after driving deep into Duquesne territory at the 15.

After two plays got the Dukes to the 28, Brumbaugh took his team to the line of scrimmage. All-American center Mike Basrak, who played an incredible contest, snapped the ball to Matsik, who tossed it back to Brumbaugh. Brumbaugh heaved a desperation toss downfield toward Hefferle, who broke to his left, away from Pickle, who was covering him on the play. Hefferle grabbed the ball in full stride and outran Pickle to the goal line for a 52-yard touchdown that gave the Dukes their first lead of the day at 13–12.

The Bulldogs were unable to mount a serious threat in the final minutes, as Duquesne held on for the dramatic victory. All a distraught Sasse could say after the game was simply, "That was a heartbreaker to lose, wasn't it?"[1] Smith also was concise in victory: "Well, I suppose I can afford to smile a little now."[2]

It was a Brumbaugh-inspired effort that led the team to victory. *New York Journal* writer Tom Thorp went as far as to call Brumbaugh the best player he had seen all season. "The only fellow I saw in the same class as Brumbaugh was Clint Frank of Yale and he wasn't quite as good," Thorp wrote. "Did you ever see a sweeter piece of work than the winning pass in the last quarter?"[3]

With his gutsy performance in leading the Duquesne comeback, Boyd Brumbaugh became a legend on the Bluff on the greatest day in Pittsburgh college football history.

Team	1st	2nd	3rd	4th	Final
Duquesne	0	7	0	6	13
Mississippi St	6	6	0	0	12

Team	Play	Score
Miss St	Pickle 8-Yard Run (Kick Blocked)	0–6
Miss St	Walters 40-Yard Pass From Armstrong (Kick Failed)	0–12
Duquesne	Brumbaugh 1-Yard Run (Brumbaugh Kick)	7–12
Duquesne	Hefferle 72-Yard Pass From Brumbaugh (Kick Failed)	13–12

#9

A Fruitless Venture

There are many oddities that dot the landscape of American sports, none more than a series of three football games that the University of Pittsburgh and Fordham University played between 1935 and 1937.

These games featured two teams who were among the best in college football in the era. But in addition to that, their three contests were unique for another reason: neither of these great teams was able to score a point in 180 minutes of play. The games truly proved to be a fruitless venture for both programs.

In the late 1920s and early 1930s, the University of Pittsburgh was considered among the elite of college football. By the time the reign of coach John "Jock" Sutherland ended following the 1938 campaign, the Panthers had won five national championships under his leadership. While Fordham coach Jim Crowley (a former member of the famed Notre Dame backfield the Four Horsemen) was a man about town who liked to hang around the great celebrities who lived in New York City, Sutherland was somewhat of a loner. Never married, Sutherland put all his focus and effort into his football team. He was described as a stern man who rarely smiled but was considered a genius when it came to formulating game plans, especially on the defensive side of the ball.

In the mid-1930s his teams were magnificent, losing only six games between 1933 and 1938. In 1935, the team finished 7–1–2 with the only blemishes being a loss to Notre Dame and scoreless ties against neighbor Carnegie Tech and the Fordham Rams—the first of the three scoreless ties, despite Fordham outgaining Pitt in total yardage, 150–73.

A year later, the Panthers had a phenomenal season that saw them go 8–1–1 and capture their first bowl victory—a 21–0 Rose Bowl victory over the University of Washington that earned them a share of the national championship. The only

Probably the second greatest running back in the history of football at the University of Pittsburgh is Marshall Goldberg (*left*), pictured celebrating a victory in 1936 with his teammates. Goldberg and Tony Dorsett are the only two Panthers players to finish twice in the top five of the Heisman Trophy voting. (Courtesy of the University of Pittsburgh Athletics)

blemishes on the season were a rainy 7–0 loss to crosstown rival Duquesne and the second of the scoreless ties with Fordham at the Polo Grounds. Defensively, the Rams were led by senior (and future legendary NFL coach) Vince Lombardi, who was part of a defensive line that was aptly named the Seven Blocks of Granite. The Rams stifled most opponents they faced, including the Pitt offense on this day as once again the two teams left the field with another 0–0 tie.

The team Sutherland put together in 1937 was most likely his best. The offense was led by a dream backfield that included Marshall Goldberg, Dick Cassiano, Curly Stebbins, and Frank Patrick, among others, who devastated opponents. Meanwhile, defensive end Bill Daddio led an impenetrable defense that came into their third annual matchup with Fordham at the Polo Grounds unscored upon in the first three games of the season. Crowley had led his club to an equally impressive start, beating Franklin & Marshall 66–0 before a 48–0 thrashing of Waynesburg. While the offensive output in the Rams' two games was much more impressive than that of the Panthers, the level of competition that Pitt had played was vastly superior than Fordham's. Crowley had built another formidable defense, this one led by Alex Wojciechowicz after losing Lombardi to graduation following the 1936 campaign.

The first two contests in this amazing trilogy were void of any significant scoring opportunities, but this one had several, which would make it perhaps the most frustrating of the three. Statistically, Pitt proved to be the superior team, but critical mistakes would prove to be their undoing as they couldn't capitalize on their dominance.

At the outset, the Rams forged perhaps their best drive of the day. They moved into Panthers territory thanks to a fake punt that saw running back Steve Kazlo rifle a 26-yard pass to fellow back Joe Granski. But Pitt soon halted the drive and the game ground into what it had become the previous two years: a series of short drives followed by punts.

As the second quarter began, Pitt had the ball at their own 10 when John Urban ripped through the line for 15 yards. But before he was tackled, the ball squirted out of Urban's hands and was recovered by Granski. While Fordham couldn't push the ball into the end zone with their advantageous field position, they lined up for a field goal attempt that the Rams hoped would end the fruitlessness. But the kick was no good, and Pitt escaped their own mistake.

Shortly after, Fordham punted to the Panthers, and Curly Stebbins returned it 35 yards to the Rams' 40. Pitt moved inside the 15 after Goldberg ran 10 yards, but then, just as Urban had before, he fumbled the ball. It rolled downfield as both teams desperately tried to pick it up. Finally, the Panthers' center Bob Dannies jumped on it, and Pitt was in great field position with a first down. They moved inside the 10, where Stebbins tossed a pass into the end zone that was intercepted by Fordham. But once again luck was on the visitors' side as the interception was negated by a holding call against the Rams. With new life, the Panthers were wary of making any further mistakes. Goldberg recalled that Matisi screamed at his teammates, "If anyone gets penalized on this play, they'll have to answer to me!"[1] The Panthers executed the perfect reverse, and Goldberg waltzed into the end zone to finally break the scoreless ice after three years. Ironically, Matisi was called for holding and the touchdown was called back.

Matisi always claimed to not have held on the play, but his teammates begged to differ. Stebbins recalled, "The next day I open the Sunday paper—the *New York News*—and there is (a photo of) the most beautiful stranglehold you ever saw. Tony is in a crouch with his left arm around the Fordham guy's leg, hanging onto him for dear life, and the Fordham guy is standing up but sort of leaning, as if he's holding onto something. I can still see the whole scene. It reminds me of the flag-raising at Iwo Jima."[2]

The true shame of it from Pitt's perspective was Matisi was on the other side of the play and the penalty had no bearing on the success of it. It was a penalty nonetheless, one that devastated the Panthers. They were stopped on fourth down and unable to score as the teams went into the locker room still tied at 0.

The beginning of the second half saw Fordham with another great opportunity, this one due to a fumble by Stebbins on the opening kickoff. The Rams moved to the Pitt 10, where the drive ended with Sutherland's defense holding firm. John Druze lined up for a field goal attempt from the 19, but the kick fell short and Goldberg picked it up at the 7. Once again Pitt had dodged a bullet, but the Panthers immediately put themselves in a bad position again when Goldberg fumbled and Druze picked it up deep in Panthers territory. The Fordham offense couldn't take advantage and turned it over to Druze once again to try to break the tie. Instead, he missed a third attempt and Pitt took over at its own 20.

Pitt would get three more opportunities to end the scoreless madness. The first came after a drive that reached the Rams' 15 before Daddio missed a field goal attempt. With the Fordham defense tiring, Stebbins, Stapulis, and Urban began carving through the Rams' line, picking up a combined 50 yards on the drive before Stebbins once again fumbled, and the ball ended up in Wojciechowicz's hands. On the next drive, the Panthers were moving again, but, remarkably, Stebbins lost another fumble, this one recovered by Joe Woitkoski.

Eventually, both teams ran out of scoring chances, and the game ended just as the previous two had. Pitt recovered, going on to win their final six games with relative ease and was named national champions for the first time by the Associated Press poll. It proved to be the Panthers' most successful season until they finally won another national title in 1976. The next season, the scoring drought between the teams at last ended as Fordham came to Pittsburgh and lost to the Panthers 24–13.

Although not being able to defeat Fordham frustrated the Panthers, in the end it didn't really hurt Pitt as they won two national championships in the three seasons. In the long run, the three ties made this series more memorable. Had the Panthers won any of the three games, the series would be forgotten in time instead of being recalled as one of the great oddities in college football history.

Team	1st	2nd	3rd	4th	Final
Pittsburgh	0	0	0	0	0
Fordham	0	0	0	0	0

Stat	Pittsburgh	Fordham
First Downs	11	4
Rushing Yards	165	87
Passing Yds	30	23
Comp-Att-Int	3–12–0	1–12–0
Total Yards	195	110
Punt Average	37	43
Fumbles Lost	5	0
Penalty Yards	20	60

#8

CARNEGIE TECH TARTANS 19, NOTRE DAME FIGHTING IRISH 0
NOVEMBER 28, 1926
MEN'S NCAA FOOTBALL

No Respect

In the history of college football, there are few, if any, upsets that rank bigger than the Carnegie Tech defeat of Knute Rockne and his Notre Dame Fighting Irish on November 28, 1926. A Notre Dame team fighting for a national championship lost to a 5-to-1 underdog just looking for some respect.

But respect was something Rockne had not given his opponent on this day. He was so sure of victory that he thought about keeping his first team in South Bend to rest them for the season finale clash against USC. After deciding to send them to Pittsburgh, he chose to remain in Chicago to see the Army-Navy game and leave the coaching to his assistants. The result of his lack of respect was a humiliating loss, one so great that ESPN named it the third greatest upset in college football history behind Centre College over Harvard in 1921 and the memorable Appalachian State defeat of Michigan in 2007 in a television special, *Greatest College Football Upsets*. It was this miscalculation by Rockne that forever will be known as the low point of his career.

In the late 1920s, Carnegie Tech and Notre Dame were on opposite ends of the college football spectrum. Tech was an afterthought on the Pittsburgh collegiate gridiron landscape and nowhere near a factor nationally, while Notre Dame was competing for national championships yearly. Though the two teams played every year, it really wasn't a rivalry. In the previous four meetings between the two schools, the Irish had outscored the Tartans 111–19.

Tech coach Walter Steffen was trying to build a competitive program that would be respected on the same level as the University of Pittsburgh. A two-time All-American at the University of Chicago and eventual member of the College Football Hall of Fame, Steffen took over the helm at Carnegie Tech in 1914. He mostly enjoyed success in his first 10 seasons at the school, although none against major collegiate competition. Steffen led a complex life, holding two positions in two different cities, one as the Carnegie Tech head coach and that of a judge on the Superior Court of Illinois, where he was elected in 1922. Despite that challenging lifestyle, he stayed on with the Tartans until 1932 when the travel became too much.

In 1926 the Tartans were enjoying one of their best seasons, bringing a 6–2 record into their season finale against the Irish at Forbes Field. Their impressive campaign had included wins over area powerhouses Pitt and West Virginia, though they'd lost to another area power, Washington & Jefferson. The other five games came against nonmajor schools. Notre Dame had a much more difficult schedule and had handled it flawlessly. They had allowed a single touchdown all season, that to Minnesota in a 20–7 win, shutting out their remaining seven opponents, including the powerful Army Cadets. They had outscored more superior teams than Carnegie Tech by a combined 197–7 margin, which led Rockne and his squad to have little, if any, respect for the Tartans as they looked toward a more imposing matchup against USC in Los Angeles the following Saturday with the national championship on the line.

Although the lack of respect prompted Rockne to temporarily consider keeping his starters home so they could rest, he eventually relented and sent them to Pittsburgh for the game. He assured Tech athletic director Clarence Overend that he would send all his players, explaining, "We are pointing for your game Saturday and will give you all we have."[1] While the legendary coach would indeed send his entire team, there was one person he wasn't going to send: himself. Claiming he was stuck in Chicago at a meeting of the Western Conference college coaches where so-called important matters kept him there, never imagining this would be anything more than a one-sided affair—with or without him on the sideline.

Rockne actually stayed in Chicago to watch the Army-Navy game. While some claimed he did it to scout the Midshipmen for their 1927 encounter, the truth that was his agent, Christy Walsh, had set up a financial opportunity with two other top coaches, Pop Warner of Stanford and Tad Jones of Yale, where all three would write stories about the Army-Navy contest to be carried in various newspapers around the nation and then pick an All-American team. Rockne wrote to Walsh, "The game in Pittsburgh will not be important enough. . . . I can (put) it in charge of someone else."[2] As it turned out, the game was a one-sided affair, just not the one Rockne had envisioned.

A record crowd of over 45,000 descended on Forbes Field to see these two squads clash. Rockne had put his one-time star player and now assistant coach Heartley "Hunk" Anderson in charge. Anderson, who eventually would replace

Rockne after a tragic plane accident took his life in 1931, had a game plan given to him by his mentor, and, come hell or high water, he wasn't going to change it. Part of it called for Notre Dame to send out the reserves to start the contest and then bring the first team back in the second quarter to crush whatever remaining spirit the Tartans had. Steffen used this to try to inspire his Tartans. He told them, "Men, Knute Rockne thinks you are so poor as football players that he's starting his second string against you, and he's so sure he'll win, he's not even here. He's in Chicago watching Army and Navy play some real football."[3]

Rockne's plan didn't quite work to perfection. While Tech had the better of the play in the early going, the first quarter wasn't much more than a punting contest, and the game remained scoreless going into the second. With the Fighting Irish first squad soon to enter the game, most thought the Tartans would quickly fall behind. But the dominance that everyone expected never materialized. And, in fact, this was the point when Carnegie Tech began to control the game.

The Notre Dame first team didn't enter the game until midway in the second period after a roughing-the-punter call against the Irish, which gave the Tartans a first down at the visitors' 45-yard line. At that point Tech started their first serious drive of the day. O'Boyle rushed for 12 yards before Howard Harpster hit Bill Donahue for a 21-yard pass that moved the ball to the Irish 18. Following a Cyril J. Letzelter run to the 13-yard line, future college Hall of Famer Lloyd Yoder put his hands up to silence the fans who were now cheering loudly. Yoder took the snap and put the ball in the hands of Donahue, who went around right end and into the end zone, giving the Tartans a surprising 6–0 lead. Letzelter's kick hit the upright so the score remained that way.

Giving up only their second touchdown of the season, the Irish were stunned. Things would get worse for Notre Dame moments later when Cooper blocked a Notre Dame punt deep in their own territory, and Tech regained possession at the 15-yard line. After an offside penalty put the ball at the 20, Harpster completed a 17-yard pass to Carleton Mefort, bringing them to the Notre Dame 3. Two plays later, Letzelter knifed in from the 1 for the touchdown. After successfully completing the extra point, Tech not only had a 13–0 lead but thoroughly dominated the Fighting Irish first team.

Through it all, Anderson stuck to Rockne's game plan, despite the fact it had no contingency plan for Notre Dame falling behind. And the second half proved to be no better than the first for the Irish. In the third quarter, the Irish offense never threatened against the stubborn Carnegie Tech defense, while Harpster added dropkick field goals (made by dropping the ball and kicking after it touches the ground) of 32 and 45 yards to increase the Tartans' lead to 19.

Notre Dame finally started a long drive early in the fourth quarter with the hope of mounting a late charge. The Irish moved the ball down to the 1-yard line after Christy Flanagan found Harry O'Boyle for a 29-yard gain. Not wanting to give the momentum back to Notre Dame, Tech's defense stood tough, turning back the Irish three times. Then, on fourth-and-goal, Yoder made one of the great defensive plays in the program's history, throwing Flanagan for a 2-yard loss that gave the ball back to the Tartans.

Carnegie Tech held on for a 19–0 win—one of the most memorable upsets in college football history. As time expired, thousands of Tartans fans stormed onto the field to celebrate a win that would be forever remembered.

For Rockne, it may have been the greatest miscalculation of his long and storied career. Had he been there, perhaps he would have made the proper maneuvers that would make the difference between winning and losing. After Notre Dame's dramatic 13–12 victory over USC the next week, it was clear the loss to Carnegie Tech had cost them what would have assuredly been a national championship. To his credit, Rockne stated afterward to the press, "Tell Judge Steffen and his boys that I congratulate them heartily and only wish that I was there to shake their hands and offer them my best."[4] While Rockne displayed good sportsmanship after the game, he showed no such respect to Carnegie Tech before this historic upset.

Team	1st	2nd	3rd	4th	Final
Notre Dame	0	0	0	0	0
Carnegie Tech	0	13	6	0	19

Team	Play	Score
Tech	Donahue 13-Yard Run (Kick Failed)	0–6
Tech	Letzelter 1-Yd Run (Letzelter Kick)	0–13
Tech	Harpster 32-Yd Field Goal	0–16
Tech	Harpster 45-Yd Field Goal	0–19

PITT PANTHERS 24, NOTRE DAME FIGHTING IRISH 22
FEBRUARY 18, 1928
MEN'S NCAA BASKETBALL

A Legend Is Born

When speaking of the greatest player ever to don a basketball uniform at the University of Pittsburgh, the conversation usually begins and ends with a six-foot guard from Uniontown, Pennsylvania, the school's lone three-time All-American by the name of Charley Hyatt. Hyatt would go on to lead Pitt to the program's only two national championships and to be named the Helms Foundations Player of the Year in 1930.

But in 1928 he was just a sophomore, and the Panthers were trying to complete their first and, as it turned out, only undefeated season in program history. Standing in their way was their toughest opponent of the year, the Notre Dame Fighting Irish. The teams would face off against the Irish in Pitt Pavilion, a basketball arena located underneath Pitt Stadium. This was not only a contest that pushed Pitt toward their first national title but one that began the legend of Charley Hyatt.

In the 1920s, Pitt was led by a man who is arguably the greatest basketball coach in school history: Henry Clifford "Doc" Carlson. Carlson's nickname suited him perfectly, since he received his medical degree from the university. A former All-American end in football at Pitt under the great Pop Warner in 1917, Doc took over the basketball program in 1922 and slowly built it to one of the premier teams in the country. He was an innovator who, among other things, was one of the first to use double teams on defense and developed a figure-eight offense that was widely copied by many of his contemporaries and that incorporated many weaves and passes to set up open shots. Of all the things he was known for, perhaps the most memorable was his irascible behavior on the sidelines and his harsh treatment of referees. His on-field attitude often

Pictured is the greatest player ever to wear a University of Pittsburgh Men's Basketball uniform, Charley Hyatt. By the time he was finished at Pitt, he was selected as a first-team All-American in each if his three seasons on the varsity team, while leading the Panthers to two national championships. (Courtesy of the University of Pittsburgh Athletics)

irritated his opponents and opposing fans alike, in an era when hot tempers weren't as accepted as they are today.

However unique or controversial his techniques were, they all combined to help Carlson and the team as they continued to improve through his first few seasons. As successful as he had been, there was nothing that pointed to the team becoming the best in the land in the 1927–28 campaign. The Panthers were coming off a mediocre 10–7 season in 1926–27, but little did anyone know that a young sophomore from Uniontown would take Pitt to the next level.

Charley Hyatt had yet to take the floor in a varsity game, but by the time his career was done, he would become one of only 18 players in NCAA history to be selected as a three-time All-American. His 880 career points were an incredible amount for the time, and he eventually was included in the initial class at the Naismith Basketball Hall of Fame in 1959. He had played well so far in this campaign, but those who didn't yet know him would certainly discover what a special player he was by the end of this contest.

The Panthers came into this game against the Fighting Irish with a 14–0 mark and had rarely been challenged. They defeated a tough Michigan team by 10 points to start out the season and destroyed the defending eastern collegiate basketball champions, the Dartmouth Big Green, 64–33, along the way.

In their 14 wins, the Panthers allowed their opponents to come within single digits on only three occasions—two of which were in back-to-back games in the final two contests of a four-game road trip in five days to begin the season.

Notre Dame was certainly having a wonderful season as well. Hall of Famer George Keogan was coaching the Fighting Irish and had the team playing well with a 14–2 record going into the Pitt Pavilion. The team had lost only to Northwestern, 25–23, and Michigan State, 26–16, but had won their last three games, including a 31–19 defeat of Carnegie Tech at the nearby Skibo Gymnasium the night before.

Since it was such a highly anticipated game, the demand for tickets was at a premium. Over 5,000 fans wanted tickets to the game in a facility that could seat only 4,000. Once the Pavilion was filled, police had the unenviable task of trying to send the remaining fans home.

It was a frigid evening in Pittsburgh, and those frustrated fans who weren't able to get tickets continued trying to push their way in through the gates while breaking glass around the stadium in the process. The police had finally restored order and the fans went back to their dorms and homes angry. The 4,000 who made it in contributed to an enthusiastic atmosphere.

The Pitt Pavilion was neither aesthetically pleasing nor a comfortable place to play or watch a game. Located beneath gate 3 at Pitt Stadium, it was cold and damp. When the Panthers practiced there, they had to wear their warm-ups to stay comfortable.

Notre Dame had played one of the toughest schedules in the country and wasn't intimidated by the undefeated home team. The Irish played a consistent, precise style of basketball in the first half, successfully moving the ball around, possessing it for minutes at a time until they found an open shot, usually right underneath the basket. But the Panthers were sloppy, constantly turning the ball over while missing what open shots they were given. Edward Smith of Notre Dame opened the scoring with an early basket as the Irish dominated the contest for the first 20 minutes. Notre Dame built a 15–8 lead as the teams went into the locker rooms at the intermission.

The capacity crowd and the Pitt players were stunned. As the teams came out of the locker room for the second half, the Panthers still couldn't find any offensive rhythm. The Fighting Irish began to play more physically, and the referees called several fouls against them. As a result, by hitting their free throws, the Panthers were able to cut into the lead. Pitt had hit two from the line to begin the half before Hyatt connected from the floor to cut the lead to 3 points.

Notre Dame's Robert Hamilton and Francis Crowe fouled out with 5 minutes left, and the Panthers saw their opportunity to finish the comeback. Hyatt tied the score before Stan Wrobleski, who was second in the nation in scoring to Hyatt, gave them a 1-point lead on a free throw with time running out.

With Notre Dame not wanting to waste what had been a fine effort to this point, Irish center Tim Moynihan hit a free throw to once again tie the score at 22–22 with 50 seconds left. Pitt captain Reed Sykes, a swift player who, along with Hyatt, was named as an All-American in 1927–28, called a timeout to try to set up the Panthers' final shot at victory. Pitt moved the ball around, trying to find an open shot, but the Irish defense was suffocating. Finally, Paul Zehfuss got the ball at the top of the lane. Trying to force a turnover, the Notre Dame defense descended on Zehfuss as the clock neared zero. Suddenly, Zehfuss saw Hyatt open under the basket and passed the ball to him. The young sophomore hit the winning shot on a layup as the buzzer sounded to end the game, giving Pitt a thrilling 24–22 victory.

The fans roared, and many came onto the floor to celebrate. Pitt had managed only four field goals but took advantage of the aggressive Irish defense to outscore them 16–6 from the foul line. The win gave the Panthers momentum to finish their quest of an undefeated season, going on to win their final six games to end the season with a 21–0 mark.

Eight years later, the Helms Athletic Foundation was founded by Bill Schroeder and Paul Helms, and it eventually began to choose national champions in basketball for the pre-NCAA tournament days dating back to 1900. For the 1927–28 season, it chose the Panthers as national champions, thanks in part to their dramatic victory over Notre Dame—delivered by a legend named Charley Hyatt, who made one of the great shots in program history to secure one of the greatest Panthers victories ever.

Notre Dame

Player	Fg	Ft	Pts
Smith	3	2	8
Donovan	2	0	4
Moynihan	1	1	3
Hamilton	1	0	2
Newbold	1	0	2
Jachym	0	1	1
Crowe	0	2	2
McCarthy	0	0	0
Totals	8	6	22

Pittsburgh

Player	Fg	Ft	Pts
Hyatt	3	2	8
Reed	1	4	6
Zehfuss	0	2	2
Wunderlich	0	3	3
Wrobleski	0	5	5
Totals	4	16	24

Team	1st	2nd	Final
Notre Dame	15	7	22
Pittsburgh	8	16	24

PITT PANTHERS 32, GEORGIA TECH GOLDEN TORNADO 0
NOVEMBER 23, 1918
MEN'S NCAA FOOTBALL

The Undisputed Champion

In the era before the college football national championship game, rarely did the two best two schools in the country meet. But on a November day in 1918, Pittsburgh college football fans were treated to just such an event when the defending national champion Georgia Tech Golden Tornado (as they were called back then), led by Hall of Fame coach John Heisman, took on Pop Warner and his Pitt Panthers to determine the sport's undisputed champion.

The 1918 college football season was unlike any other—for all the wrong reasons. It was toward the end of World War I and also the year of the Spanish flu pandemic. More than 500 million people worldwide were infected by the flu, which killed 675,000 in the United States alone. Consequently, many colleges either canceled their football seasons or cut them down significantly. The University of Pittsburgh cut its 1918 slate to only five games, but four were against national powers.

The team who took the field for that abbreviated schedule was led by one of the great coaches in the history of the game, Glenn Scobey "Pop" Warner. Warner was quite an innovator, as he came up with such things as the famed single-and double-wing formations as well as huddling before each play and using an unbalanced offensive line. He was also so popular in football history that the famed Pop Warner Youth Football League is named after him. Warner came to the Panthers in 1914, and the program instantly became one of nation's best. Pitt would go undefeated in the legendary coach's first three seasons, as he won his first 26 games while leading the program to two national championships in 1915 and 1916. In 1917 the Panthers went 10–0, outscoring their opponents by a 225–25 margin. But as great as they were, they weren't considered better than coach John Heisman's Georgia Tech club.

Before Jock Sutherland there was Glenn Scobey "Pop" Warner. Coaching at the university between 1915 and 1923, Warner was 60–12–4 while capturing the school's first three national championships. Warner began his career at the university by winning his first 30 games before losing to the Cleveland Naval Reserves in the final game in 1918. (Courtesy of the University of Pittsburgh Athletics)

To say that Heisman's 1917 club was the dominant team in the nation would be a vast understatement. Georgia Tech defeated their opponents by an average margin of 53 points. The Golden Tornado defense allowed only 17 points all season, while what they called the "Jump Shift" offense was able to easily move through opponents all season.

An innovator offensively, Heisman, who the famed trophy is named after, may have actually saved the game of football when he brought the forward pass to the game. Football was a contest of savage violence in the early years of the twentieth century, and many players were actually being killed every year. Between 1900 and 1905 at least 45 died, prompting even the president of the United States, Teddy Roosevelt, to investigate the issue. Heisman promoted throwing a forward pass, a maneuver that came into his consciousness after seeing a punter try it out of desperation following a botched play. Heisman claimed that it would "scatter the mob," or spread the players around the field, instead of everyone bunched together at the line waiting for the violent collision.[1]

Heisman's innovative play, along with his lethal Jump Shift offense, helped Georgia Tech go 9–0 that season, including a 98–0 victory over Carlisle. The 1918 season was proving to be even worse for the Golden Tornado's opponents. Georgia Tech had won their first five contests of the year, increasing their overall winning streak to 33-games, and remarkably eclipsed the 100-point plateau on three occasions, including a 128–0 embarrassment of North Carolina State two weeks before they came to Pitt. The Tornado had amassed an incredible 424 points in those five games while not allowing a single point.

Warner's team also was playing well. While the Panthers' numbers were not as impressive as those of Georgia Tech, they had played arguably a tougher schedule to that point, beating two national powerhouses in Washington & Jefferson and Penn by a combined 71–0.

Originally, the Panthers were supposed to play Syracuse in a rescheduled game on this date after an earlier contest was canceled due to the pandemic. But wanting to face off against the best team in the nation to prove who the national champion should be, Pitt convinced Georgia Tech to come to Forbes Field for a game on November 23 and canceled the game against the Orangemen completely. By day's end, it would be a move Heisman and his squad would truly regret.

The game pitted the famous Jump Shift offense against Pop Warner's impenetrable defense. It was apparent early on that the Panthers were no ordinary opponent. After stalling on its first drive of the day, Pitt punted and then pounced on Georgia Tech's fumbled return at the Tornado's 42-yard line. Pitt moved quickly toward the end zone, with R. A. Easterday finding Tom Davies for 12-yard pass completion, followed by a 12-yard George McLaren run that put the ball at the 14. The drive stalled there, and Davies missed a 17-yard field goal attempt to keep the game scoreless.

After that, the Panthers' defense stood firm, forcing the first Golden Tornado punt of the contest, after the high-powered Georgia Tech offense managed only one first down. Easterday took the punt back 20 yards as Pitt started its next drive at the Tech 37. Not wanting to throw away a second opportunity, the Panthers once again utilized the type of play Heisman made famous, as Davies hit Easterday for a 20-yard touchdown toss. Davies connected on the extra point, and Pitt was in front 7–0.

Once again the Panthers' defense halted the Jump Shift offense. After Tech punted, the home team appeared to have great field position, but a 15-yard penalty against Pitt on the play forced a rekick. Instead of taking advantage of the second chance, Tech fumbled the snap on the ensuing play at their own 21, and the Panthers recovered. An interception on the next play denied Pitt a chance to increase the lead, but after the Panthers forced yet another punt, Davies returned it 50 yards for a score that doubled their lead to 14–0 early in the second quarter. While Georgia Tech was able to move the football somewhat easier following the punt return, it never seriously threatened to score for the remainder of the quarter, and the teams went to the half with the home team still ahead by two touchdowns.

Pitt's lead and command of the first half had been surprising, to say the least. Having no points at the half was an extreme concern to Heisman and his troops. Despite being one of the preeminent coaches in the history of college football, Heisman was in a rare position of coming up with a strategy at the half to get his team back in the game. The problem was he was facing a man who was equally legendary in the game's history.

The Panthers received the opening kickoff of the second half, and Ralph Gougler sprinted 45 yards to the Georgia Tech 45. After moving to the 32, the Pitt offense appeared to be stopped, losing 3 yards on the next two plays. On third-and-13, Warner reached into his bag of plays and pulled out a perfect one. McLaren took the snap and threw it to Davies on a lateral, who tossed it downfield to Easterday, catching the Golden Tornado by surprise. Easterday caught the ball and took it in for a quick touchdown that gave the Panthers a 20–0 lead after Davies missed the extra point.

Georgia Tech's dwindling chances for victory would completely disappear before the third quarter ended. Warner called for another double pass, again from McLaren to Easterday to Davies, and it went for a 34-yard gain and a first down at the Tech 5. Two plays later, McLaren ran it into the end zone to all but end the affair at 26–0.

Georgia Tech was trying everything it could to get on the scoreboard, but it turned out to be a fruitless venture, as the Panthers stopped them at every opportunity. It was bad enough the Golden Tornado was behind by four scores, but Pitt would add insult to injury on the last play of the game. With time running out, Tech punted, and Davies received the ball at his own 45. He ripped down the field through the defeated visitors into the end zone that made the score 32–0 as the gun sounded to end the game.

It was a contest in which the Panthers thoroughly humiliated their guests, holding them to just 18 yards of offense. Warner was delighted with his defense's tremendous effort. "Our defense was better than it had been this season," he said. "Georgia Tech's favorite plays were stopped, and their failure to gain in the early stages of the game, or to make any impression on our team took the heart out of them."[2]

Heisman was conciliatory but still upset with his team's effort. "Our boys lost their signals and their heads," he said. "They were beaten by a better team but did not do as well as they might have. However, I am not trying to detract from the glory due Pitt. The Panthers are a wonderful combination. They are strong in every department, and I believe the best football combination in the country."

While Pitt lost their final game of the season to the Cleveland Naval Reserve 10–9 to end its 32-game win streak, the victory against Georgia Tech showed the country that the Panthers were the best, as they were selected as the national champions for the third time in four seasons.

Team	1st	2nd	3rd	4th	Final
Georgia Tech	0	0	0	0	0
Pittsburgh	7	7	12	6	32

Team	Play	Score
Pitt	Easterday 20-Yd Pass From Davies (Davies Kick)	0–7
Pitt	Davies 50-Yd Punt Return (Davies Kick)	0–14
Pitt	Easterday 35-Yd Pass From Davies (Kick Failed)	0–20
Pitt	McLaren 3-Yd Run (Kick Failed)	0–26
Pitt	Davies 55-Yd Punt Return (Kick Failed)	0–32

Stat	Georgia Tech	Pittsburgh
First Downs	4	8
Rushing Yards	18	62
Passing Yds	0	126
Comp-Att-Int	0–5–3	6–13–2
Total Yards	18	188
Punt Average	42	36
Penalty Yards	25	40

#5

California Dreamin'

The late 1920s and 1930s was an exciting time for fans of the University of Pittsburgh football team. The Jock Sutherland era was at its apex, with the program capturing five national championships in a run in which the Panthers posted a remarkable 111–20–12 record. For all the success the Panthers enjoyed, there was one topic that caused the team and fans alike nightmares: Pitt's struggles in the Rose Bowl.

At the time, the so-called "granddaddy of them all" was played between two of the best teams in the nation; it wouldn't strictly match the champions of the Pac-12 and Big Ten conferences until 1947. Pitt earned their first Rose Bowl invite in 1928, and the Panthers suffered a heartbreaking 7–6 loss to Stanford. Pitt's next two trips to Pasadena were nothing short of a California nightmare.

In 1929 the Panthers played a very strong schedule and comfortably beat eight of the nine teams they played by double digits. The only one who gave them issues was the University of Nebraska, whom they defeated 12–7. It was a magnificent season led by consensus All-Americans Joe Donchess and Ray Montgomery as well as by Toby Uansa and Thomas Parkinson, who both also were first-team All-Americans.

They secured a bid to the Rose Bowl to play an 8–2 USC club who many thought would provide Pitt a challenge but still not defeat them. Coming into Pasadena, the Hall of Fame coach thought his superior depth would be the difference. As it turned out, the one clear advantage the Trojans had, outweighing Pitt on the line, began to take its toll. USC ran up a 26–0 lead at the half, eventually crushing Sutherland's team 47–14. Luckily, bowl games back then were considered nothing more than an exhibition, and in 1933 historian Parke Davis

This picture was taken at the Rose Bowl in Pasadena, California, in 1937 as the University of Pittsburgh took on the University of Washington. Pitt would eventually win the game, 21–0, the first bowl win in school history after losses in their first three Rose Bowls. After the victory, they captured a piece of the school's seventh national championship. (Courtesy of the University of Pittsburgh Athletics)

put together his list of national champions from 1869 to 1932 for the *Spalding's Football Guide* and named the Panthers the national champions for 1929.

Three years later, in 1932, scoreless ties against Ohio State and Nebraska where the only blemishes on an otherwise outstanding season as Pitt went 8–0–2, once again securing a bid to the Rose Bowl and a rematch against the Trojans. Many felt Colgate was a better opponent for USC than the Panthers, and ticket sales were struggling because of it. Sutherland had a new travel plan in hopes of bringing in his team fresher for this encounter. It called for a 10-day stay in Tucson, but the Rose Bowl committee wanted them to cut it short so they could help promote the game in Pasadena. As a result, the Panthers coach was irritated, and he took his frustrations out on the squad, practicing players so hard that they were worn down by game time. Eventually the critics were proved correct, as the USC once again destroyed their eastern guests, this time 35–0.

Fast-forward four years, and the powerful Panthers were having another spectacular season. They started off slowly in 1936, losing to crosstown rival Duquesne 7–0 and tying Fordham 0–0 for the second consecutive year to drop their record to 4–1–1. They finished the year with impressive wins over Penn State, Nebraska, and Carnegie Tech to end the campaign 7–1–1. Rumor had it that Pitt was pegged for a Sugar Bowl matchup against the second-ranked LSU Tigers, with Alabama going to the Rose Bowl against the Pacific Coast Conference champion Washington Huskies.

Washington felt Pitt was the best opponent to play, as the Panthers were awarded the first Lambert Trophy, presented annually to the best team in the East. The Rose Bowl committee agreed and extended a bid to the Panthers to come out to Pasadena for a fourth Rose Bowl appearance. No one would have blamed their fans for having doubts about another trip west, but Sutherland was determined to finally give his team and their fans the chance to experience a Rose Bowl.

Sutherland decided against the plans and practice schedule the team had followed in the previous two trips to Pasadena. Instead of stopping several times to practice on the way there, they would leave the first day of Christmas break, December 16, and stop only once before arriving in California to practice. It was an idea he'd devised the year before when they traveled to Southern California for a regular-season matchup with USC, a game they won 12–7. Since it served them well then, he was confident it would once again.

Washington also came into this contest at 7–1–1. After losing to perennial national power Minnesota in the first game of the season 14–7, the Huskies dominated most of their foes the rest of the way, a 14–14 tie at Stanford being their only other blemish. They finished the season against nationally ranked USC and Washington State, shutting out both to complete their magnificent season. Coach James Phelan's Huskies finished fifth in the nation, and, like his counterpart Sutherland, Phelan was confident they'd emerge victorious.

More than 87,000 people packed into the famed facility, and many expected Washington to administer the same type of beating that USC had done on two occasions. The Huskies, like the Trojans before, had a huge weight advantage over Pitt, but unlike the previous trips to the Rose Bowl, the Panthers were better prepared and much more fundamentally sound in their blocking. Defensively, the going would be just as tough. Washington utilized the forward pass much more than most teams at that time, and Pitt had little trouble halting it, allowing Washington to penetrate no further than the Pitt 18-yard line for the entire game.

Early on, Sutherland's squad showed things would be different. For starters, running back Bobby LaRue was having the game of his life. After the Panthers took over an early possession on their 45-yard line, LaRue ran through a defender and into the open on the left side of the line for a 30-yard sprint to the

Washington 10. Four plays later, Frankie Patrick burst into the end zone from 1 yard out for the opening touchdown of the game. Daddio added the extra point and Pitt had an early 7–0 advantage.

The Huskies unleashed their passing attack on the Panthers and drove to the Pitt 18. It was there that they attempted three straight passes, all incomplete, and turned the ball over to Pitt on downs. Late in the second quarter, the PCC champions were once again driving into Panthers territory, but an interception by Steve Petro, the lineman who was starting his first varsity game, ended the attempt just before the half ended.

Sutherland's team had been here before, leading in the third quarter of the 1930 Rose Bowl against Stanford but unable to put their opponent away. This time, that would be no problem. Unlike the Stanford contest, Pitt was dominating this game, running through Washington with ease.

The second half started with Goldberg losing a fumble at his own 29 and giving Washington great field position. But on the next play, Donald Hensley picked off a pass, ending the Huskies' scoring threat. LaRue promptly took a handoff and raced between the tackles for 43 yards. The long run seemed to deflate the Washington defense, as Patrick took a handoff for 19 more yards before LaRue burst through the Huskies' defense and raced to the Washington 3. Patrick took the ball into the end zone on the next play to give Pitt a two-touchdown lead.

In the fourth quarter, as Sutherland put in his second-team defense, the Huskies marched deep into Pitt territory. But they were stopped by one of the great defensive plays in Pitt history. After Sutherland put his starting defensive squad back in, Pitt's defensive lineman Tony Matisi hit Washington quarterback Byron Haines while he was attempting to pass. The ball popped up in the direction of Daddio, who secured it and rambled down the right side 71 yards for the touchdown.

With the score now 21–0, victory was secure. Pitt held off the Huskies the rest of the way to secure not only a shutout but also the first bowl win in the history of the program and a share of the national championship—the fourth under Sutherland. While it should have been a joyous moment, the bowl experience in 1937 was anything but for the team. Angry the school had given them no expense money (compared to the new suits and $100 each Washington player received), the Pitt players would eventually vote to turn down a bowl bid the next season. This precipitated a conflict between the program and the administration, who was not only upset the players turned down a bowl bid but didn't like the criticism they received from other schools, suggesting the stipends the university was giving its football players were excessive and the school planned on cutting them drastically. Those issues would eventually culminate with the end of the Sutherland era following the 1938 campaign—and with it, the championships the school celebrated.

Regardless of the bitter way it turned out, the Panthers had finally ended their Rose Bowl jinx, and the program and their fans had a wonderful California experience to help rinse away the nightmares of Rose Bowls past.

Team	1st	2nd	3rd	4th	Final
Washington	0	0	0	0	0
Pittsburgh	7	0	7	7	21

Team	Play	Score
Pitt	Patrick 1-Yd Run (Daddio Kick)	0–7
Pitt	Patrick 3-Yd Run (Daddio Kick)	0–14
Pitt	Daddio 71-Yd Interception Return (Daddio Kick)	0–21

Stat	Washington	Pittsburgh
First Downs	8	11
Rushing Yards	48	243
Passing Yds	95	51
Comp-Att-Int	5–11–3	2–4–2
Total Yards	143	294
Punt Average	29	43
Fumbles Lost	1	1
Penalty Yards	0	20

#4

WASHINGTON & JEFFERSON PRESIDENTS 0, CALIFORNIA GOLDEN BEARS 0
JANUARY 2, 1922
MEN'S NCAA FOOTBALL

The Scoreless Victory

For most, a scoreless tie is nothing more than a frustrating, unsatisfying result to a hard-fought game. But when an extreme underdog finds a way to hold the prohibitive favorite to a scoreless tie, it takes on a whole new meaning.

For the favorite, it ends up as a bitter memory, but for the underdog, it feels like a victory. The 1922 Rose Bowl was just such an experience.

The University of California was the defending national champion in 1921, while the Washington & Jefferson College Presidents were an up-and-coming team, though still considered second-rate behind the University of Pittsburgh in the region. The 1921 season changed the perception of W&J, as the Cal Bears found out in the Rose Bowl.

Located in Washington, Pennsylvania, about 32 miles outside of Pittsburgh, Washington & Jefferson today is one of the better Division III programs in the country. In the early part of the twentieth century, the Presidents battled some of the best teams college football had to offer. And in 1921, they had emerged as one of the powers in the game—a team who had no real superstars to speak of, except for their head coach, Earle "Greasy" Neale.

Nicknamed "Greasy" after a neighborhood kid called him that in response to Neale calling him "dirty," the coach had been one of the great athletes of the early part of the twentieth century. A star at West Virginia Wesleyan, baseball, not football, was his favorite sport. "My first love was baseball," he said, "and my consuming ambition was to become a big-leaguer. The football I played as a youngster was merely a fill-in to keep busy until it was warm enough for baseball."[1]

Neale eventually lived his dream with an eight-year major-league career with the Reds and the Phillies, the highlight of which was playing in the famed 1919

Alfred Earle "Greasy" Neale was certainly a wonderful football coach, being elected to the NFL Hall of Fame as the championship coach of the Philadelphia Eagles. He was also a tremendous collegiate player, leading the W&J Presidents to the 1922 Rose Bowl, and a good Major League Baseball player. Pictured here in his Cincinnati uniform, Neale hit .259 in nine seasons as well as .357 for the Reds in the 1919 World Series. (Library of Congress Prints and Photographs Division, the Bain News Service Photograph Collection, LC-B2-4992-14)

World Series (known for the infamous Black Sox scandal), in which he hit .357 for Cincinnati. While he was playing baseball in the spring and the summer, he would coach college football in the fall. He had coached at Muskingum, Marietta, and his alma mater before finding his way to W&J in 1921. Neale was a great innovator, developing such plays as the triple reverse and fake reverse, as well as the man-to-man defense.

Known as a great teacher, Neale was elected to the Pro Football Hall of Fame for his fabulous career leading the Philadelphia Eagles to their first two NFL championships. When he was inducted, the selectors honored Neale "for the example he set and his influence as a teacher of men and for the integrity of his character throughout his career."[2]

This was never more evident than in 1921 with the Presidents. He led them to a 10–0 season that included victories against Syracuse and local rivals West Virginia and Pittsburgh. The leader of the team was Russ Stein, a first-team All-American who joined his brother Herb at Pitt, becoming the first pair of brothers to be named All-American in the same season. The Presidents also had halfback Hal Erickson and reserve back Charlie "Pruner" West, who late in the season became their starting quarterback. West would eventually become the first African American quarterback ever to start a Rose Bowl game.

As good as the Presidents were in 1921, they received little consideration for the Rose Bowl, despite the fact they had defeated some of the best teams the East had to offer. To say they were a second choice would have been a misnomer. Iowa, Cornell, Penn State, Princeton, Yale, Harvard, and little Centre College (enjoying a surprising season of their own) all turned down bids to Pasadena to face the powerful Cal Bears before W&J accepted.

The Presidents were thrilled to be playing in the prestigious game, and their trip to California helped make the experience legendary. Travel to California was expensive for the small school, so athletic director Bob Murphy mortgaged his house in order for the team to make the cross-country trip without using money from the college. But as a result, Murphy could only take the bare minimum 11 players on the trip. This caused issues when end C. L. Spillers came down with pneumonia on the trip and had to be left in Kansas City for treatment. According to the story, another player, J. Ross Buchanan, had stowed away on the train and was given Spillers's ticket.

Once they finally made it to California, the Presidents found they had earned little respect from the experts there. Sportswriter Jack James wrote the famous line, "All I know about Washington and Jefferson is that they are both dead."[3] With an enrollment of only 450 students, it was the smallest school ever to play in the game. With only 11 players at Neale's disposal, it was no surprise that the undefeated California Bears, who had outscored their opponents by a 312–33 margin, entered the game as a prohibitive 14-point favorite. It's hard to pinpoint the exact explanation for what happened next. Perhaps it was overconfidence by the Bears, or the fallen rain that slowed down the speedy PCC champions, or the fact that these 11 players from western Pennsylvania just had the game of their lives. Whatever it was, this contest would prove to be anything but a one-sided affair.

From the outset, the Presidents' defense, which shut out WVU and Pitt during the season, was superior to Cal's potent offense. The Bears were famous for end runs that went for long yardage, for power running plays up the middle that seemingly never failed to gain yardage, and for long passes from the arm of Brick Mueller. Each time they tried their famed plays, they were met by an aggressive W&J defense that never bent. Over the course of the game, the Presidents held the vaunted Cal offense to 49 yards rushing, zero passing, and only two first downs, while the Presidents' offense seemingly had its way with the Cal defense.

More than 40,000 fans looked on with amazement as the western champions seemed beaten at almost every turn. It started early, as the Presidents ripped through the Bears' defense, driving from their own 25 to the Cal 35, when it appeared they were finally stopped. Facing fourth down, punter Wayne Brenkert lined up to kick but instead took the snap and ran around right end. The blocking was perfect, and he easily raced into the end zone to presumably put W&J ahead, 6–0. But an offside penalty negated the score, and a couple plays later, Cal picked off a pass and returned it to the Presidents' 36. Was this to be the turning point that would finally vault the favorites to the victory that was predicted? The answer turned out to be no, as a fake field goal attempt by Cal moments later resulted in an incomplete pass, and W&J regained possession. Cal would move once again deep into the visitors' territory as the first half was coming to an end, reaching the W&J 19, and another incomplete pass a kept the contest scoreless.

As the second half went on, the Presidents continued to control the action, as it became apparent the huge favorites suddenly seemed to be hoping the game remained scoreless. In the fourth quarter, Brenkert hit the freshman Kopf with a 30-yard pass that set up a field goal attempt by Stein. The kick sailed wide of the goal posts, but Stein would get a second chance to win the contest shortly after.

Following a Cal punt on the next series, Erickson returned it 20 yards to the Bears' 40. Kopf ran for 9 yards on two plays and then Stein rushed for 3 more, but the drive was stopped and Stein lined up at the 38 for another try to win the game. This time the field goal attempt was blocked as the Presidents saw another scoring attempt fail. It would be the last opportunity of the day for either team.

Even though the underdogs should have been thrilled with the outcome, their coach, while proud of his team, was not satisfied with a tie. "We should have won, but it's all in the game," Neale said afterward. "My boys have been underrated all through the season, and I knew the stuff they had in them. The mere fact that everybody figured we were soft for California didn't bother us for a bit. We showed that we were there."[4]

Even though Washington & Jefferson had no respect before the game, they certainly did afterward. Years later, when William Boand developed his method for selecting national champions by mathematical calculations, a method that is included in the NCAA's official record book as a major national champions selector, he named this Washington & Jefferson team as co–national champions for 1921, along with Cal and Jock Sutherland's Lafayette team. Stein would be inducted into the Rose Bowl's Hall of Fame as was the bowl game's first African American quarterback West.

Washington & Jefferson's makeshift team that day was the last to play in the Rose Bowl with no substitutes, and while it goes down in history as a tie, those who witnessed it would always know it was a symbolic victory for W&J.

Team	1st	2nd	3rd	4th	Final
W & J	0	0	0	0	0
California	0	0	0	0	0

The Phoenix

In Greek mythology, the Phoenix is a large bird that dies in a burst of flames before it is born again, rising from its own ashes. In the football lore of the University of Pittsburgh, the program burst into flames after 1963, falling into a losing era that had never been seen at the school before or since. It needed a young coach from Iowa State by the name of Johnny Majors to help the team regenerate from the ashes and rise again. It was on this day in 1977, more than a decade after its fall, that the resurrection was complete, as Panthers football won its ninth national championship.

To appreciate the heights the Panthers had reached in the 1977 Sugar Bowl, it's important to understand where they had been just a few years earlier. In 1963 it looked like the Panthers had finally turned the corner in the university's push to become relevant on the gridiron once again. John Michelosen had led the team to a surprising 9–1 mark as Pitt ended the season ranked third in the country. Following the campaign, the school administration decided to make the academic requirements more stringent for athletes, which eventually affected their ability to recruit effectively against other programs.

The repercussions of the new rules were immediate, as the program quickly spiraled below .500. Michelosen was replaced by Dave Hart in 1966, and Hart produced three consecutive 1–9 campaigns. Between 1964 and 1972, Pitt was a miserable 22–68–2.

By 1972 the University of Pittsburgh was at a crossroad when it came to its once proud football program. Chancellor Wesley Posvar was faced with one of three options: end the program, take it down to a lesser division, or loosen the tough requirements to compete with other successful programs and try to rebuild it into what it once was. He chose the third option.

After making his decision, he needed a coach who could work miracles. Someone who could take the embarrassment that was Panthers football and make it rise from the ashes like a Phoenix. The man he chose was Majors.

A tireless worker who'd turned around the program at Iowa State, Majors took the Cyclones to their first two bowl games in school history. He embraced the challenge in front of him. In his first year, he worked around the clock to secure one of the greatest recruiting classes in school history, while invigorating a fan base that had been devastated by what the program had become.

From the rubbles of a 1–10 season in 1972, the young coach immediately breathed life into it, starting with a stunning 7–7 tie against University of Georgia, the same program it would face for the national title four years later. Majors' first season ended with a 6–4–1 record, good enough for a bid to the Fiesta Bowl. While there was excitement after his first campaign, the program seemed stuck in neutral for the next two years. Then a stunning win against nationally ranked Notre Dame and a dominant victory against the University of Kansas in the 1975 Sun Bowl gave this team confidence they could compete with the college football elite.

The Panthers took the momentum they garnered in 1975 and ran with it a year later, rolling to an undefeated regular season, despite the fact they lost their two top quarterbacks to injury for large periods of the season. Robert Haygood tore ligaments in his knee against Georgia Tech in the campaign's second game and was lost for the season, and Matt Cavanaugh broke his fibula three weeks later against Louisville. Luckily for the Panthers, Cavanaugh would return a few weeks later. Helping atone for the quarterback's injuries, Tony Dorsett had a season for the ages, breaking the NCAA Division I single-season and career records for rushing yards while capturing the Heisman Trophy. The defense also proved to be phenomenal.

After they defeated Penn State to cap an 11–0 season, the Panthers were ranked first in the nation and accepted a bid to play in the Sugar Bowl on New Year's Day against the fourth-ranked Southeastern Conference champion Georgia Bulldogs. For Majors, it was a chance to complete the stunning turnaround that had started four years earlier in a game against the same opponent.

The two teams had very different philosophies of how to prepare for a bowl game. Georgia coach Vince Dooley believed in discipline. His team followed a curfew leading up to the game, and the coach kept a close eye on his players all week. Johnny Majors, however, let his players take in all New Orleans had to offer, establishing no curfew until two days before the game. Majors felt his players should be rewarded and wanted them to have fun. The Georgia players (who shaved their heads in team unity) as well as the Bulldogs' coaches and fans all thought Pitt's lax policies would hurt the team on game day and the Panthers wouldn't be focused. As it turned out, they were sorely mistaken. As Panthers tight end Jim Corbett put it, "Curfews and bald heads don't win bowl games."[1]

From the beginning of the game, Pitt looked like the focused team. Majors had his offense running plays in the I formation, something he rarely did during the season, and the maneuver seemed to catch the famed Georgia "junkyard defense" off guard. The Panthers began their second drive of the game on their own 20 and quickly moved downfield. Passes of 13 yards to Gordon Jones and 36 to running back Elliott Walker set up the Panthers at the Georgia 10. Two plays later, Cavanaugh ran it in from the 6 to give the Panthers an early 7–0 lead.

In the second quarter, the Panthers' defense took over and turned the expected close contest into an rout. First, Arnie Weatherington picked off a Ray Goss pass at the Pitt 26. Cavanaugh found Willie Taylor for 15 yards and then Jones on a slant down the middle. Jones sprinted the remainder of the way for a 59-yard scoring pass to give the Panthers a two-touchdown advantage. Fellow linebacker Jim Cramer then intercepted a pass from Matt Robinson, who Dooley put in for Goss, at the Panthers' 33. After Corbett pulled in a 10-yard reception, Dorsett finally broke through the Bulldog defense for 22 more yards. Willie Taylor then caught a 14-yard pass from Cavanaugh before Dorsett broke the game wide open with an 11-yard scoring run that made the score 21–0 at the half.

Georgia had been completely dominated in the first half, but as the third quarter began, they caught their first break of the game. Walker fumbled on his own 25, and Georgia defensive end Lawrence Craft pounced on the football. Unfortunately for the Georgia faithful, the Bulldogs' offense continued to sputter against the Panthers' defense, moving only 3 yards before settling for a field goal to cut the deficit to 21–3.

Any thoughts of a comeback essentially ended in the next few minutes. First, Dorsett ripped off a 67-yard run that preceded a Carson Long field goal to restore the Pitt's 21-point lead. Then Al Chesley picked up a Goff fumble at the Georgia 23, and shortly after, Long, who had already set the NCAA career-scoring record for kickers earlier in the season, was successful on another field goal to cap the scoring at 27–3. Pitt's third-string quarterback Tom Yewcic, who did a great job during the regular season when the other two quarterbacks were injured, came in for Cavanaugh, who was named the game's MVP, to finish the one-sided victory.

As the clock hit zero, the Georgia fans sat stunned as Pitt celebrated their national championship. An emotional Majors, who after the contest announced that he accepted the head coaching job at his alma mater, Tennessee, said, "We came here so we could play for the national championship. After the game I told our team that I could never hope to relive another four years like the past four years."[2] In the end, his statement was correct—it would be tough for anyone to duplicate what Majors had done at Pitt. Raising a program from the ashes like the Phoenix was truly his greatest feat.

Team	1st	2nd	3rd	4th	Final
Georgia	0	0	3	0	3
Pittsburgh	7	14	3	3	27

Team	Play	Score
Pitt	Cavanaugh 6-Yd Run (Long Kick)	7–0
Pitt	Jones 49-Yd Pass From Cavanaugh (Long Kick)	14–0
Pitt	Dorsett 11-Yd Run (Long Kick)	21–0
GA	Leavitt 25-Yd Field Goal	21–3
Pitt	Long 42-Yd Field Goal	24–3
Pitt	Long 31-Yd Field Goal	27–3

Rushing—GA

Player	Att	Yds	Ave	Td
McLee	14	48	3.4	0
Goff	17	76	4.5	0
Pollard	5	16	3.2	0
Davis	1	3	3.0	0
Robinson	1	-1	-1.0	0
Flanagan	2	-7	-3.5	0

Rushing—Pitt

Player	Att	Yds	Ave	Td
Dorsett	32	202	6.3	1
Walker	11	35	3.2	0
Cavanaugh	12	15	1.3	1
Yewcic	2	11	5.5	0
Sindewald	2	3	1.5	0
Sims	3	12	4.0	0

Receiving—GA

Player	Rec	Yds	Ave	Td
Davis	1	19	19.0	0
Pyburn	1	14	14.0	0
McLee	1	13	13.0	0

Receiving—Pitt

Player	Rec	Yds	Ave	Td
Taylor	4	72	18.0	0
Jones	3	80	26.7	1
Walker	1	36	36.0	0
Corbett	1	10	10.0	0
Dorsett	1	-6	-6.0	0

Passing—GA

Player	Comp	Att	Pct	Yds	Td	Int
Robinson	2	15	13.3	33	0	1
Goff	1	4	25.0	13	0	3
Flanagan	0	2	00.0	0	0	0
Davis	0	1	00.0	0	0	0

Passing—Pitt

Player	Comp	Att	Pct	Yds	Td	Int
Cavanaugh	10	18	55.6	192	1	0

#2

A Two-Man Show

For years, many great players took the court for the Duquesne men's basketball team, pursuing a national championship that never would come to fruition. Players like Ed Milkovich, Paul Widowitz, Chuck Cooper, and Jim Tucker led extremely talented teams that had hopes of finally ending a 15-year quest with a long-awaited title. A national semifinal and regional final finish in the NCAA tournament to go along with two NIT championship games and three semifinal appearances between 1940 and 1954 all ended in disappointment.

After the 1953–54 club, arguably the greatest in school history, stunningly lost to Holy Cross in the 1954 NIT finals, it was feared that the Dukes' elite status in college basketball was about to end. After all, the 1954–55 squad, despite having two of school's greatest players in Dick Ricketts and Sihugo Green, was not expected to reach the level of the previous teams. Instead, this two-man show wound up leading the school to the title it had so long desired.

While Ricketts and Green returned the next season, the Dukes lost three pivotal players to graduation in Jim Tucker, Fletcher Johnson, and Sid Dambrot. The news got even worse for coach Dudey Moore when starting guard Lou Iezzi was lost for the 1954–55 season due to illness, and 6'5" Tom Peszko was ruled academically ineligible. This left Moore with only his two stars, along with guards Mickey Winograd and Jim Fallon and forward Dave Ricketts, Dick's brother, as his only viable options to lead the team. To compete, Ricketts and Green would have to be at their best. And they showed they were with victories against fourth-ranked Dayton and defending national champion LaSalle in the Madison Square Garden Holiday Festival, which resulted in the Dukes moving to second in the Associated Press poll. But when either Ricketts or Green was injured or ill, things were very different.

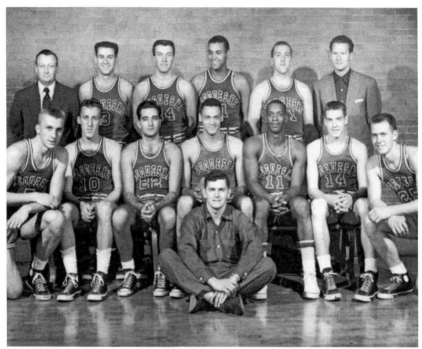

The 1955 Duquesne Dukes hold the distinction of being the only western Pennsylvania Division I team to capture a national championship in a tournament when they defeated the Dayton Flyers in the finals of the National Invitation Tournament. (Courtesy of Duquesne University Athletics)

Green missed the Steel Bowl Tournament final, which was an annual regular-season college basketball tournament in Pittsburgh, with appendicitis, resulting in a 71–64 Duquesne loss to George Washington. Meanwhile, a bad ankle injury suffered by Ricketts in the contest against LaSalle caused him to struggle in losses to St. Francis (Pennsylvania) and Dayton in the regular season.

Luckily, both players were healthy for the majority of the season, and the Dukes finished the year at 19–4. While it was permissible at one point for a school to play in both the NCAA and NIT tournaments, the NCAA prohibited that practice in 1952, forcing schools to choose one or the other. Both committees were courting Duquesne, trying to convince the Dukes to play in their respective tournament. Eventually, Moore and his Dukes decided they were loyal to the NIT and went on to Madison Square Garden as the tourney's No. 1 seed.

Despite unsubstantiated reports that Green had suffered from a toothache, the stomach flu, and even a stepped-on toe, he was ready for the NIT, as the Dukes easily moved past Louisville and Cincinnati in the first two rounds to face ninth-ranked Dayton in the finals. It was not an advantageous matchup for the Dukes, as Dayton coach Tom Blackburn and his seven-foot center Bill Uhl had defeated Duquesne in two of their three meetings during the regular season. Blackburn knew if they were to make it three out of four, his Flyers would need to nullify either Ricketts or Green. But it was a strategy that was easier said than done, as this magnificent twosome would be at their best, putting on the show of a lifetime in the first half.

The Flyers were certainly one the hottest teams in the nation, finishing the season on a 17–1 run, and on average their roster was 3 inches taller than Duquesne. What they didn't have was an answer to stop the Dukes' duo. Moore had his team playing very aggressive defense, and only Uhl, who led the team with 25 points in the game, was able to find his scoring touch. A massive crowd of 18,496 fans—the largest of the season at Madison Square Garden—were in awe at what they were seeing from Ricketts and Green. The two combined for all of Duquesne's points in the first half, as the Dukes vaulted out to a 35–30 halftime lead.

Duquesne fans, who far too long had to hear cries of "wait 'til next year," were now 20 minutes from seeing their dream finally become a reality. But for all of Ricketts and Green's dominance, the Flyers were only 5 points down. If Blackburn could have come up with a strategy to slow down the two All-Americans, the Duquesne faithful may have had to wait another year for the elusive championship. Fortunately for the fans from the Bluff, the Dukes played even better in the final 20 minutes of regulation.

Green took his game to the next level, scoring 10 of the team's next 15 points (with Ricketts, of course, scoring the other 5) to stretch the advantage to 54–45. Finally, with 7:40 gone in the second half, Winograd knocked down a free throw to become the first Duquesne player other than Ricketts and Green to score. While he finished the contest with only 6 points, Winograd was nonetheless a pivotal part of the victory, holding the Flyers' star Jack Sallee—who scored a combined 50 points in his previous two games against the Dukes—to only 2.

Instead of allowing their opponents back in the game, the Dukes kept pushing and adding to their lead. Ricketts and Green led the way, combining for 56 of the team's 70 points. As the game finally ended, the Duquesne players, coaches, and fans looked up and saw a sight they never had before: the Dukes on the winning side of a national championship game.

When the team returned to Pittsburgh, more than 5,000 fans met the Dukes at the airport and rushed the runway as the plane carrying the victorious champions came to a stop. Another 1,000 fans looked on and cheered from the terminal.

Ricketts and Green went on to become consensus All-Americans, marking the first time two players from one school had received the honor in the same

Duquesne fans waited 15 long years before they could finally celebrate a national championship. Pictured here are a group of fans preparing to drive to New York City in 1955 to finally see their school capture that long-awaited title. (Courtesy of Duquesne University Athletics)

season. The two also are the only players from one school to be selected as the first overall pick in the NBA draft in consecutive seasons. But even with all their awards and honors, it was their performance in the 1955 NIT finals that will always make Ricketts and Green legends on the Bluff, as they delivered the lone national basketball championship in school history.

Duquesne

Player	Fg	Ft	Pts
Green	13	7	33
Da. Ricketts	0	0	0
Di. Ricketts	7	9	23
Fallon	1	2	4
Winograd	2	2	6
Severine	1	2	4
Totals	24	22	70

Dayton

Player	Fg	Ft	Pts
Sallee	1	0	2
Horan	6	8	20
Pastin	0	0	0
Uhl	10	5	25
Sicking	0	0	0
Fiely	2	0	4
Harris	1	2	4
Dieringer	0	2	2
Riazzi	0	0	0
Jacoby	0	0	0
Almashy	0	0	0
Walsh	0	1	1
Totals	20	18	58

Team	1st	2nd	Final
Dayton	30	28	58
Duquesne	35	35	70

PITT PANTHERS 24, GEORGIA BULLDOGS 20
JANUARY 1, 1982
MEN'S NCAA DIVISION I FOOTBALL

The Last Waltz

In 1981 Jackie Sherrill was leading one of the best football programs in the country as the Panthers secured a spot in the Sugar Bowl. Sherrill's contract was about to expire, and negotiations had reportedly been nonexistent—which eventually chased Sherrill to Texas A&M, where he signed the richest contract in college football history up to that time. As it turned out, without Sherrill going forward as head coach, the 1982 Sugar Bowl marked the end of the last championship era the school has enjoyed. But if it had to come to an end, there was no better way to do it.

After coach Johnny Majors left in 1976, the school didn't want to return to the losing days of years past, so athletic director Cas Myslinski knew he needed the right man to keep the winning atmosphere alive. He looked no further than one of Majors's chief assistants: Jackie Sherrill, who had left Pitt after the 1975 campaign to take over as head football coach at Washington State.

Sherrill didn't have a great season, as the Cougars finished only 3–8, but Myslinski felt he was the right man for the job. Sherrill proved to be an outstanding recruiter, bringing in a class to Pitt in 1977 that might just have been the best in college football history. It included names like Jerry Boyarsky, Hugh Green, Russ Grimm, Ricky Jackson, Mark May, Bill Neill, Greg Meisner, Benjy Pryor, and Carlton Williamson. These players helped form a phenomenal run for the Panthers, as they went 22–2 between 1979 and 1980, winning a piece of the national championship in the latter season.

The phenomenal recruits kept coming. In 1979 the group included tight end John Brown from Burrell High School, who would turn into one of the program's best ever. And joining him was quarterback Dan Marino, who lived only blocks from Pitt Stadium and who was arguably the most touted recruit

Quarterback Dan Marino grew up only a few blocks from Pitt Stadium before accepting a scholarship to play there. In 1981 he threw for a school record 2,876 yards (since broken), including a clutch 33-yard pass to John Brown to win the 1982 Sugar Bowl 24–20. (Courtesy of the University of Pittsburgh Athletics)

ever to be brought in by the school. These two would be pivotal parts of a 1981 team who, despite losing several key players to graduation in 1980, was able to win their first 10 games. As a result, the Panthers ascended to the No. 1 spot in both major polls as the regular season was coming to an end.

Except for a tight 29–24 win over Boston College and their freshman quarterback Doug Flutie, Pitt soundly defeated every team on their schedule. Among the victories was a revenge match against 11th-ranked Florida State, which was the only team to defeat the Panthers the year before. All the Panthers had to do to get another shot at the national championship in 1981 was defeat 11th-ranked Penn State at Pitt Stadium.

While Penn State was a very good team, Pitt had an outstanding defense and an offense led by Marino, who was on his way to setting school record in both yards, with 2,876, and touchdowns, with 37. Against the Nittany Lions, he led them to a 14–0 start and the Panthers were on their way to pulling ahead by three touchdowns when an interception, as it turned out, curtailed their championship hopes. Penn State tacked on 48 unanswered points in a 48–14 humiliation at home.

The Panthers were devastated but still had a Sugar Bowl bid in their pocket. The now 10th-ranked Panthers would face the defending national champion Georgia Bulldogs, who had a phenom of their own in sophomore running back Herschel Walker, who had accumulated 1,891 yards and 18 touchdowns in 1981. Pitt looked at it as a chance for redemption and, as it would turn out, a way to end this final championship era in a memorable manner.

Even though the Panthers had a 1,000 rusher of their own in Bryan Thomas, the spotlight was on Walker. Fans wondered if he and the Bulldogs would carve up the once feared Pitt defense the way Todd Blackledge had for Penn State. Walker's notoriety was also a good inspiration for the Panthers' defense to stop the All-American runner, as it was for Thomas, who proved to be superior this day.

Averaging 282 rushing yards per game going into the contest, Georgia quickly learned that this was perhaps the best defense it had faced all season. Pitt thoroughly dominated Georgia in the contest statistically, but turnovers by the Panthers' offense made the game much closer than it should have been.

After a scoreless first quarter, Georgia forced a fumble by Tom Flynn on a punt return at the Pitt 49 early in the second. While Pitt held Walker in check for most of the game, on this drive the Panthers couldn't contain him. The Bulldogs drove 51 yards, capping it with an 8-yard touchdown run by the future Heisman Trophy winner to give Georgia a 7–0 lead.

Sherrill guessed that the deep pass would be difficult against the tough Bulldogs' defense, so he helped design a game plan that would feature short passing and the running attack of Thomas and Wayne DiBartola. Other than the turnovers, it worked spectacularly. Short Marino passes led to a 41-yard field goal by freshman kicker Wayne "Snuffy" Everett to cut the deficit to four as the teams exited the field for the first half.

Georgia's confidence seemed to slip as Marino led the Panthers on an 80-yard drive to open the second half. He completed three passes for 48 yards, the final 30 on a touchdown toss to Julius Dawkins to gave Pitt its first lead of the day, 10–7. But the lead was short-lived. Soon after, Thomas fumbled a pitch at his own 10, and Georgia recovered. Walker ran the ball into the end zone from there, and the Bulldogs were once again on top at 13–10 after a missed extra point.

The game had turned in to a back-and-forth affair, as Walker returned the favor—coughing up the ball at his own 23. Panthers defensive end Michael Woods recovered it, giving Pitt great field position. Thomas carried the ball three times, getting down to the Georgia 6. From there, Marino rolled out and hit Brown with a short touchdown toss that put the Panthers up, 17–13.

But Georgia bounced back. Aided by a 23-yard run by quarterback Buck Belue and a 24-yard Walker burst, Belue hit Clarence Kay with a 6-yard scoring strike to give Georgia the lead back at 20–17. Now the Bulldogs hoped their defense, ranked second in the nation going into the game, could hold on to secure the win.

It looked like it had just done that when the Bulldogs stopped Flynn short of a first down on a fake punt with 5:26 remaining in the contest and Georgia regained possession. Now the Pitt defense rose to the occasion, forcing a punt, and the Panthers took over at their own 20 with 3:46 left.

With Georgia playing a prevent defense to protect against the big play, Pitt stuck to its strong running attack and short passes to get them down the field. Twice the Panthers faced fourth down, one play away from certain defeat. The first time was at the Georgia 46. Needing 4 yards for a first down, Marino did something he rarely did: scramble up the middle for 8 yards. Minutes later, the second fourth down became arguably the greatest play in the program's history.

Pitt faced fourth-and-5 at the Georgia 33 with 42 seconds left. With so little time left, a running play didn't seem to be an option. "We considered a run," Sherrill said later, "but I thought we had to pass with time running out. I thought the best thing we could do was give Danny multiple patterns and let him pick out what was best."[1]

The plan was to send Thomas and DiBartola on 10-yard patterns, hoping that Marino would hit them with a short pass to get a first down. But when Marino brought the team to the line, he saw an eight-man front intent on stopping the run. The young quarterback decided a 10-yard pass was no longer an option, since he knew he needed to keep the running backs in the pocket to block. He was now intent on going for the win on that play and called an audible.

Sprinting toward the end zone were speedy wide receivers Dwight Collins and Julius Dawkins, as well as Brown, who'd come to Pitt with Marino three years earlier. Marino had several options, but he rifled his pass toward Brown. The perfectly thrown pass landed in Brown's hands in the end zone. The Panthers' fans in the Superdome erupted, as Pitt had now taken a 24–20 lead with 35 seconds left. With Georgia now in desperation mode after regaining possession, Belue tossed the ball downfield on the next play, and the pass was picked off by Pitt cornerback Troy Hill, clinching the Panthers' magnificent victory.

It was an outstanding way to end the season. The Panthers ended up fourth in the Associated Press final poll and second in the United Press International poll, while being awarded the national championship by the National Championship Foundation. The Panthers also set themselves up as the favorite to win the title in 1982.

Jackie Sherrill replaced Johnny Majors in 1977 and was able to help establish Pitt as one of the preeminent football programs in the country. He holds the school's all-time winning percentage record at .842 with a 50–9–1 mark in five seasons. Unfortunately, a disagreement with the school following the 1981 campaign led to him moving to Texas A&M. In his final game on the Panthers' sideline, he led Pitt to an exciting 24–20 win over Georgia in the Sugar Bowl. (Courtesy of the University of Pittsburgh Athletics)

But the joy soon turned to frustration. Sherrill, whose five-year contract was about to expire, wanted more control over the program, because he was frustrated about not being consulted on travel plans and scheduling. He had met with members of the Pitt administration on two occasions and each time he was told that it wasn't the time to discuss the matter. With tensions between Sherrill and Pitt rising, Texas A&M came into the picture, offering the coach a generous contract. Deciding Pitt wasn't interested in retaining him, he took the offer and went to College Station, Texas. Pitt replaced him with the popular Foge Fazio, but it turned out he wasn't the right man for the job, and once again the program stumbled into futility.

In the end, the 1982 Sugar Bowl proved to the last waltz for the Majors/Sherrill era, but it concluded the way it should have—with a magnificent play to deliver a magnificent victory that gave the Pitt Panthers one last day in the sun.

Team	1st	2nd	3rd	4th	Final
Georgia	0	7	6	7	20
Pittsburgh	0	3	7	14	24

Team	Play	Score
GA	Walker 8-Yd Run (Butler Kick)	7–0
Pitt	Everett 41-Yd Field Goal	7–3
Pitt	Dawkins 30-Yd Pass From Marino (Everett Kick)	7–10
GA	Walker 10-Yd Run (Kick Failed)	13–10
Pitt	Brown 6-Yd Pass From Marino (Everett Kick)	13–17
GA	Kay 6-Yd Pass From Belue (Butler Kick)	20–17
Pitt	Brown 33-Yd Pass From Marino (Everett Kick)	20–24

Rushing—GA

Player	Att	Yds	Ave	Td
Walker	25	84	3.4	2
Belue	7	45	6.4	0
Stewart	4	12	3.0	0

Rushing—Pitt

Player	Att	Yds	Ave	Td
Thomas	26	129	5.0	0
DiBartola	13	68	3.6	0
Marino	4	11	2.8	0
Flynn	1	0	0.0	0

Receiving—GA

Player	Rec	Yds	Ave	Td
Walker	3	53	17.7	0
Brown	1	8	8.0	0
Buckler	1	6	6.0	0
Kay	1	6	6.0	1
Stewart	1	5	5.0	0
Scott	1	5	5.0	0

Receiving—Pitt

Player	Rec	Yds	Ave	Td
DiBartola	8	64	8.0	0
Dawkins	6	77	12.8	1
Brown	6	62	10.3	2
Thomas	6	58	9.7	0

Passing—GA

Player	Comp	Att	Pct	Yds	Td	Int
Belue	8	15	53.3	83	1	2

Passing—Pitt

Player	Comp	Att	Pct	Yds	Td	Int
Marino	26	41	63.4	261	2	3

Notes

#49

1. Ray Fittipaldo, "National Title Resting at CCBC," *Pittsburgh Post-Gazette,* Mar. 27, 1997.
2. Fittipaldo, "National Title."
3. Jim Equels Jr., "National Champions," *Beaver County Times,* Mar. 24, 1997.
4. Equels, "National Champions."
5. Equels, "National Champions."

#47

1. Chuck Newman, "Dukes Nip Cats by 57–54," *Philadelphia Inquirer,* Mar. 6, 1977.

#46

1. Bob Healy, interview with author, November 2017.
2. Healy, interview.
3. Healy, interview.

#45

1. Jack LeDoux, "10,000 to See Tangerine Game," *Orlando Sentinel,* Jan. 2, 1950.
2. "Tangerine Bowl Football Returns to Saint Vincent," Official Athletics Site of Saint Vincent College, http://athletics.stvincent.edu/news/2017/1/26/tangerine-bowl-football-returns-home-to-saint-vincent.aspx, Jan. 26, 2017.

#44

1. "Maurice Stokes," *2017–18 St. Francis Basketball Media Guide,* 11.

#43

1. Jack Sell, "Duke-Tennessee Game Cancelled over Player," *Pittsburgh Post-Gazette,* Dec. 24, 1946.
2. Sell, "Duke-Tennessee Game."
3. Sell, "Duke-Tennessee Game."

#42

1. Charley Feeney, "Klausing, CMU, Face Goliath," *Pittsburgh Post-Gazette,* Nov. 18, 1978.
2. George Lobsenz, "CMU Backers Going Bananas," *Daily News,* Nov. 17, 1978.
3. Charley Feeney, "CMU's Klausing, Puts OK on Overtime Work," *Pittsburgh Post-Gazette,* Nov. 20, 1978.

#41

1. Craig Meyer, "Why Did Pitt and Penn State Break Tradition for 16 Years?," *Morning Call,* http://www.mcall.com/sports/college/psu/mc-penn-state-pitt-rivalry-what-it-means-20160908-story.html, Sept. 8, 2016.
2. Jenn Menendez, "In Renewal of Intrastate Rivalry Pitt Powers Past Penn State, 42–39," *Pittsburgh Post-Gazette,* http://www.post-gazette.com/sports/Pitt/2016/09/10/Pitt-Panthers-vs-Penn-State-Nittany-Lions-square-off-at-Heinz-Field/stories/201609100140, Sept. 10, 2016.

#40

1. "Looking Back at Jerome Lane's Backboard-Shattering Dunk," ESPN.com, http://www.espn.com/video/clip?id=18550666.
2. "Looking Back," ESPN.com.
3. "Looking Back," ESPN.com.
4. "Looking Back," ESPN.com.

#37

1. "Unusual Circumstances Bring Kentucky to Robert Morris for NIT," WTAE Pittsburgh, http://www.wtae.com/article/unusual-circumstances-bring-kentucky-to-robert-morris-for-nit/7460370, Mar. 13, 2013.
2. "Unusual Circumstances," WTAE.
3. "Unusual Circumstances," WTAE.
4. Associated Press, "Robert Morris Stuns Kentucky 59–57 in NIT," Robert Morris Colonials, http://rmucolonials.com/news/2013/3/20/70289.aspx, Mar. 19, 2013.
5. AP, "Robert Morris Stuns."

#35

1. "Jackets Had Sights Set for No. 1," *Pittsburgh Press,* Dec. 11, 1966.

#34

1. "Post Game Notes," *Hartford Courant,* Mar. 16, 2003.

#33

1. Scott Newman, "Pitt Gets a Thrill from 31–31 Tie," *Pittsburgh Press,* Oct. 1, 1989.
2. Kelly Carter, "Nehlen Cuts Postgame Talk," *Pittsburgh Press,* Oct. 1, 1989.

#32

1. Douglas Looney, "More Than a Win," *Sports Illustrated,* https://www.si.com/vault/1990/12/17/123290/more-than-a-win-for-allegheny-the-division-iii-title-wasnt-what-mattered-most, Dec. 17, 1990.

2. Mike Debraggio, "Reliving the Moment," *Allegheny Magazine,* http://sites.allegheny.edu/magazine/football-championship/reliving-the-moment/, Winter 1991.

#31

1. Eddie Beachler, "Pitt, Duquesne, Westminster Fives Accept Cage Bids," *Pittsburgh Press,* Mar. 11, 1941.

2. Beachler, "Pitt, Duquesne, Westminster Fives Accept Cage Bids."

#30

1. Chris Huston, "Q and A with Pittsburgh Panthers Great Hugh Green," cbssports.com, https://www.cbssports.com/college-football/news/q-a-with-pittsburgh-panthers-great-hugh-green/, Dec. 6, 2012.

2. "Pitt Bound for Gator Bowl," *Pittsburgh Press,* Nov. 16, 1980.

3. Bob Smizik, "Pitt Puts Its Number One Foot Forward," *Pittsburgh Press,* Dec. 30, 1980.

4. Smizik, "Pitt Puts Its Number One Foot Forward."

#29

1. Marino Parascenzo, "Pitt's '76 Hopes Rise in Sun Bowl Victory," *Pittsburgh Post-Gazette,* Dec. 27, 1975.

2. Parascenzo, "Pitt's '76 Hopes Rise in Sun Bowl Victory."

3. Russ Franke, "Pitt Attack Runs on Solar Energy," *Pittsburgh Press,* Dec. 27, 1975.

#26

1. Associated Press, "Fields Shines Down Stretch, Carries Pitt to First Elite 8 in 35 Years," ESPN.com, http://www.espn.com/mens-college-basketball/recap?gameId=294000022, Mar. 27, 2009.

#25

1. Jacqueline Kantor, "Local Trio Says Losing Teammate Brought Women's Basketball Team Closer Together as It Plays in Elite 8," Pennlive.com, http://www.pennlive.com/sports/index.ssf/2015/03/california_university_of_penns.html, Mar. 23, 2015.

2. Kantor, "Local Trio."

#23

1. "Carl A. DePasqua: Head Coach," *1970 Pitt Football Media Guide.*

2. "The Pitt Panther Is Back," *1970 Pitt Football Media Guide.*

3. Colin Dunlap, "In 1970, Pitt Had an Improbable Comeback against West Virginia," *Pittsburgh Post-Gazette,* http://www.post-gazette.com/sports/wvu/2010/11/25/In-1970-Pitt-had-an-improbable-comeback-against-West-Virginia/stories/201011250287, Nov. 25, 2010.

4. Dunlap, "Improbable Comeback."

5. Dunlap, "Improbable Comeback."

#22

1. Bill Heufelder, "Dorsett, Pitt, Tip Scales 24–7," *Pittsburgh Press,* Nov. 27, 1976.

2. Heufelder, "Dorsett, Pitt, Tip Scales 24–7."

3. Douglas S. Looney, "Tony Does His Number One More Time," *Sports Illustrated,* Dec. 6, 1976.

#18

1. Phil Axelrod, "Confident Panthers Never Had Doubts," *Pittsburgh Post-Gazette,* Oct. 13, 1976.

#17

1. Alex Kirshner, "West Virginia vs. Pitt 2007: 'We Blew It against the S*****est F***ing Team in the F***ing World,'" SBnation.com, https://www.sbnation.com/a/2007-college-football-season/pitt-west-virginia.

#16

1. George Von Benko, "1963 No Bowl Team," Pittsburgh Sports Report, http://www.pittsburghsportsreport.com/2003-Issues/psr0310/03100110.html.

#15

1. Associated Press, "Pitt Stuns No. 2 Clemson on Chris Blewitt's 48-Yard Field Goal," ESPN.com, http://www.espn.com/college-football/recap?gameId=400869485.

2. AP, "Pitt Stuns."

#14

1. Scott Dochterman, "Late 3-Pointer Carries Vulcans to National Title," *Pittsburgh Post-Gazette,* Mar. 28, 2004.

2. Dochterman, "Late 3-Pointer."

#13

1. Joe Starkey, "Class of '73 Keyed Pitt's Magical Season," *Tribune Review,* http://triblive.com/x/pittsburghtrib/news/s_467818.html, Aug. 27, 2006.

2. Jerry DiPaola, "Pitt Star Dorsett Recalls 303-Yard Performance against Notre Dame," *Tribune Review,* http://triblive.com/sports/college/pitt/5000131–74/dorsett-dame-notre, Nov. 5, 2013.

#12

1. "Dukes Reach Indianapolis for NCAA Court Tourney," *Pittsburgh Press,* Mar. 21, 1940.

#11

1. David Finoli, *When Pitt Ruled the Gridiron* (McFarland Publishers: Jefferson, NC, 2015).

#10

1. Luther Voltz, "Sasse, Smith and Players Talk after Game Is Ended," *Miami News,* Jan. 2, 1937.
2. Voltz, "Sasse, Smith and Players Talk after Game Is Ended."
3. Henry McLemore, "Thorpe Says Brumbaugh Best Back He Has Seen All Year," *Miami News,* Jan. 2, 1937.

#9

1. Gordon Edes, "0–0, 0–0 and 0–0: For Three Consecutive Years in the 1930s, Pittsburgh and Fordham Were Fit to Be Tied," *Los Angeles Times,* http://articles.latimes.com/1987–09–05/sports/sp-1516_1_curly-stebbins, Sept. 5, 1987.
2. Edes, "0–0, 0–0 and 0–0."

#8

1. Bruce Gerson, "A Victory for the Ages," *Carnegie Mellon Today,* http://cmtoday.cmu.edu/entertainment_artsculture/a-victory-for-the-ages/, Nov. 22, 2016.
2. Associated Press, "Upset Special: With Rockne gone, Irish Took a Michigan-like Tumble," ESPN.com, http://www.espn.com/espn/wire/_/section/ncf/id/3006504, Sept. 5, 2007.
3. AP, "Upset Special."
4. Chester Smith, "Rockne Sorry He Wasn't Here to Shake Hands with Steffen and His Players," *Pittsburgh Gazette Times,* Nov. 28, 1926.

#6

1. Bill Pennington, "John Heisman, the Coach behind the Trophy," *New York Times,* http://www.nytimes.com/2006/12/08/sports/ncaafootball/08heisman.html, Dec. 8, 2006.
2. "Georgia Tech Hardest Team Pitt Has Met," *Pittsburg Press,* Nov. 24, 1918.

#4

1. "Greasy Neale, 81, Coached Eagles," *New York Times,* http://www.nytimes.com/1973/11/03/archives/greasy-neale-81-coached-eagles-40year-career-in-football-led-to.html, Nov. 3, 1973.
2. "Greasy Neale," *New York Times.*

3. "1922 Rose Bowl," Washington & Jefferson College, http://www.washjeff. edu/1922-rose-bowl.

4. "Washington and Jefferson Plays Vaunted California Bears to Scoreless Tie," *Philadelphia Inquirer,* Jan. 22, 1922.

#3

1. Pat Livingston, "Panthers Humble Pore 'Lil Boys," *Pittsburgh Press,* Jan. 2, 1977.

2. Russ Franke, "Pitt: How Sweet It Is!," *Pittsburgh Press,* Jan. 2, 1977.

#1

1. Bob Smizik, "Panthers, Lions Claw Out Bowl Wins," *Pittsburgh Press,* Jan. 2, 1982.